War and the Cultural Turn

For Peter Ward

War and the Cultural Turn

Jeremy Black

polity

The right of Jeremy Black to be identified as Author of this Work has been asserted in accordance with the UK Copyright, Designs and Patents Act 1988.

First published in 2012 by Polity Press

Polity Press
65 Bridge Street
Cambridge CB2 1UR, UK

Polity Press
350 Main Street
Malden, MA 02148, USA

ISBN-13: 978-0-7456-4833-0 (hardback)
ISBN-13: 978-0-7456-4834-7 (paperback)

A catalogue record for this book is available from the British Library.

Typeset in 10.5 on 12 pt Times
by Toppan Best-set Premedia Limited
Printed and bound in Great Britain by MPG Books Group Limited, Bodmin, Cornwall

The publisher has used its best endeavours to ensure that the URLs for external websites referred to in this book are correct and active at the time of going to press. However, the publisher has no responsibility for the websites and can make no guarantee that a site will remain live or that the content is or will remain appropriate.

Every effort has been made to trace all copyright holders, but if any have been inadvertently overlooked the publisher will be pleased to include any necessary credits in any subsequent reprint or edition.

For further information on Polity, visit our website: www.politybooks.com

Contents

Preface

In making the case for a culturally aware approach to military history, it is necessary to avoid the opposite dangers of dismissing and blindly accepting culture as an explanatory concept. In this book, I try to throw light on different, but overlapping uses of cultural analysis, or rather analysis in terms of culture. These different uses and sites of debate reflect the very varied definitions of culture in military terms, and also the extent to which these definitions have been utilized. The net effect is that culture as a descriptive and analytical tool lacks coherence. Moreover, it lacks constancy, as there is a marked tendency to adapt practices to the crisis of conflict, and that in a situation in which crises tend to take an unexpected form. Such adaptation may be hidden by institutional continuity and the maintenance of tradition, but neither is incompatible with change.

As a result, it is helpful to present culture as itself changeable, rather than being a constant force that imposes a set of practice on its subjects. Culture thus acts as a variable within a system of military activity and norms that is composed of variables, such as technology and international relations, each of which affects the other. Individual military cultures are shaped not only by these externalities but also by the nature of the military cultures of other states, for processes of emulation are particularly important, with competition leading to imitation as well as conflict. Thus, the idea of a form of cultural purity or rejectionism does not describe the willingness to adopt and adapt.

Adoption may lead to the borrowing of weapons, training, organizational structures, tactics, or doctrine, and adaptation may lead not only to this borrowing but also to the development of anti-weapons, anti-tactics, anti-strategy and so on, in order to lessen the advantages of opponents. These anti-processes can be described in terms of culture, not least with reference to the gap in method between the process being opposed and the response, and indeed such a description informs part of the use of culture as a descriptive and analytical term; notably with reference to Iraq and Afghanistan but, more generally, in response to radical Islam.

It is, however, necessary to distinguish between what can be classified as cultural responses and, on the other hand, the particular responses to specific functional circumstances. Looked at differently, each can affect the other, but that does not mean that there is not an element of difference. Moreover, it is important not to assume that the relationship between cultural and functional responses is (or was) in some fashion invariable.

The Preface provides the opportunity to add a personal note. Convention dictates that this takes the form of acknowledgements, and, indeed, I have been very fortunate in being able to discuss these and related matters with others in the fields of military studies and military history. I have also profited greatly from the comments of George Boyce, Guy Chet, John France, Mike Pavkovic, Patrick Porter and Dennis Showalter on an earlier draft of all or part of this book. The opportunity to give papers on this and related topics at the Naval War College in Newport, Rhode Island, at the universities of Oxford, Reading and Washington, on a Far Eastern tour in early 2011, and to ICAP has also been most welcome. It is a great pleasure to dedicate this book to Peter Ward, a good friend and keen navalist. His friendship and company on Devon walks and at Devon meals are much appreciated.

That, of course, is the conventional terminus, but I feel it might be interesting to reflect on how this subject has impacted on me over recent decades. I have been lecturing on military history for over three decades, and the subject has certainly changed greatly. When, in the 1980s and 1990s, I mentioned or advanced cultural perspectives, I very much felt that I was an isolated figure. The emphasis, instead, was on technology and on a teleological course of development that led towards industrial warfare and a total war capacity. This approach was accentuated with the notion of the Revolution in Military Affairs (RMA) and the idea of paradigm shifts towards modernity and then beyond. In my *Causes of War* (1998), I advanced an alternative reading in terms of a revolution in attitudes to the military, but it had no impact. In *War and the World. Military Power and the Fate of Continents* (1998), I concluded that 'technology will not be able to provide barriers to protect "civilization"', but that assessment sank without trace. Far more typical of attitudes was the warning that 'the Admiral is committed to the RMA' which I was given in 2000 when invited to speak at the Naval Strategy School in Monterey, California.

The initial success of the coalition forces in Iraq in 2003, brought technological triumphalism to a crescendo, only to be followed by a reaction in which cultural factors were thrust to the fore. Much of the discussion over the last decade of both warfare and military history has adopted the language of culture in an attempt to make sense of a situation in which technological interpretations, still more technological determinism, does not carry so much credence as was the case in the 1990s and early 2000s. Indeed, it has also been argued that the rediscovery of culture is a response to imperial crisis, the crisis of Western power-projection.[1] Armies, such as the American and British, are paying more attention to cultural factors, with culture playing an explicit role in recent doctrine, and the military have revived an interest in cultural anthropology. This development poses problems as well as offering valuable prospects.

In short, the causes of the cultural analysis appear to be a form of presentism, with military history swept along in the flow of a new current of concern with the present-day. Looked at differently, this concern has provided military historians with an opportunity to prove their relevance. The last has an institutional focus, as, partly due to the lack of support for military history in many universities, much of the work on military history is conducted within military education institutions, such as West Point. This situation encourages a determination to prove the relevance of the subject[2] as, possibly, do the assertive psychological characteristics of those who tend to teach military history.

The use of cultural factors, however, has generally been similarly indiscriminate; and, indeed, some of those who pushed 'technology' with zeal and without sophistication have transferred to 'culture' with similar zeal and simplicity. This book is written because I am troubled about the misuse of cultural explanations just as I was concerned about their earlier neglect. I also feel that any single approach to military history and military studies is necessarily flawed. The scholar, like the analyst, needs to keep alert to questions and ambiguities, and to avoid the misleading rush to apparently certain answers.

At the same time, there is an attempt to offer an interpretation of important issues over time and space. To do so, I first provide a general chapter that outlines the major themes, and then chapters that focus on individual themes in the context of a period of particular interest. Thus, abstract theoretical discussion and concrete case studies are linked, showing how both can be mutually enriching. Moreover, especially in chapter 7, there is an understanding and presentation of military history itself as a form of cultural analysis that can, in turn, be subject to such an analysis. The last leads to the obvious conclusion, that there is no one way to approach this subject; but that point does not lessen its significance.

1

Introduction

The German philosopher Georg Wilhelm Friedrich Hegel (1770–1831) would have been delighted, for the discussion of military history has revealed a classic case of the thesis and antithesis that he saw as important to the quest for truth via the dialectic. More particularly, if the emphasis on technology that reached an apogee in the 1990s and early 2000s, with interest in a supposed Revolution in Military Affairs and a related 'transformation' of the military, represented the thesis; so a stress on cultural factors was the antithesis, or was used in this fashion. Moreover, this thesis and antithesis also had a clear chronology and a pronounced geographical emphasis. The clear chronology was an emphasis on technology in assumptions from the Vietnam War, up to and including the invasion of Iraq in 2003; and, in contrast, although there were already valuable discussions of the cultural theme prior to 2003,[1] a stress on culture thereafter. The variety of issues and concepts summarized as the cultural aspects of war is a subject that has attracted considerable attention over the last decade, offering a different way of assessing capability to that focused on weaponry.[2] In part, this attention reflects the more general extent to which cultural influences have notably emerged clearly in the writing of history, including military history.

The geographical emphasis related to this changing chronology and, in particular, the presentism it offered. For example, whereas the stress during the Vietnam War of the 1960s and early 1970s was on elements of Vietnamese and/or Communist culture and ideology that sustained opposition to the American intervention, the emphasis, from 2003, was on aspects of Islamic culture and fundamentalist ideology. In each case, there was an attempt to understand why the output of the world's most technologically advanced and resource-rich military, that of the USA, a military with a high standard of professionalism, was unable to achieve the outcome of a settlement on its own terms. The key issue appeared to be that of the failure to make America's opponents internalize a set of values in which they accepted the American understanding of relative capability. Thus, the cultural factor apparently became a way of understanding both the role and success of will-power and the wider political context.

Defining Terms

The danger, however, is that culture becomes, like technology, an over-used term as well as one that is difficult to define, a danger that the multiple uses of it outlined in this book makes clear, notably the sprawling character of this chapter, which seeks to introduce many themes. Constructing a workable concept of culture poses many problems, and anthropologists and archaeologists in practice use the term culture in such an all-embracing sense that it has become almost meaningless and could simply be read as society.

One difficulty with concepts of culture is that they also change across time, and, consequently there is no permanent concept of culture, let alone one that works across all languages and, of course, cultures. Hence, a poor choice is offered: either to superimpose one particular concept upon any aspect of the past which happens to come under review, or to retain the changing concepts of culture that are to be found in the sources. The first offers analytical clarity, but fails to note differences in concepts of culture; while the second approach reduces the communicability of what is being described.

Moreover, taking note of changing concepts of culture also entails noting the degree to which some cultural norms and consequences contradict others. For example, individual states, such as the contemporary USA and Britain, have strategic cultures that contain contradictory elements as battles over doctrine and resources make clear. Drawing attention to the complexity of usage is a valuable contribution that historians can offer, not least as their grasp of the past is different to that of anthropologists and political scientists who have provided much of the work in the field. Nevertheless, the perspective of these other subjects is of great value. In particular, anthropologists have emphasized the degree to which culture is a contested sphere, one that lacks coherence and, instead, is characterized by struggle. By challenging the concept of culture as an overarching, one-dimensional and fixed set of objective ideas, we approach closer to reality, but also underline the problems of analysis and exposition.

The over-use of culture as both a descriptive term and an interpretative method is another aspect of a more general poverty of historiography in the field of military history, one, moreover, that the ethnogenesis apparently offered by some cultural interpretations highlights. There has been a lack of attention to this poverty, but, in 2002, Dennis Showalter, a leading American military historian, pointed out that 'Military history is arguably the last stronghold of what historiographers call the "Whig interpretation"...[it] sees the development of warfare as progressive.'[3] This perceptive comment drew valuable attention to the culture of military history, a culture that, in turn, offers a useful angle on one of the leading concepts in military studies and history, the cultural turn in military history.

A theme in this book is that culture is dynamic, not static, as both a reality and as an analytical process. Culture needs to be tackled as a dynamic and problematic phenomenon, whereas the standard approach in military history is to employ less refined and less problematic concepts of culture as an apparently overarching, one-dimensional and fixed set of objective ideas, a practice long challenged within the social sciences.

A Range of Sub-Cultures

Some scholars have argued in favour of the need to consider particular cultural elements in warfare, especially the way in which understandings of appropriate military conduct, victory, defeat, and causality, are all culturally conditioned. Thus, the response in Egypt of the ruling Mamluks to firearms in the late fifteenth and early sixteenth centuries is seen in terms of a warrior culture that preferred an emphasis on individual prowess. For others, culture in military history focuses on perception and expectations, especially the perception of opportunities, of problems, of options, and of success. The determination of the Ottoman rulers of Turkey (and much else) to gain prestige as defenders of Islam against Christians and Sunni orthodoxy against the Safavids of Persia (Iran) can be presented in this light. Others have sought to employ cultural issues in warfare as explanatory factors in large-scale, overall or synoptic theories allegedly explaining military history.

The last approach includes (although it is not limited to) the eloquent, if somewhat simplistic and triumphalist, account of Western military success that, in part, reflects the misleading looseness of cultural definitions. This account is seen in particular in the work of Victor Davis Hanson, such as his *The Western Way of War: Infantry Battle in Classical Greece* (1989) and *Carnage and Culture: Landmark Battles in the Rise of Western Power* (2001). Hanson presented Western military advantage as resting on particular ideas and institutions that were rooted in Hellenic traditions. The most vulnerable aspect of Hanson's argument was its meta-cultural approach, a sweeping view of a shared civilization across time and space. Nevertheless, within Hanson's argument, there was a notion that repays serious consideration, namely that democracies have a particular military culture of their own, and that there is a relationship between regime type and military performance.

A similar argument was made for 1944–5 by Max Hastings, when he contrasted Anglo-American military culture with more brutal German and Soviet counterparts, arguing that being citizen soldiers meant that fighting quality was lower, a point with which Hanson would definitely have disagreed. Hastings suggested that the result of the Western allies' measured approach to war, coupled with German determination, ensured that much of Eastern Europe was exposed to Soviet brutality and tyranny; yet, also, that the ability of Anglo-American forces to maintain their military culture rested in part on the Soviet willingness to take very heavy casualties.[4]

Hanson's book was prompted by a particular political juncture, and can be seen as an expression of a culture of American discussion, but the book was also part of an ongoing debate over the linkages between wartime efficiency and political culture. Hanson's work thus offered an interesting parallel to that of Samuel Huntington.[5] Indeed, it can be seen as a consequence, or even rationalization, of the latter for military historians. At the same time, as a reminder of the need for care in locating scholarship, more recent work has also argued for a positive synergy between democracy and military effectiveness in the case of Athens, at once a democracy and an empire.[6]

Culture is a much employed term. There is the culture of society as a whole, including why people fought and how they responded to the issues of conflict, on which there has recently been excellent work for the American Civil War (1861–5). There is also the definition of military culture as a specific form of institutional culture[7] and, linked to this, a focus on organizational culture of particular militaries, a topic that overlaps with sociology. This category, which includes issues such as hierarchy, discipline and the responsiveness of subordinates to responsibilities, illustrates the widespread applicability of the concept of culture and of related terms and vocabulary. For example, in assessing the effectiveness of the naval dockyards during the later Anglo-French wars, Roger Morriss considered administrative culture in the shape of ideas, structures, practices and mores, providing an important way of assessing control and organization.[8] A particular aspect of administrative ethos and practice has been discussed in the shape of the 'culture of secrecy'.[9] In another direction, an important review article of 2007 referred to 'the new emphasis on culture, especially the history of memory', and discussed the significance of the subsequent presentation of war.[10]

Strategic Culture

There is also the concept of strategic culture, employed to discuss the context within which military tasks were 'shaped'. This concept, which overlaps with that of strategic landscapes, and focuses on issues in international relations studies, owed much to a 1977 report on Soviet strategic culture for the Rand Corporation by Jack Snyder. As such, the concept provided a way to help explain a system for which sources were manipulated for propaganda reasons and accurate reports were few. This situation describes that of many states in the past. The idea of explaining a system in terms of a culture captured the notion that there were relevant general beliefs, attitudes and behaviour patterns, and that these were in some way integral to the politics of power rather than being dependent on the policy circumstances of a particular conjuncture.[11] Roger Barnett, a supporter of the concept, argues that strategic culture leavens 'collective memory with cumulative experience'.[12]

Strategic culture continues to be the concept of choice when considering China; in part because its intentions are of key concern to the USA as it assesses how best to respond to China's increasing power. For example, a recent pamphlet from the Strategic Studies Institute of the American Army War College focuses on the topic of China's strategic culture, concluding that it provides a means to accurate assessment: 'To craft any intelligent, effective policy towards China, the US national security community must have a clear contextual understanding of the historical and cultural factors that define China's strategic thinking, and that can best provide an impassioned assessment of China's goals and intentions.'[13]

However, strategic culture as an approach does not offer precise answers. For example, in what is principally an essentialist approach, it has been argued that China's strategic culture was primarily defensive and focused on protecting its frontiers, but there has also been a critique of the notion of a defensive, Confucian, strategic culture, and, in its place, an argument that there have been long-standing expansionist strands in Chinese strategic culture, notably at the expense of steppe peoples.[14] The room for different assessments emerges on this point, which, more generally, suggests that the very building blocks of larger theories have to be handled with care. For example, the standard interpretation of Ming China (1368–1644) is that the military establishment scarcely enjoyed a central place, not least because the military was nominally hereditary, whereas the norms of civilian society were merit-orientated. Moreover, the civil service bureaucrats who were powerful under the Ming had scant commitment to the goals of the military and, as a result, the prestige of military service was limited. This situation led to a lack of interest in war, let alone expansionism, and to only limited commitment to the state of the military.[15] However, there is also room for a reinterpretation stressing the extent to which emperors had an important military role or sought such a role.[16]

The issue of Chinese bellicosity is seen to be of considerable pertinence at present, not least because of concerns over Taiwan,[17] although it may also be asked how far a discussion of Chinese war-making in, say, the eighteenth century is of relevance today, in what is a very different political context, both domestic and international, as well as with regard to the nature of war. To turn back, the tension between early and late Ming war-making in the periods 1370–1450 and 1550–1644 is notable, the former being far more focused on power projection, as is that between late Ming and the attitudes of the Manchu, who seized power in the 1640s and 1650s. Given these variations, it may be asked whether there is any relevance in comparing Manchu and modern attitudes.

Islam as a strategic culture raises a host of similar points: notably, for the early twentieth century, the tension between pan-Arabism and pan-Turkish ideas. The variation in Islamic strategic cultures and the capacity for development of individual ones is also clear from the experience of the last two decades. To refer to Islamic war-making is to neglect differences between the militaries of particular states, both in the past and at present. Thus, strategic culture lacks meaning if it is pretended that there is some inherent, semi-timeless characteristic. Instead, like organizational culture, strategic culture takes on value by referring to a particular period. These concepts have to address historical context, specifically the issue of coherence and consistency in face of the contested character of national and service interests, the range of debate, and the roles of politics and contingency.

More generally, it is necessary to identify and probe the problem of plurality, diversity and contradictions within strategic cultures. For example, there is the question of the strategic culture of individual military services, which, in part, are shaped by their assessment of their domestic role. There is also the issue of the extent to which war and, more particularly, combat led to the development and/or bringing to fruition of particular characteristics, such as the victory disease seen with Allied generals in the autumn of 1944. That situation created a systemic problem for Dwight Eisenhower, the Supreme Commander of the Allied Expeditionary Force, as subordinate commanders eschewed good discipline in their grab for battle laurels,[18] although he can also be faulted for patronage politics. In an instance more generally relevant for military history, subsequent perceptions of the campaign in 1944 owed much to aggressive memorizing.[19] The same was true of the memoirs left by British commanders in North Africa in 1941–2; and would have been the case for many campaigns had the commanders put pen to paper.

National Exceptionalisms: The Cases of the USA and Canada

The use of culture as an argument for essentialism approximates to earlier and current discussions of distinctive ways of war, including the thesis that national military behaviour is learned behaviour.[20] Moreover, the self-proclaimed role of the military, especially army, as the defender of national unity, notably in Brazil, Chile, Indonesia, Pakistan and Turkey, helped ensure an exceptionalism that linked (and reflected) both the state and the military.[21]

American exceptionalism is a particularly influential idea, one that often draws on views of the American character and constitution, notably with a presentation of citizen soldiers and a militia tradition, a presentation that, in fact, underplays the extent of professionalism.[22] The concept of exceptionalism, and the related notion of a distinctive way of war, however, is one that causes problems across the range of historical enquiry, as well as providing valuable insights. As far as military history is concerned, an emphasis on exceptionalism is an aspect of the diversity of circumstances and variety of developments that can be seen to play an important role, not least in subverting the frequent schematic attempts that are made to assert the existence of a single model. This process of schematicism by exceptionalism has been accentuated by the theoretical stress on cultural dimensions, particularly the ideas of cultural responses to conflict as well as organizational and strategic culture, as these are, by their nature, if they are to be analytically helpful, distinctive, and based on particular states.

The USA has attracted strong interest in so far as exceptionalism is concerned. This interest is linked to the long-standing debate about an 'American way of war', a theme pushed hard by many American scholars,[23] but also contested. For example, the extent to which the colonists adapted to the nature of war against native Americans has been debated. On the one hand, North America has been presented as a space where European-style tactics continued to prevail.[24] It has also been argued that the interior was overcome in part due to the devising of a distinctive way of war based on irregular and total warfare directed against hostile populations, as in the destruction of native crops and villages.[25] The emphasis on difference serves political-cultural goals as it looks back to the politically attractive argument that America won independence because it rejected *ancien régime* notions of conflict, and that its distinctive socio-political system thereafter assured a continued difference. More recently, an emphasis in the discussion of American exceptionalism has been on technology and its linkage to culture.[26]

This supposed *sonderweg* [unique path] can be clarified through such explanation. Furthermore, the discussion of American exceptionalism can be contextualized by considering other states. To focus on Canada might appear surprising, as, in considering the USA, contrasts are more commonly made with other leading powers, particularly Britain, for the distinctive strategic culture of which there is a developed literature.[27] However, it is valuable to look at Canada alongside the USA, not only because it throws light on the latter, but also as it indicates the extent to which a state that is not the leading power in the military system can still make a major contribution in war and be a worthwhile subject for analysis. Canada's role has attracted much attention from its military historians, which is well deserved as, from 1917 to the mid 1960s, Canada made a major contribution to world history, as also did India. These contributions focused on war, yet are largely neglected both in writing on war at the global level and in modern Canadian and Indian consciousness. This situation is a reminder of the roles of contingency and changing political culture in military assessment.

Canada's contribution can be divided into three episodes: the First World War, the Second World War, and the early years of NATO. As far as the First World War was concerned, the Canadian contribution was crucial in the last two years of the war, when Canadian units played a key role in the evolution of effective offensive tactics on the

Western Front, particularly artillery–infantry co-ordination, and also in providing a key component in the drive for victory. The Canadian contribution in 1918 was particularly important. At that stage, the strategic situation was very critical for the Allies, indeed far more so than in the last campaign of the Second World War. Russia had been knocked out of the war, and its resources were now open to German exploitation. The USA had come into the war, but, as yet, only a portion of its military had been deployed in France and, partly due to inexperience, their fighting effectiveness was modest, as their early operations showed. The French military was exhausted. As a consequence, British and Dominion forces played a key role in 1918, and, within them, the Canadians were crucial. More generally, Canada was also important during the war in the development of munitions production, in the supply of food to Britain, in the naval protection of North Atlantic maritime routes, and in the financial resourcefulness of the British imperial system. These capabilities were important to the strategic geography of the war.[28]

In the Second World War, Canada again played a crucial role, although the Canadian government was initially reluctant to provide troops for the Western Front, in part because of the heavy losses in the First World War. Lessons learned, politics and socio-cultural factors were all linked in this reluctance. Canadian forces were particularly important in the crisis of 1940, when the British military and strategic situation collapsed, with the fall first of Norway and then of France. In this situation, it was very important to have Canadian forces available to act as an operational reserve, able to counter any German invasion landing in southern England. Also in 1940, Canadian troops were deployed to occupy Iceland, helping to thwart the possibility that this Danish colony would become a German submarine base. As the Canadian forces in 1940–1 rested on the defensive, their role is underrated in the popular consciousness; a characteristic problem with operational military history, especially if written with this consciousness in mind; but such defensive roles are vital. So also was the defensive role represented by convoy protection, which was more effective, although apparently more mundane, than the interest in hunter-killer tactics. The Canadian navy focused on convoy protection, rather than the big-ship capabilities and surface ship-killing tasks of the British and American navies. Although less dramatic than the latter, and challenged by serious factional tensions within the navy,[29] the Canadian role was vital. The rapidly expanded navy became the third biggest in the world, and, without its effort, it would have been impossible to maintain maritime routes across the Atlantic in the face of a savage German submarine offensive. Another aspect of the Canadian war effort that tends to be overlooked was the British Commonwealth Air Training Plan, which was established in 1939, and which became the key location for training.

The Canadians also played a major role in offensive operations. Political pressure to be seen to be doing something, always a significant factor in the politics of strategic culture, led the army to take a major role in the poorly planned attack on Dieppe in 1942, in which the majority of the attacking force was killed, wounded or captured by the German defenders. More successfully, in 1943–5, Canadian forces made an important contribution in the Italy campaigns, while, in 1944–5, they played a key role in those in north-west Europe. Canada's contribution to the Allied cause, as well as to the survival of Britain itself, in the Second World War was far greater than its manpower. Crucial food and munitions were also provided, as was financial support. The Canadian government provided large amounts of money to Britain in grants and loans, and, per capita, the Canadians provided more assistance than the Americans.[30]

In turn, the Canadians played a major role in the early years of NATO, particularly as France, Britain and Portugal were heavily engaged in imperial defence, while Germany had been disarmed. The Canadian contribution remained crucial until the late 1960s, when Canada began to make a smaller defence effort, while France and Britain recentred their military efforts from their colonies on to Western Europe, and Germany by then had a substantial military.

An emphasis on the role of Canada serves as a reminder of the extent to which images of a nation's military trajectory can be misleading. In this case, in particular, recent American criticism, notably in the 2000s, of Canada for neutralism and a lack of military vigour, cannot serve to provide a reliable account of Canada's military past.

In turn, this point invites attention to the position for other states. In the case of the USA, as of Canada, there is, for example, the misleading emphasis on the volunteer military tradition and the citizen soldier, and the related critique of professionalism, an emphasis that was particularly strong in the nineteenth century, and that still had echoes in the twentieth. The regular American army, however, was always much bigger than its Canadian counterpart, while the American navy rose to be a major force on the world scale between 1890 and 1920, and therefore its nature became different to that of the American army in this period. From 1940, in turn, the American army became a large-scale professional force, although at that time, the Canadian forces also moved from being primarily militia-based to becoming a permanent regular institution.

The variable nature of the historical interpretation of American military history is not simply a matter for scholars, but, instead, is more centrally located first in public history and, secondly, in political clashes past and present. In the case of the USA, these proved stronger than in anglophone Canada, although once the Québec dimension is added the situation is very different. From the outset, there was division within the USA over the direction of military policy, and this was centrally linked to anxieties about the character of the republic. Support for a strong military was seen as betokening centralist, indeed autocratic, tendencies, and as un-American. In contrast, the Federalists pressed the case for thinking of America as threatened by Britain, France and Spain, and therefore as needing a strong defensive capability. Thomas Jefferson was particularly associated with the first view, and Alexander Hamilton with the second.

This tension persisted, albeit in different forms, in the nineteenth century, being reshaped in response to events and their perception, for example the war of 1812. A major difference over the role of regulars as opposed to militia was seen then and over the following decades. This was related to criticism of West Point as a European-style institution, and to differences over foreign policy, not least the desirability of expansionism within North America.

To a considerable extent, the public political dimension of differences over military tasking and force structure became less acute within the USA after the Civil War (1861–5). During the following 140 years, there was more political consensus on these issues than in the first eighty years of the republic, in large part because of widespread support for (eventual) participation in the two world wars and the Cold War. This participation was made more acceptable by presenting it as defensive moves in response to aggression, the approach also adopted in the extrapolation of the reaction to the 2001 attacks into a war on terror. However, the potential for dispute within American public culture and the political system remained high as was shown, for example, by the eventual response to large-scale engagement in the Vietnam War.

The situation was different in Canada, although there was a contrast between military mobilization in Québec and in anglophone Canada in both world wars. This was very much seen in the 1942 conscription plebiscite, where the no vote was 73 per cent in Québec, and, in contrast, the peak in the no vote elsewhere was 30 per cent in New Brunswick, and the no vote was only 16 per cent in Ontario.

Political difference can also be seen in terms of the use of force in domestic politics. This was most obvious in the case of the American Civil War (1861–5), and, compared to that, the situation was very different in Canada. The contrast might have been less apparent, however, had Québec separatism gone further, and, from a Québec perspective, force, or the threat of force was applied: in the original British conquest of French Canada in 1758–60 most obviously, as well as in the nineteenth century, when troops were deployed in the mid nineteenth century during the Fenian raids crisis, and, more recently, when the prospect of force was an aspect of the debate over Québec separatism. Indeed, in the 1960s, this issue led to interest in the acquisition of wheeled personnel carriers by the Canadian army, and to comparable preparations for countering civil disobedience.

In the absence of such action, however, the use of force was relatively modest in Canada. Troops were employed against the regional opposition of the *Métis* in the late nineteenth century, and, more centrally, there was deployment of troops against strikers in the 1890s to 1920s, notably the widespread labour activism in 1919, especially in Winnipeg. Thereafter, the use of the military was modest, and most of the strikes were not met by violence. Nor was there any equivalent in Canada to the deployment of regular troops to further civil rights in the 1950s in the USA, nor to the use of National Guard forces in response to ethnic rioting in the 1960s. This difference can be emphasized or, conversely, the stress could be on the limited use of force in both countries from the 1970s, for example in 1992 in the face of the serious Los Angeles riots.

Mention of similarity in some aspects, however, has to take note of fundamental differences in both political and strategic culture. Canada was part of an imperial military and political system, which entailed far more co-operation than is often appreciated. This co-operation was seen, in particular, first in the defence of Canada against real or potential American attack, and, subsequently, in the major role Canada played in the two world wars. The emphasis is generally on Canada coming to independence with, in particular, stress on the delay in Canada declaring war on Germany in the Second World War, but the reality, from far earlier, was of the shared responsibilities that were an aspect of an imperial system that rested on such co-operation. This was particularly important in the British imperial system due to the small size of the British regular army and the reluctance to turn to conscription. Canadian troops served in the Boer War in South Africa (1899–1902) while 2,000 Canadian troops were lost when the outnumbered and vulnerable garrison of Hong Kong fell to the Japanese in December 1941.

The contrast with the USA, an independent state from 1776, is readily apparent. Furthermore, American independence was amplified, first, by America's tendency to shun participation in military alliances prior to 1917 and, secondly, by its major rise in population and economic strength, such that, whatever the per capita commitment to war, the Americans were able to devote resources that were far greater in aggregate terms than those of Canada.

This contrast returns attention to the nature of exceptionalism but, again, it is possible to note repeated parallels between America and Canada in the twentieth century. Important elements included the emphasis on power projection rather than home security, the generally peaceful nature of the Home Front, the need to adjust to the exigencies of alliance politics, and the impact of socio-cultural changes on assumptions about war-launching and war-fighting. At the same time, a chronological perspective on these parallels suggests that exceptionalism should be seen not as a set pattern of distinctive development, but as a pattern that was open to change, the point that emerges repeatedly in discussion of strategic culture. There was no clear tasking for the American military nor, indeed, for America as a major power. Instead, any consideration of the variety of tasks that had to be fulfilled, combined with the counterfactuals entailing other tasks considered by contemporaries that might have enlarged this list, suggests that there was no distinctive American tasking, on land or sea. In 1840–70, for example, there was war with Mexico and civil war, but conflicts with Britain and France were also possible, both linked to the Civil War and, in the cases of the Oregon Question and Mexico, separate to it. The ability of the USA, like that of Canada or any other state, to shape its military options, and thus accentuate and sustain distinctive features, indeed exceptionalism, has to be considered alongside a stress on the role of constraints in this development. This point underlines the complexity of the factors involved in what might constitute an exceptionalism, as well as the need to discuss American (or Canadian) developments not in terms of a clear contrast with those of Europe but rather as aspects of a diverse Western military history.

A major difference, however, is that Canadian forces always were more colonial than their American counterparts in their mentality, in the sense that the Canadians drew their inspiration for ideas about war and force structure from a predominant foreign model. The model was Britain up to 1945–50, and the USA more commonly thereafter, the latter an increasingly normal situation for Western powers after 1950. Another difference stemmed from the extent to which, in recent decades, Canadian forces were, and are, more alienated/marginalized than their American counterparts from the dominant political system at home, a political point that repays consideration when organizational culture is discussed. Moreover, military institutions have been greater players in Washington decisionmaking than have their Canadian equivalents.

The political context for America and Canada was one of contrasting strategic cultures. From the start, the USA often believed it had external threats from which it must defend itself through force. It always used its armed forces in a classic fashion as a tool of state, under its direct national control, to achieve hard-headed (but not necessarily clear-sighted) state interests: the USA expanded across the continent from 1783 to 1900 because it defeated or overawed its neighbours. In turn, in 1917 and, even more, 1940–1, the combination of real dangers and its own latent power forced the USA into abandoning isolationism and becoming the world's dominant state.

During the nineteenth century, Canada could never have defended itself against the USA; but Britain did so. Meanwhile, as part of the imperial system, Canada loaned its forces to Britain, which greatly affected the nature of Canadian militarism[31] and meant that, in both world wars, Canada was immediately drawn in (and its resources tapped intensively and fast), unlike its isolationist neighbour. Per capita, Canada mattered more in those wars than the USA did; and in 1917–18, mattered more absolutely on the Western Front than the American army did. Moreover, between 1940 and 1960, Canada punched far above its weight in terms of military power, and diplomatic influence, and it mattered to the world. Since the early twentieth century, meanwhile, Canada has been protected from external danger by its neighbour, which is its guardian and therefore the greatest threat to its autonomy.

Seen from a different perspective, which underlines the problems with employing the concept of strategic culture, Canada has not used its forces explicitly to pursue state interests without a policy of loaning them to some international organization, be it the British empire, the UN or NATO, each of which Canadians thought could help maintain a liberal political and economic order across the world. Since Confederation in 1867, Canadians have never used Canadian forces in direct service of their interests, not even in the emblematic case of 1939. Instead, they define their interests as being those of the world community. In fact, Canadians never have had to be responsible for their own security, yet power and strategy have been central to their survival. That is, Canadians actually mattered a lot and projected much power, but never for simple reasons of state (or national) interest; and always this projection created political problems at home, especially with regard to Québec.

Admittedly, however, both the USA and Canada have always found it hard to admit that their forces are being used to pursue narrow selfish interests; hence, there is a high degree of rhetoric surrounding their usage.[32] Neither state likes to believe it is thinking or acting in a realist fashion, even when it is doing so.

Considering Canadian and American developments within a diverse Western tradition offers some guidance to their future character, more particularly if that is seen in the long term. However, politics is the art of the short term, if not generally the episodic, and, from that context, it is the contrast in the public cultures of the two states that are readily apparent. Although isolationism retains a powerful purchase in the American public, government is able to draw on support for commitments presented as necessary, and it is not essential to locate these in multilateral envelopes. The post-1945 Canadian public culture of force has been different, and this contrast has to be set alongside the possibility of discerning similarities at the functional level. Yet, an emphasis on the way in which events can shape military cultures underlines the extent to which there is nothing fixed in apparent national differences and invites a sense of indeterminacy when considering the future.

With reference to ideas of national exceptionalism, the concept of strategic culture does have to address the fact of the heavily contested character of national interests, as well as the impact of contingency and the issue of consistency in the policies of particular states. Thus, there have been long-standing competing strands of thought within the evolution of the American army, strands that link differences in strategic and institutional culture.[33] The same is true of other armies.

In Quest of Symbols

There has been considerable scholarly interest of late also in symbolic aspects of the military and of war; although, by their nature, it is even more difficult to assess the relative importance of these aspects than when comparing several aspects of realist interpretation. Yet, a past failure to give due weight to the cultural contexts of warfare has ensured that much military history has devoted insufficient weight to these symbolic aspects, which include modes of fighting as well as a ritualization of combat and conflict that can affect, as well as reflect, tactical, operational and strategic goals.

It is also possible to present wars in a 'cultural' context as different from the more 'realist' conventional wars of the rivalry of states, not least by emphasizing psychological elements, such as honour,[34] in the causes and conduct of war. This emphasis on non-'realist' and non-materialist factors is especially important in understanding the causes of war. Rather than treating the latter in terms of rational drives and/or the operation of an international system, it is possible to draw attention to the cultural drives that make war seem welcome and desirable or, at least, less threatening.[35]

Cultural imperatives and weaponry have also been linked for much more recent times, as in the argument that the B-17 bomber embodied the dreams of glory of American air power enthusiasts, or Rachel Holloway's account of President Ronald Reagan's 'reinvigoration of the technological sublime', notably with his support for a Star Wars capability.[36] The current Iranian interest in missiles and atomic weaponry can be seen in the same light. There is a symbolic commitment to the issue that is separate to that of rational assessment. In the case of Saddam Hussein of Iraq, this symbolic value led him to claim, prior to his overthrow in 2003, the existence of weapons of mass destruction that had not in fact been manufactured. These claims provided a strategic culture that was based on an invented force.

The overlap of reality and fiction is particularly pertinent in the case of new and advanced weaponry. More generally, the role of cultural assumptions in the optimistic response to the whole idea of air capability, and the extent to which these assumptions vary within the organizational cultures of individual militaries, are clearly important to particular national cultures of air power.[37] There is no reason why this approach should not be more generally applied.

A Western Way of War?

'Culture', however, is a term also so widely and loosely used[38] as to have its analytical value at least in part compromised, a point that requires discussion whenever culture is deployed as a descriptive or, even more, explanatory category. Furthermore, the idea of a culture of warfare was politicized in the early 2000s in that the notion of a specifically Western way of war, moreover a particularly successful one, became an aspect of the American culture wars. This was especially the case with the bitter debate over the views of Victor Davis Hanson, an American military historian who actively developed this interpretation, notably in his *Carnage and Culture: Landmark Battles in the Rise of Western Power* (2001). These views apparently influenced Vice-President Dick Cheney[39] and greatly helped Hanson's career.

For some commentators, the notion of a Western way of war is a hostile response from within America to political correctness and multi-culturalism in American education. That view, however, is overly simplistic: it ignores the wider resonances of the subject, not least discussion about cultural factors outside the USA, as well as the extent to which concern, both there and elsewhere, with cultural issues was a response to conflict with non-Western forces, especially the experience of the Korean and Vietnam Wars. The last was a theme most recently revived, with different opponents, in Afghanistan and Iraq. Thus, the stress on the cultural dimension is, in part, a result of an awareness of multi-culturalism in global military affairs, even if the response to this awareness can lead to arguments of particular cultural superiority.

To take another approach, there is a contemporary political aspect to this discussion, as belief in the special effectiveness of a Western cultural type of war-making provided encouragement to those encouraging American interventionism in the 2000s, such as Hanson, and will maybe, under different circumstances and with other writers, continue to do so. The notion of a specifically Western way of war, however, flagrantly simplifies the West, and thereby ignores diversity within the West, including what has been a frequent reluctance to engage in battle; and this notion also seriously simplifies the non-West, both by consolidating it as a unit and by simplifying it as a force. Thus, for example, the dichotomy of a Western preference for open battle versus Oriental trickery is doubly flawed. This dichotomy is also an aspect of the divide between the sometimes oversimplified notions of culture used within military history and the more promising approaches elsewhere within the intellectual marketplace. Similar points can be made about ideas of an Islamic way of war.

A Variety of Cultures

The looseness, and therefore flexibility and extendability, of the cultural interpretation of war, however, can in itself be instructive, as it encourages a focus on the impact and role of ideas and assumptions. These, in turn, affect the very process of military history. For example, the study of combat styles has been seen as indicating the possibilities that a borrowing from other disciplines offers military history.

Furthermore, returning to more functional considerations of the cultural dimension, the varied nature of assumptions affecting military capability and its assessment encourages a departure from the more structured, and apparently clear cut, ranking of militaries that arises when the focus, instead, is on weaponry and organization. In practice, these issues are not separate, as cultural factors help to explain why particular weapons, such as firearms, or organizational systems, for example conscription, are adopted or discarded in individual states (or cultures) with contrasting consequences. These factors have been employed to discuss developments such as the willingness or otherwise to adopt handguns in Mamluk Egypt and seventeenth-century Japan. Such developments were linked to an important goal and means of military culture, namely honour and reputation.[40]

More generally, even though 'culture' is used somewhat loosely as an analytical term, it provides a valuable way of bringing together the varied dimensions of warfare – organization, tasking, 'war and society', and the 'face of battle'; each of which indeed has a highly significant cultural dimension, and a dynamic character to that as well. For example, the change in the French army with the French Revolution can be related to a shift from a 'battle culture of forbearance' to one of attack in which tactical order played a smaller role.[41] An emphasis on culture also offers a more relativist mode of explanation in military history, notably by comparing the strategic and organizational cultures of competing states and their militaries, rather than by measuring them against an absolute or, apparently, universal scale of technological capacity or proficiency, as in the generally misleading attempt to assess which is the 'best' army in the Second World War. As an example of organizational factors, views on military promotion up the ranks, and the related practices, reflect cultural factors. In the Second World War, the British army showed a tendency in promotions to value personal recommendation over specialist expertise or operational experience, a value that matched the nature of the norms in British society.

The pursuit of the idea of the 'best' army, or of better armies, as in the work of Max Hastings on 1944–5,[42] reflects problems with the idea of employing cultural classification in the shape of national distinctiveness, as it is unclear that differences at the aggregate, national, level are more pertinent than variations within armies, for example between individual divisions[43] or between élite *Wehrmacht* units and the bulk of the German divisions, which tended to be far less well equipped and to fight with less determination. This stress on an élite can be discussed in functional military terms of the allocation of troops and *matériel*, but also reflected the assumptions of the *Wehrmacht* and the ideology of the Nazi regime, each of which can be considered in cultural terms. Similar points can be made about many other militaries, and indeed about the forces of individual societies as a whole. Thus, under Saddam Hussein, there was a contrast between the élite Revolutionary Guards and the bulk of the army. This point is also pertinent for irregulars. As a result, it is unhelpful to discuss aggregate military characteristics without also underlining differences.

This is an instance of a more general relativist approach, one that needs to be open to the variety of military cultures across the world, past and present (and, planners note, future as well). This openness means not only an interest in non-Western developments, but also an understanding of their variety and complexity – as well as the avoidance of misleading approaches to the respective capability of West and 'non-West', and to warfare between them. This openness challenges model-based approaches that emphasize apparently scientific analysis, and that are designed to demonstrate universal laws. To do so, these approaches focus on a limited and readily defined group of conflicts and military systems. Such an openness to the variety, and importance, of cultures is at variance with the pronounced dominance of Western assumptions, paradigms and examples in military history. Thus, one instance of 'cultural' analysis limits another, which is a consequence of the widely ranging nature of the use of the language of culture. In short, the cultural approach also relates to the practice of military analysis, its subject, content and themes, and this point should be an important theme in discussion of the cultural angle.

Across both time and space, the cultural specificity of particular types of warfare emerges as a building block for analysis, indeed the key building block. As such, this cultural specificity displaces attention from a crudely functionalist account of military capability, effectiveness and success, one based on the appropriate use of resources and technology and on the maximization of the latter. Instead, the idea of the appropriate is discussed in terms of the assumptions and ideology, in short, culture, of particular societies. However, that in part begs the question of the scale of units of analysis, say from Islam to a particular Muslim tribe, and also the degree of continuity that is anticipated, and thus used to underline a form of cultural essentialism.

The Presentist Culture of Military History: The Case of the Revolution in Military Affairs

Military history is not in some fashion separate from contemporary discussion about war; nor from the general currents of historical thought. Indeed, the combination of both help shape it, although any account of that shaping has to allow for the partly autonomous nature of the particular discipline and of the writers, publishers and readers involved in it. Indeed, this interplay requires an explicit discussion, because there is a misleading tendency to push these factors to the background. Instead, the perception and analysis of military history are both products of shifting assumptions. Thus, culture is both an analytical construction (or, rather, a number of different constructions), and also a perception that reflects changing moods.

The historical moment for the modern cultural assessment is clear cut; although there were also earlier such assessments that are of considerable interest and that provide valuable insights on recent and current developments. This historical moment is that of the last decade and, in particular, of the unravelling of the confidence displayed in the 1990s about the extent to which embracing and shaping technological developments provided the opportunity for carrying through a Revolution in Military Affairs (RMA) that allegedly constituted a paradigm shift in military capability and effectiveness, in short a transformation. Far from being restricted to technology, the RMA rested on a holistic interaction between it and the concepts and force structure that would provide maximum effect.[44]

The belief in the RMA was particularly strong in the USA, and remains significant, although the term usually employed now is that of transformation.[45] This belief was also embraced elsewhere, in part as a way of responding to the USA, at least by maintaining the interoperability seen as necessary for taking part in joint operations. This belief accorded with ideological drives and demands of the period, but also with specific political and military requirements, and with the struggle (debate is too mild a word) over resources within the military and the related military–industrial complex. These factors were interrelated, which underlines the problem with separating out only one theme for analysis. For example, political conjuncture was important as the demise of the Soviet Union and the end of the Cold War led to pressure in the West for a 'peace dividend' in the shape of lower military expenditure. This pressure interacted with a reluctance to raise taxes or increase borrowing. The net effect was one in which branches of the military sought to demonstrate their particular value in order to preserve their position.

Before considering these points, a note on the mixed relationship between academics and the RMA is relevant. In part, there were the issues of influence and relevance, issues that also play a role in discussion of cultural factors today. The wealthiest military, that of the USA, sponsors conferences and also treats history as an important aspect of its military education, not only for those entering the military but also for internal promotion, especially to, and in, command ranks. Without suggesting any undue influence, and, as an outsider, it is striking how very free debate is within much of the American military; this situation can obviously affect the subject of linked academic discussion in the USA. There are related pressures elsewhere, including in Britain. Indeed, against a background of a serious fiscal situation, cultural factors can serve there (and elsewhere) as an explanation of apparently how best to compensate for a relative lack of resources, with relevant situational awareness, for example, seen as a crucial force multiplier.

The 'space' for would-be objective academic debate is limited in many countries, in part because military analysis has not developed in the universities, a situation that owes much to an anti-militaristic ethos[46] and to political developments,[47] and in part because the pressures within, and from, the military are very much for analysis to accord with current military doctrine. The extent to which this is the case is underplayed in anglophone discussion, because the cultural norm in most English-speaking states is one of free enquiry; but, aside from the significant limitations in practice in anglophone states, this situation is not more generally relevant.

As far as the USA was concerned, the belief of the 1990s and early 2000s in the RMA made historical and cultural aspects of military analysis appear far less relevant, if not completely irrelevant. The conviction that a paradigm shift in capability had occurred, or was occurring, or would occur – and there was a disturbing lack of precision on these points – was, at once, historical and cultural in nature and, paradoxically, a denial of such factors, as if the paradigm meant moving beyond history. In practice, belief in *the* RMA, or *a* RMA (and, again, there was a worrying lack of precision comparable to that of the 'end of history' or the 'clash of civilizations'), represented another iteration of a pronounced trophe in modern Western culture, namely that which put a stress on change and an emphasis on machines and, in doing so, reflected and sustained the assumption of a hierarchy of military proficiency defined by technology. There was a definition of past ages in terms of their material culture, notably the Stone, Bronze and Iron Ages, and a stress on past revolutions in capability stemming from new technologies, particularly the stirrup, gunpowder, steam energy and nuclear power. Reference was made to these past changes when discussing the current situation. The fixation on technological progress is central to that of a focus on what is seen as progress that is very important to the American cultural imagination. In particular, the RMA resumed the earlier stress on the transformative character of air power.[48]

This technological focus, however, represented a serious misreading of military capability and proficiency, and indeed of military history, although it was scarcely a new focus. The emphasis on technological change was one that had become particularly strong with nineteenth-century industrialization, which itself demonstrates the contingent nature of intellectual analyses and cultural moods. However, this emphasis was already in play earlier, not least with the self-conscious awareness of differing military forms that can be seen with, and from, the European Renaissance of the fifteenth century. This awareness helped underline both the possibility of major change through time and also the extent to which this change could be linked with a powerful cultural relativism between different developments in competing societies.

Christendom and Islam

A crucial point in the last was the reading, indeed re-reading, of the long-standing clash between Christendom and Islam. Although, in practice, conflict was not continual, while Muslim societies devoted more time to conflict with each other rather than with the West (and Western states did the same), this clash could be read in existential terms, indeed, to employ Samuel Huntington's phrase from the 1990s, as a clash of civilizations. As a consequence, there was a long-standing concern among European commentators to explain how best to protect Christendom from the advance of Islam. This concern owed much to the extent to which Christendom appeared to be in retreat from the twelfth century on, repeating the earlier cataclysm seen with the original Islamic advances in the seventh and eighth centuries. In the eleventh century, William of Tyre observed 'War is waged differently and less vigorously between men who hold the same law and faith. For even if no other cause for hatred exists, the fact that the combatants do not share the same articles of faith is sufficient reason for constant quarrelling and enmity.'[49] Jerusalem, a key reality, as well as symbol, of Christianity, lost in the seventh and regained again at the close of the eleventh century, was conquered anew for Islam in 1187, and the Crusader states in the Near East were finally extinguished with the fall of Acre in 1291.

By then, Byzantium, the Eastern Roman empire, was a fraction of its former strength, and, in the fourteenth century, the Ottoman Turks invaded the Balkans, turning back to finish off Constantinople (Istanbul) itself in 1453. Subsequent Ottoman progress was not without serious setbacks, for example at Belgrade in 1456 and Rhodes in 1480, but seemed inexorable and, indeed, an apocalyptic threat. By 1520, when Süleyman the Magnificent came to the Ottoman throne, the Ottomans were in control of most of the Balkans and had recently, in 1516–17, conquered the Mamluk empire, adding Egypt, Syria and Palestine to their dominions and, as rulers of the Hejaz, becoming the protectors of the sacred sites of Mecca and Medina. The 1520s brought the total defeat of the kingdom of Hungary and in 1529 the Ottomans besieged Vienna, albeit unsuccessfully.

This advance, like the brief occupation of Otranto in southern Italy in 1480–1, in practice proved the effective limit of an advance that had seemed to overrun the Continent, although not the limit for the range of Ottoman capability in Europe, for Cyprus (1570–1) and Crete (1645–68) were to be prominent among later gains. Like many measures of military effectiveness, the question of how best to respond to the Ottomans coincided with the rebirth of interest in the Classical past during the Renaissance. That renewal encouraged a new cultural fixing of the apparent relationship between Christendom and Islam with a search for ready reference between Antiquity and Modernity. This search, which was dramatically seen in the painter Albrecht Altdorfer's depiction of the victorious Macedonians of Alexander the Great at the battle of Issus (333 BCE) as modern European warriors, led to an adoption by Renaissance writers of the Classical Greeks' account of their confrontations with Persia, notably the Persian invasions of 490 and 480 BCE. These invasions were presented in terms of resistance to a brutal and expansionist power and, crucially, a power with far greater military resources, both on land and at sea. A far from nuanced account of Persian power was offered. In reality many Greek states did not resist the Persians in 480 BCE, and some allied with the Persian emperor Xerxes, but that was not a narrative welcome in the Renaissance, other than in suggesting the need for vigilance against backsliding in the Christian camp.

For the Renaissance, the emphasis again was on virtue rather than weaponry, crudely culture not technology; although it is dangerous to use generalizations for movements such as the Renaissance or the (later) Enlightenment without noting a diversity of tendencies and variety of circumstances. Nevertheless, whereas gunpowder was shared with the Ottomans, who had particularly successful siege cannon as well as effective *janissary* infantry armed with handguns; this sharing was not the case, it was claimed during the Renaissance, of the Christian virtue displayed in resistance to them. Thus, culture served Christian commentators as an explanation both of conflict and of respective capability.

At the same time, this cultural dimension did not lead to a reliance on zeal nor on any sense of superiority. Instead, there was a determined attempt to employ information and experience as aspects of a clearly understood learning curve. If this does not apply the term culture overly loosely, this process can be regarded as a key aspect of the Western response. It was present, in particular, with developments in ballistics and fortification, as well as in the use of information to help conceptualize and understand the working of a multi-polar international system. The understanding and use of information emerges as a sphere in which cultural and technological factors overlapped.

It would be mistaken to imagine that this process was solely seen in the West, and, if less is known about its characteristics and extent in other cultures, the situation is better than was the case even thirty years ago.[50] Non-Western powers, such as Ottoman Turkey, Ming China, Tokugawa Japan and Mughal India, could make effective use of information, which is a key constituent and employment of power, and in significant respects this usage vied with those of the West until at least the eighteenth century. This capability can be presented as an aspect of the culture of power.

The Chinese information system proved highly effective in planning the deployment of power in the eighteenth century, against both Tibet and the Dsunghars of Xinjiang, into the Eurasian 'Heartland', to employ a later term which itself has a cultural resonance. Chinese usage of information rested on an effective communication system. Aside from improving the flow of information, and, crucially, providing the predictability that made the use of information an integral part of planning, the communication system – roads, canals and, fundamentally, supply depots – made it possible to move large quantities of resources. As a result, eastern China was able to support power projection into the 'Heartland' by moving resources to the internal frontier, a movement that, in part, rested on cultural/ideological assumptions about a necessary military superiority in this area so as to preserve the order of being focused on the superior position of the Chinese emperor.

Thanks to an effective system, Indian rulers accumulated information about the situation both within their own territories and externally. This system was to be taken over the British alongside their understanding and, thus successful use, of military labour markets, and local economic and financial systems. The Ottomans benefited from the presentation of information in a relatively sophisticated fashion, both on the empire and on lands further afield. Ottoman land and revenue surveys and descriptions of frontiers afforded the Ottoman government knowledge of its resources, as well as helping to delineate the otherwise porous frontier of the empire.[51]

The context within which the relationship between West and non-West was judged changed from the 1680s, with consequences for the conceptualization of power. Whereas the Ottoman failure in besieging Vienna in 1529 was one essentially arising from the problems of campaigning at the distant edge of empire, and was not marked by the defeat of the main Ottoman army, the situation was very different in 1683. Furthermore, whereas Ottoman failure in 1529 did not prevent Ottoman advances and successes until 1566, the situation was radically different after 1683. This was true both in the early years, and also in the century 1690–1790 as far as the trend of success was concerned: Ottoman successes occurred, notably in 1715 in southern Greece and in 1739 in northern Serbia, but could not reverse the key Western triumphs, particularly the conquest of Hungary.

Information Culture and the Rise of the West

This changing context lessened the need for any Western Thermopolyae complex in which vulnerable and greatly outnumbered forces relied on willpower in mounting resistance, as with the Spartans at Thermopolyae against the Persian invaders in 480 BCE. Nevertheless, combining notes of heroic resolution, Christian martyrdom and racial superiority, this theme of resistance against the odds appealed to Western public opinion, as with the prominence given to the successful British defence of the South African outpost of Rorke's Drift against Zulu attack in 1879, and also equivalents for other countries.

Instead of considering how to maintain a threatened military position, the emphasis in the West from the eighteenth century was on how best to advance control and to secure advances, an emphasis that encouraged a more technocratic approach. Moreover, an aspect of this was provided by the conviction that Western superiority pertained both in knowledge and in its application; and this superiority was regarded as utilitarian and also as providing evidence of greater moral worth, as well as racial, religious and cultural superiority.[52] The use of knowledge was linked to the stereotyping of opponents and thus to the rationale of warfare and conquest, as in the British wars with the Xhosa in southern Africa between 1834 and 1853.[53] The conviction of such Western superiority, a cultural factor, needs underlining, since the modern tendency to counterpoint technological and moral factors has to be reconsidered in light of the worth placed on technology and, indeed, the extent to which it is in part a social construction.

The latter point can be highlighted by assessing the cultural aspect of the information systems that were central to Western capability and power-projection, while accepting that such an analysis risks a new Whiggish approach to the rise of the West. Thus, a relative lack of commitment to maritime activity and naval strength in the eighteenth century, which can be regarded as a cultural slant true of most, but not all, Islamic societies, impoverished the non-Western empires, not as land powers at the time but in so far as information acquisition and assessment were concerned. In particular, navigational/astronomical methods and empirical, knowledge-based, practices of organizing new, and reviewing existing, information were important to the West. Maritime activity played a major role in developing a technical intelligentsia, as with the School of Mathematics and Navigation, which opened in Moscow in 1701, an institution important to Peter the Great's effort to create a Russian navy. These methods and practices of information were increasingly integrated from the late eighteenth century. The issues of that era were confronted in the West within the context of an intellectual culture organized on the basis of a self-conscious rationalism devoted to the new.[54]

War helped to enhance the drive for information, as its different levels involved particular requirements. The tactical dimension required an understanding of terrain, both of the details and of what they entailed. The operational dimension necessitated an appreciation of territory and such questions as what resources could be obtained from particular areas. The strategic dimension required a grasp of the relationship between control over territory and the understanding of how best to conceptualize and achieve the goals of victory. Operations at sea led to pressure for an increase in information, not only charting of waters and coasts, but also currents and winds, and on a global scale.

The representation and reproduction of such information also became regular and more fixed. Thus, the density of the information matrix was enhanced in response to specific requirements and, once enhanced, became normative. In turn, this process encouraged the idea that information definition and acquisition were both dynamic processes.

On the world scale, the West became distinctive for a successful interest in information both largely divorced from spiritual references, an important cultural point, and set in the guiding context of global information systems. This separation was natural in a society increasingly impressed by the idea that authority should take scientific form. The development was seen in the long-term impact of Cartesian thought and, subsequently, in the major attempt in Britain to reconcile revealed religion with the insights gained by Newtonian science – a science with Europe-wide prestige. This understanding of religion ensured that it did not act as a brake on new systems of understanding, nor as an ideology of conservatism.

In turn, science was both institutionalized at the state level in Europe and inserted into education systems. In the nineteenth century, Western spiritual renewal, in the form of evangelicalism, was largely compatible with utilitarianism, scientific attitudes and imperial expansion. The debate over geological knowledge and the Darwinian controversy are both instructive.

Although science offered apparently fixed answers, the process of scientific exposition entailed an inherent changeability stemming from new validation. For example, advances in measurement encouraged higher standards of accuracy and precision. In a Western culture that had embraced change, there was a continuous process of improvement and testing. In naval capability, the period from 1850 to 1910 brought the testing of new systems of armament, propulsion, firepower and communications, as well as experimentation with underwater and aerial warfare. The characteristics of particular combinations of material for use in armour, for example nickel-steel, were tested, as were oil-fired engines. The change in information systems from 1810 to 1910 was a greater transformation than in any previous century.

More generally, the emphasis on observation, experimentation and mathematics, seen also in astronomy, chemistry, physics and other branches of science, provided encouragement for information-gathering and for the use of data to help both decisionmaking and cycles of testing policies or products, and then amending them. As a consequence, there was a relative strengthening of Western capability and effectiveness,[55] not least through the borrowing of Western concepts of information by non-Western states such as Japan, which thus affirmed Western norms in measurement, for example of the Meridian and of time.

Across the world, the development of formal Intelligence processes, systems and institutions ushered in a new world of information acquisition and analysis. Information became Intelligence in a reflection of military value and use. Information was also a crucial adjunct to international capitalism, for example in the search for raw materials and, more generally, comparative advantage, to integrated production systems, and to multi-nationals. The role of capitalism was a product of the long-term relationship between information and commercial élites, and, again, cultural preferences were important, in this case in the shape of a willingness to reshape the social élite in order to participate in financial and industrial entrepreneurship. In trading states, the levers are controlled by complex commercial élites interested mostly in controlling flows and nodes. Surplus value comes from tapping into, creating and controlling flows of raw materials, goods, capital and labour (usually skilled). States are funded by taxes on these flows.

In territorial states, in contrast, and this was the case for most Islamic states, much smaller élites, composed mostly of landowners, controlled the levers and were interested primarily in extracting surplus values from direct ownership or taxation of land. Non-Western states, such as Persia/Iran and what later became Saudi Arabia, were essentially territorial powers, with limited élites extracting tax revenue from land (a process also later seen with oil), rather than commercial powers extracting revenue from trade flows. Once (some) Western powers understood how to restructure their organization around these flows, these powers were quickly able to surpass the ability of territorial states to generate surplus. The latter began an increasingly steep relative decline; this was the situation in the nineteenth century, notably for Persia.

The techniques available to the West were only very slowly or poorly adopted by most non-Europeans, and the contrast provided a dynamic edge to the Information Revolution. In historical order, this had a long genesis, but was particularly important in the nineteenth century. Thus, double-entry book-keeping, the development of national debts, atlases stressing routes and ports (nodes and flows), and insurance, were followed by packet boats (commonly used outside Europe from the 1820s), the telegraph (first terrestrial, then submarine), limited liability companies as a means of unlocking and organizing resources, and radio.

Within the West, the consequences of the Enlightenment and the American and French Revolutions included a new culture of strength: the changing understanding and use of information to advance power both internationally and domestically. 'Rationalism' as statecraft cannot be divorced from political contexts, nor these contexts from the reconceptualization of states and societies in terms of malleable entities that could, and should, be directed by information; the last very much seen with the French Revolution, but also, more generally, with nineteenth-century Western states. These ideas contributed to the growing development of a specifically Western information system, notably in comparison with the situation elsewhere and with reference to key issues at the point of contact, both in warfare and in imperial control.

The discussion of the understanding, and therefore, use of information as a form of cultural history underlines the wide-ranging and porous nature of the cultural definition, a characteristic that poses a major problem in terms of analytical rigour, if not value. There is also, again, a marked danger of adopting a Whiggish approach, but such Whiggism was (and is) itself a cultural characteristic (and product), and, at times, a resource or problem, the latter when it helped lead to a failure to understand other societies. Western capability as an aspect of an advancing and allegedly superior civilization was a theme that linked the post-Vienna (1683) situation to the confidence seen by American commentators from the Second World War to the Vietnam War.

Organizational Culture: The Whiggish Account Contested

Whiggism is also seen in the standard approach to military organization, that which emphasizes state control, bureaucratization and professionalism. However, the role of private contracting[56] and, even more, the history of private warfare[57] suggests that this account, and the cultural and intellectual values it represents, can be questioned.

The increased reliance by states on private military and security contractors is notable in recent decades, and is the case with both conflict and post-conflict situations. This development represents a significant change in the nature of military activity and one that challenges previous assumptions about the appropriate nature of military organization. In large part, the increased reliance on private military services is an aspect of the situation of flux in military activity that has characterized the years since the end of the Cold War.[58]

Historically, the role of private organizations reflects a range of factors, none of which has been of consistent importance. These factors include the extent to which states did not monopolize power, the role of military professionalism in warfare, and the extent to which this professionalism was a form of contracted labour, and one in which there was no necessary privilege for state employers.

Looked at differently, there were two main forms of military service; that for pay, in which there was a degree of volition; and service that was compulsory. The latter might be rewarded with money, but the cash nexus was not the main rationale. Compulsory military service was generally for the benefit of the state and at the behest of the ruler. Such service was therefore 'national', although that is to employ a terminology that was anachronistic for most of history, with the important exception of service from foreign captives. The range of the latter included those acquired as slaves from abroad, often an important source of manpower; and also combatants captured in war, and the latter practice continued across history. Frederick the Great (II) of Prussia used captured Saxon troops in the Seven Years War (1756–63).

Voluntary service for pay was of the essence of mercenary payment, but it has been redefined across history in order to ensure that such service is seen as virtuous if for one's own state/country/people/lord, and very much not so if for someone else's. This construction means much in the modern world, and helps locate private military service and organization in an ambiguous light, but the situation is far less secure in terms of historical judgement. Thus, a distinction between troops serving for pay and those serving for reasons of patriotism or ideology, does not capture the nature of military service across most of history because it rests on a social politics that is true for the modern world, but not earlier.

Opportunity and need co-existed in the past, as they do today. Private military service was frequently a matter of providing a service that could not so readily or securely be obtained by a particular employer. In antiquity, the Egyptians hired Numidian javelin throwers, the provision of whom could reflect payment but also other aspects of the complex relationship between powers, notably with overlordship mediated by the practicalities of ensuring support. Similarly, the Greeks hired slingers from Rhodes, archers from Crete, and light cavalry from Scythia and Thessaly. Christian heavy cavalry, which was not matched in Moorish al-Andalus (Andalusia) nor in North Africa, was in demand in the Middle Ages for military service in conflicts between Moorish states, providing a clear case for the appeal of hiring professionals across cultural lines.

Aside from issues of loyalty, as with the Carthaginian mercenaries after defeat by Rome in the First Punic War,[59] the professionalism of mercenary units willing to fight for any master was not able to compete with the large and effective professional state army of Republican and, later, Imperial Rome. The latter, indeed, represented a very different ethos and type of military structure, one that put its focus on scale as well as professionalism. This stress on numbers was antipathetical to the nature of private warfare, which could not match it.

This situation continues to the present day, with a contrast between warfare involving large numbers of effective troops – a situation in which there is scant role for mercenaries – and warfare involving smaller numbers: a situation in which mercenaries are more apt to flourish. This latter characteristic helps to explain why mercenaries have made a partial come-back in recent years. Like private military contractors in general, they are an aspect of the more widespread move of the modern state and contemporary warfare away from the numbers involved in the mass capability provided by conscription.

Mercenaries served (and serve) to ensure the diffusion of expertise and, crucially, new techniques. It was, and is, however, not necessary to rely on private markets and contractors to ensure such diffusion, as it can be provided by allied states. Indeed, military assistance of this type was common within and, in part a constituent of, alliances, imperial systems and practices of international military training and advice. Such assistance was a key means by which states exercised influence. This assistance and influence could, and can, be provided by the regular military, but states also used, and use, other formats for military assistance, including Intelligence agencies and private concerns. In part, reliance on these means was, and is, a matter of secrecy and in part a question of expertise and/or ease of use. In this, the provision of military advice and training was frequently linked to that of equipment, and the two should be seen as part of the same story. Alongside this private strand in state assistance, and overlapping with it, came the private strands arising from the activities of entrepreneurs and from the desire by local rulers and groups for military assistance from those who could provide it.

Across time, but, more particularly, in the nineteenth century, states increasingly became the expression of organized violence, a process that owed much to the ambition of governments to monopolize the use of such violence, at the expense, notably, of stateless mercenaries and pirates. The monopolization of violence became a definition of statehood as a functional rather than a legitimist understanding of rulership became more common. For example, in the nineteenth century, there was a decline in the number of private military practices as new norms were established.[60] Military entrepreneurship, the practice of hiring and being mercenaries, became less frequent, and this decline influenced relations between states and also those between states and non-state bodies. Subsidies and indirect recruiting were replaced by foreign aid and direct recruiting. The Crimean War (1854–6) was the last in which the British government recruited units of European foreign mercenaries for war service, namely the German, Swiss and Italian Legions.[61] As a different instance of increased government control, the red-shirted volunteer force with which Giuseppe Garibaldi conquered Sicily and Naples in 1860 was absorbed into the Italian army. When, in 1862, he subsequently formed a private army to capture Rome, then an independent Papal state, it was defeated by the Italian army. Such independence was no longer tolerable.

Similarly, authorized non-state violence, for example by privateers and by mercantile companies with territorial power, was eliminated in a piecemeal fashion, mostly in the nineteenth century. This process owed something to the degree to which these groups provoked inter-state conflicts, by being outside full state control, and much to a sense that they were anachronistic to states and societies that increasingly placed a premium on, and identified themselves through, rationality. This rationality was conceived of in terms of system, that is clearly defined organization and explicit rules of conduct, and state-directed systems. In 1898, the British government purchased the properties and claims of the Royal Niger Company, which brought it control of southern Nigeria and of the Company's army, the Royal Niger Constabulary. Moreover, the Jameson Raid on Transvaal in 1895, in order to try to stir up opposition there to Boer rule, was strongly criti-cized in Britain as well as unsuccessful.

Aside from authorized non-state violence, unauthorized non-state violence, particularly piracy and privately organized expeditions designed to seize territory, was also in large part stamped out in the nineteenth century. This process both demonstrated and enhanced the ability of states to monopolize power.[62]

Monopolization of violence was also linked to the internal paci-fication, and thus control, of societies. This pacification and control was a gradual process, the scale and scope of which varied greatly, and one that was to be challenged and, in part, reversed after 1945 with the rise of terrorism and other violent challenges to the author-ity of the state. Nevertheless, governments sought to prevent the use of organized violence for the pursuit of domestic political objectives, and also took steps against feuds.

At the personal level, the activity of the state was less insistent, but measures were, nevertheless, taken to abolish, or at least limit, duel-ling, and to restrict the ownership of arms. The last greatly restricted the scope for unauthorized private military forces. In particular, arms that had a battlefield capability were monopolized by governments on land and at sea, as were fortifications. Thus, the restriction of the ownership of arms was co-terminous with the greater emphasis on conscription in the nineteenth century, underlining the determination of governments to control both the practice of mass recruitment and its consequences. Nationalism was a significant aspect of the politics of this process.

From the perspective of these changes in the nineteenth and early twentieth centuries, the situation today seems very different, but it is important to put the rise of private military companies,[63] in the context of a series of interlinked changes. First, need is a key issue. A spiral of economic weakness, social breakdown and political instability poses problems not only for states but also for companies seeking to operate in unstable states. This situation is more generally significant because much of the world's raw-material production and reserves are located in such countries. As a result, production and shipment facilities have to be protected, whether oil platforms, and now shipments, off the Nigerian coast, oil pipelines in the Caucasus, or copper mines in Bougainville. This need has led to a major rise in private military companies providing corporate stability. These companies play a crucial role in protecting not only assets but also the transfer of capital flows for their clients.[64] Such private security is particularly important in Africa and is a fast-growing industry that benefits from a lack of regulation which is also very troubling.[65]

At the same time, this process is an aspect of the professionalism of force that, more generally, can be seen with the abandonment of conscription. This development has led to a change in the availability of military protection and, in part, private security and para-military companies have risen to fill the gap. The privatization of war appears less obvious from the perspective of high-spectrum capability, notably rocketry, satellites and air power, although much of this capability is produced and maintained by companies that are dependent on private investors and pension funds. At sea, private companies are hired to protect ships and oil facilities from pirates, guerrillas and terrorists, but the options for naval conflict are securely within the state ambit. Indeed, the key questions of naval capability, those of Chinese developments and their challenge to the USA and India, bear scant reference to the question of privatization.

This point underlines the extent to which the idea of 'war among the people' as the pattern for future conflict[66] may well be yesterday's story. Such conflict will continue, and may well become more serious in the only partly controlled large urban spaces of the world, such that vigilantes and organized vigilantism become a more significant aspect of conflict.[67] However, 'war among the people' is unlikely to describe the nature of confrontation between the major states. Paradoxically, this situation may provide more opportunities for private security and para-military companies, as well as for para-military police forces. Many militaries may need to focus on the consequences of confrontations and arms races between states. Thus, civil security and control, domestic and foreign, will appear a different task requiring another solution.

Africa may well be a key area where mercenaries are employed, as in the unsuccessful attempt to overthrow the government of Equatorial Guinea in 2004;[68] but it is also important to consider American influence, not least as the USA is currently the major provider and client of private military services. First, it is the world's leading economy, and therefore able to afford such activity, an ability enhanced by the extent of debt financing and the willingness to borrow. Secondly, the USA has particularly far-flung strategic and economic interests, indeed interests that span the world. Thirdly, the USA has a relatively small military for the size of its population or, rather, it has the world's most expensive military but much of this expenditure is devoted to new-spectrum weaponry, and the manpower available is limited at least in so far as commitments are concerned. This situation has been greatly exacerbated by the ending of conscription under President Nixon. Fourthly, as a free-market economy with a considerable degree of governmental de-centralization, there are 'spaces' for private, non-state activity that are greater than in other leading states, while there is also a tradition of light regulation that in theory reflects the limited extent of governmental authority and that in practice, even in that light, can be very limited. This situation creates a challenge to attempts to create global codes of conduct.

These trends came to a head after the end of the Cold War, in order to provide an environment in which private military services flourished. In particular, the end of the Cold War led to the government's attempt to find and exploit a 'peace dividend'. Under President Clinton (1993–2001), the size of the American military was cut by one third and weapons procurement was reduced. Operational pressures, however, mounted. American force reductions made it increasingly likely that a major commitment would be launched with inadequate strength and/or would entail the calling on of additional resources: coalition allies, local allies in the country of operation, or private military services. President George H. W. Bush's intention that the USA would be able to launch two Desert Storm (1991 Gulf War)-scale operations concurrently had to be abandoned, which led to pressure for greater effectiveness from smaller forces and also to concern about the ability to call on allies. In part, these factors drove a key aspect of American military policy up to 2003, the commitment to the potential of and for what was seen as a Revolution in Military Affairs stemming from new technology and organizational methods.

This form of war-making came to a head in Operation Iraqi Freedom, the American-led and dominated campaign in Iraq in 2003, a campaign characterized by the deployment of far fewer troops than those used in 1991 and than had been called for by the American army. The subsequent insurgency in Iraq led to a major pressure on American manpower, one accentuated by the spread and length of the insurrection. This pressure encouraged the privatization of some military functions, although contractor activity in combat service support had existed in the Korean and Vietnam wars and had grown greatly in the 1990s.[69]

In Iraq, there was the additional factor that lines of authority were unclear, with the Americans finding it difficult to maintain effective administrative structures, in large part because they had seriously misunderstood the nature of Iraqi society and politics and lacked a feasible post-conquest political strategy. In the absence of an Iraqi military and police upon which they could rely, the Americans sought to provide security by means of contracts with private security companies. By the end of May 2009, there were 32 private security companies operating in Iraq, and 132,610 'contractors', of whom 36,000 were Iraqis. In 2004, the British company Aegis Defence Services won a $293 million contract from the American army to co-ordinate the work of all the security companies involved in reconstruction in Iraq. The Aegis CEO, Lieutenant-Colonel Tim Spicer, had been linked to the Sandline affair in 1998, selling arms in war-torn Sierra Leone, contrary to a UN embargo.

The most prominent private security company was Blackwater Worldwide, now known as Xe. This company was founded by Erik Prince, a wealthy veteran with political connections to the Republicans. He had personally financed the formation of Blackwater in 1997, and the company provided numerous guards in Iraq in 2003. These guards were involved in some key episodes there, notably an ambush in Fallujah in 2003 in which four of them were killed. Their burnt and mutilated bodies were hung from a bridge; and both the ambush and the American military response were key episodes in the acceleration of the insurrection.

Blackwater became highly controversial in Iraq, and came to signify the world of private security companies. As such, it characterized a sense of lawlessness on the part of the coalition presence. This outcome was unwelcome, and ironic, as the Americans had repeatedly attempted to advance and define a legal basis for their presence and activities. As an aspect of the American presence, the private security companies enjoyed immunity from Iraqi law until the beginning of 2009. Their activities proved particularly controversial on 16 September 2007: seventeen Iraqis died in a shoot-out involving a Blackwater convoy in Nisour Square, Baghdad, while, that month, Nouri al-Maliki, the Iraqi Prime Minister, unsuccessfully pressed for Blackwater to be expelled from Iraq. Providing another aspect of the cultural question, the demeanour and behaviour of the company's employees proved highly provocative. They were heavily armed, wore body armour, and drove fast through the streets in armoured vehicles with tinted windows. As a consequence, the Blackwater employees appeared alien. Their conduct was also threatening, notably their tendency, in response to the danger from suicide bombers, to level weapons at civilians who came too close, especially at civilian vehicles.

The reputation of Blackwater was further tarnished in affidavits lodged in a Virginia court on 5 August 2009 as part of a motion lodged by lawyers representing sixty Iraqi civilians suing Blackwater for alleged crimes. Two former employees claimed that, alongside bad conduct, such as the use of excessive force and the employment of illegal exploding bullets, Blackwater adopted a political stance. One of the affidavits stated that Erik Prince, Blackwater's founder and owner, and the chairman of the board, saw himself 'as a Christian crusader tasked with eliminating Muslims and the Islamic faith from the globe'; that his companies 'encouraged and rewarded the destruction of Iraqi life'; that Prince deliberately sent men to Iraq 'who shared his vision of Christian supremacy, knowing and wanting these men to take every available opportunity to murder Iraqis. Many of these men used call signs based on the Knights of the Templar, the warriors who fought the crusades'; and that Blackwater employees routinely employed racist and derogatory terms. This affidavit linked the issues of organization and cultural assumptions.

Indicating that Blackwater was outside the control of the state, one of the affidavits claimed that Blackwater was guilty not only of these criminal activities, but also of direct defiance of the American government in the shape of tax evasion, of destroying incriminating videos, e-mails and documents, and of murdering or having murdered 'one or more persons who have provided information, or who were planning to provide information, to the federal authorities about the ongoing criminal conduct'.[70] The Iraqi response was instructive. Tahsin al-Shekhli, a spokesman for the Defence Ministry, was quoted as saying 'The company is mainly made up of mercenaries who lack high standards and discipline like official forces of international institutions. They needlessly massacred Iraqi citizens, and in cold blood.'[71]

The need for numbers of skilled personnel greater than those that can be provided by the regular military will remain an urgent problem for the USA. Similarly, such companies offer an important capability to other powers, such as Australia.[72] The development of an international approach to the regulation of private military companies and private security companies in situations of armed conflict represents a convergence of issues of force and legality. This convergence can be seen as reflecting a cultural preference for control in the shape of codes of international law addressing the relationships between state and sub-state actors, and establishing clearly the patterns of responsibility and accountability. A Whiggish approach to organizational culture and related norms scarcely exhausts the issue; and, instead, the unpredictable nature of change emerges.[73]

Responding to Circumstances

The role and acceptability of private military contractors indicate the complexity of the relationships between military cultures (in the sense of assumptions about the use of power) and general cultural characteristics. This point is also true of the willingness to endorse technology as a proof and enabler of virtuous, and thus necessary, power. Linked to this comes the question of the extent to which cultural norms lead societies to respond optimistically or pessimistically to international circumstances. There is also the question whether cultural characteristics such as optimistic, pessimistic, offensive and defensive in practice entail a response that is as much about perception as reality. Defensive societies may be more likely to resort to a cultural pessimism and vice versa, but such pessimism did, and does, not have simply one manifestation. In particular, such pessimism can encourage a defiant search for military elements that might be likely to redress what appear to be adverse circumstances, as well as launching wars designed to prevent a deterioration in circumstances, as Germany did in 1914, Japan in 1941, and Israel in 1967; not to suggest any equivalence between their political systems. Both technology and cultural factors, such as bravery, can be seen as redressing elements, with a classic instance of these cultural factors being the proclaimed role of individual fighting prowess as opposed to the firepower offered by allegedly less noble societies. That technological accounts of military proficiency can arise from both optimistic and pessimistic analyses of international circumstances indicates the complexity of the situation being addressed when the culture of war is considered.

This complexity underlines the conceptual poverty, or at least limitations, of much modern discussion of military history. There is a tendency to revert to the same, very small, group of thinkers, both in military and in naval history, and that is not terribly helpful because the usual suspects, whether Clausewitz or Cobbett, Jomini or Mahan, Sun Tzu or Mao, were writing with reference to the particular contexts of their time and indeed were very much guided by their own experiences and problems. As a result, it is important to understand military writers as products of their place and time, and the same point can be made about subsequent attempts to use these writers.[74] This is especially true of Clausewitz who, despite attempts to present him as of lasting value,[75] is best explained in terms of the trajectory of Prussia's circumstances, and the character of German philosophy during his lifetime. The alternatives to understanding writers as products of a specific environment are grim, notably supposedly timeless searches for universal truths of leadership, strategy or whatever; and the idea of fixed cultural characteristics can be seen as an aspect of this concept of universal truth, and as similarly lacking in context.

Moreover, the supposedly timeless answers generally turn out to contain a large dose of presentism, which is an abiding fault with military analysis. For example, in his *The First Total War: Napoleon's Europe and the Birth of Warfare As We Know It* (2007), David Bell drew a parallel between hopes, in France in 1789–90 and in the West in 1989–90 that the age of war was over; hopes that in each case were rapidly superseded. He then found parallels between the warfare, arguing that the insurrections facing the Revolutionary and Napoleonic French prefigured the situation in Vietnam and then 'the uncannily similar situation that unfolded in Iraq after the American victory in 2003'.[76] In practice, this comparison was weak, for insurrectionary war was not the prime problem facing the Revolutionaries nor Napoleon.[77] As a result, the comparison is unhelpful unless presented (as Bell failed to do) in a far more 'open' or suggestive fashion.

Each of the analytical approaches, the context and the consistent, suffers from the difficulties of explaining change other than in fairly simple terms, which, more generally, is a problem with the cultural theme. Indeed 'the culture of war' is essentially a static concept. As such, those who employ it face the problem of deciding how best to understand change, and notably without resorting to Whiggish platitudes and/or to a structural account that lacks sufficient room for agency. Is it to be assumed that change in a military system is a constant process as it adjusts to circumstances? Alternatively, is it the case that the idea of a culture of war implies a fundamental conservatism, and that change is only accounted for from the pressure of external forces, notably if there are serious discontinuities in the context and, more particularly, if a serious defeat is involved? The impact on the Safavids of Persia (Iran) of defeat at the hands of the Ottomans in 1514 can be seen as an instance as it led them to take a greater interest in firearms.

Of course, a perception of failure does not have to lead to a change of course as it can result, instead, in a determination to avoid the recurrence of similar problems. Arguably, this was the case with the American army after the Vietnam War, as the lesson learned was one of focusing on the Cold War in Europe, and not on counterinsurgency operations in the Third World. The customary approach is to argue that this was a mistake as the army should have trained for such operations,[78] the resulting mistake helping to lead to serious problems from the aftermath of the conquest of Iraq in 2003 onwards.

Such an approach is seductive, but also entails problems. First, there is the assumption, in this case as in others, that success can be ensured provided the correct method is followed, in short that strategic issues are swallowed by operational problems, and operational by tactical, such that resolving the lower level solves the higher one. Such an approach is a cardinal fault in much military analysis, especially among those who do not wish to address strategic issues and, more particularly, the politics of tasking. Secondly, there is the related focus on fulfilling the task irrespective of constraints.

Both of these assumptions can be queried, not least by adopting the counter-argument that it is best to frame strategic goals with reference to what can most readily be achieved, and with a high level of certainty. To do so entails not assuming that problems can be resolved by the application of effort but, rather, concentrating on those areas in which there is a clear capability advantage, most obviously, in the case of the West today, the maritime sphere and naval capability.

Cultures of the Moment

This point could be readily argued irrespective of the current emergency, but the latter gives it bite, and also underlines the degree to which scholarship has additional value if it can aid discussion of the present situation, and help look towards the future, in short embrace the presentism that so often proves a problem if it is argued in an over-determined fashion. Put simply, we need to address failure, failure in the shape of acute fiscal crisis in the USA and Britain, as well as a more general failure of strategic understanding. Much of this fiscal crisis has nothing to do with military overstretch (even if that is a potential consequence of the fiscal situation), and, as a result, comparisons of modern America with say sixteenth-century Spain, in large part, are misleading, except (valuably) as aids to thought. Instead, a combination of unprecedently high levels of social welfare, poor fiscal management, consumerism, low taxation, and an inability to match planning to economic developments, have set much of the framework.

Yet, within that context, the wars in Iraq and Afghanistan have also created major problems. Vast sums of money have been spent at a time when this expenditure has involved an increased indebtedness that has challenged national security, and arguably more profoundly than terrorist activity, although the latter of course is vicious, dangerous and needs robust action to counter it. Moreover, instead of securing rapid outcomes, Western forces became involved in lengthy presences that entailed not only significant human costs but also serious issues of commitment to particular force structures, doctrine and operational and tactical means. In short, a specific expeditionary posture was allowed to challenge not only the overall capacity of the army to discharge other functions but also the balance between the services.[79] How far this situation can be related to the culture of war is unclear, but possibly the most profound link was that of the desire on the part of the Bush administration to do something decisive after the serious terrorist attacks of 2001 on New York and Washington, and the related preference for action, a preference that can be discussed in terms of threatened masculinity and potency. In short, action causes reaction and bellicosity helps explain war.

This point adds a cultural element to the current issue of force structure. There is not only a danger, in both America and Britain, that crucial long-term military capabilities will be sacrificed to the exigencies of the army in its difficult current commitment, but also the risk of a focus on action in the shape of counter-insurgency operations, rather than on the capacity for action in the form of military strength, for example naval capability. The latter does not provide satisfaction in a situation in which there is a demand for action, but it represents a far more potent form of power, not least because it is easier to choose whether to apply it, and without that choice being dictated by opponents.

The culture of the societal context was displayed by the nature of public discussion in Britain in 2009–11, discussion that indicated a reluctance to engage with preparedness short of conflict. This reluctance reflected both the emotional character of much of the public discussion and the extent to which army advocates found the media more receptive. Indeed, the symbolization of individual military casualties, notably in terms of the public parade of hearses through the streets of Wootton Bassett in front of crowds both grieving and respectful,[80] as well as the Prime Minister reading the names of the dead in the House of Commons, and the focus of television and radio on individual casualties and on their families, created a potent situation that greatly affected the nature of the defence debate. Individual loss did not so much crowd out debate as set the tone.

In part, this situation is a feature of a wider failure in Western society, and maybe more so in (Western) Europe than in the USA to engage with the issue and implications of risk, a failure that reflects a more individualistic, hedonistic and atomistic society than heretofore, and also one that finds it easiest to respond to problems in an emotional fashion, with expertise and rational discussion both treated with suspicion. Thus, the defence debate in Britain in 2009–10 risked at one point becoming restricted to the provision of more helicopters to support operations, with the misleading impression created that this step would somehow solve problems by ending casualties among troops moved by road, instead, for example, of focusing at the tactical and operational level on the development by the Taliban of a capacity to mount new types of attack. In political terms, this media campaign provided an opportunity to dodge the question of strategic viability by focusing on a particular issue of procurement that could be afforded.

There was also a political failure to address the question of whether the policy of forward-action in South Asia could be sustained in the long term; and also 'should' in the sense of the threat this policy posed to overall force structure and doctrine.[81] Thus, a key cultural problem, the failure to address strategic questions seriously, was repeated yet again and, arguably, was matched in the case of the military by an unwillingness to accept the limited effectiveness of Western forces. The 'can do' attitude/culture of the military encouraged a framing of tasks in Afghanistan in the 2000s that paid insufficient attention to the possibility of failure.

Possibly, such discussion is one of the more important aspects of the cultural turn in scholarship, in that analysis of military matters can be more aware of this dimension of military policy and its consequences for strategy. There is, for example, a cultural as well as an intellectual challenge when discussing military preparedness and indeed operations short of fighting, let alone of full-scale war. As far as the public is concerned, this challenge owes something to the long-term difficulty of understanding deterrence as a concept; not only nuclear deterrence but the deterrence that naval and air power can offer. Deterrence involves trying to influence the attitudes of potential opponents and, as such, it is often difficult to show a clear cost-benefit analysis of the type enjoined by financial controllers. In turn, it would not be misusing the cultural approach to note that this preference for cost-benefit analysis is a direct product not only of the dominance of bureaucratic procedural methods in Ministries of Defence, but also of their particular character. To look at the situation from the perspective of an individual service indicates the extent to which cultural assumptions are bound up in any discussion of its relevant value.[82]

As a result of the combination of the need to show a role with the desire to prepare for action, navalists are encouraged, in defending their corner, to emphasize more concrete factors than deterrence, notably the volume of trade moved by sea. These factors are indeed highly pertinent, and more so as they also direct attention to the vulnerability of other powers, notably China. Turning to the challenge posed by China serves also as a reminder of the cultural elements bound up in strategic analysis, as a comparison between China and Islamic fundamentalism has more than just a 'realist' dimension.

One of the key arguments for Western naval power is that, in so far as China, or any other state, is a potential threat,[83] then this threat can be lessened by the extent to which they are dependent on oceanic trade. For example, China is obtaining more oil than hitherto from distant Atlantic sources, notably Equatorial Guinea, Nigeria, Angola and Cameroon. However, this focus on tangibles reflects, in part, a lack of willingness to engage with intangibles. These intangibles include the deterrent character of power and the extent to which it contributes to providing the presence necessary to maximize the political choice to prevent or calm incidents that might affect security.

Focusing on the complexities of the present helps throw light on the misleading clarity that some discern when they look at the past because it clarifies the problems faced by policymakers confronting the risk and risks of the future, and by analysts seeking to assess influence in decisionmaking. There is at present the fundamental choice for America and Britain between focusing on what we can do best or engaging in commitments that expose serious military and political limitations. To follow the latter course, which includes the Afghanistan commitment, and also, as a result, make poor choices about future military capabilities is reckless; but the culture of discussion by the American and British military is generally disinclined to underline the risk of pursuing current plans. Yet, again to throw light on context, this situation reflects the specifics of the strategic situation over the last decade as much as any particular characteristics of Anglo-American military culture.

Culture: Malleable, Nebulous, but Useful

This last point underlines the extent to which culture is malleable and affected by particular conjunctures. That is not the same, however, as suggesting that cultural norms can be stretched and ignored as states pursue their material strategic interests,[84] because such an assessment of interests itself reflects norms. Nor is it the case that the malleable character of culture extends to the point that actors simply reinvent their culture to fit their strategy, such that culture is more a weapon than a script.[85] Again, this approach underplays the role of norms,[86] let alone the argument that organized collective violence owes much to the impact of philosophical ideas on the minds of generals and others.[87]

What follows is an interlinked series of chapters that focus on differing types of culture in particular chronological periods. This approach has been taken to indicate the variety of the cultural turn, and, in doing so, to suggest that culture as a descriptive and analytical term, is both nebulous and part of the realist world, at once frustratingly malleable and actually quite useful.

2

The Culture of Gloire: The Royal Military

There is no one way of studying the cultural dynamics of warfare and, if what follows is a historian's way, that does not mean that there is only one historical approach. Yet, the historical approach is significant because there are only two datasets to use for an experiential discussion: the past and the present. The latter is tremendously important because it is in the present that impressions are registered and these impressions play a central role in the development of ideas, whether or not that approach is criticized as presentism. Nevertheless, there are practical difficulties with using the present, notably that it is only with the benefit of hindsight that the relative significance of events in the present can be established.

History is of greater importance than simply for validating the present and views of the present, although that use of it plays a significant role in military history, and notably so with military education. In addition to the value of looking at the past to see patterns of change that may be used in order to provide ballast for current arguments, there is the role of studies of the past in providing the perspective on, and dispassionate treatment of, what is otherwise a passionate matter.

The study of war and the military across history both throws much light on past societies and also provides insights into long-term aspects of warfare. These aspects indeed may be termed the culture of war if that is not further to overload the cultural term (and turn).

The Causes of War

The role of culture is well exemplified in this chapter, for it deals with the causes of war, as well as with the way in which warfare was conducted. These causes are an important element, as much of the response to war was established in light of the goals it was expected to further. The literature on causes and goals has varied greatly in accordance with particular emphases in the study of international relations. Debates on the latter are of great value, but also face the problem that theorists in international relations tend to look at the past as an isotrophic surface, equal in all parts, which is the approach that is most appropriate if universal rules of conduct are being deduced. In contrast, a cultural interpretation is not inherently opposed to such universal rules of conduct, but it is prone to stress variations, both chronological and geographical, alongside similarities. Indeed, the term cultural arises in part as a description of the causes, nature and consequences of these variations, and as an analysis focused on these variations.

As far as the origins of conflict are concerned, cultural interpretations tend to emphasize the results of particular states of social development, these states usually understood in terms of stages. Thus, there is an emphasis on anthropological factors when discussing societies presented as relatively simple, indeed primitive,[1] while, for more developed societies, the dynamics that are discussed are placed in a cultural reading of the nature of power. For example, in Aztec Mesoamerica (Mexico) warfare played a central role in sustaining a natural order that encompassed gods and men.[2]

Moreover, the emphasis, in cultural interpretations, is not on the 'state' as an essentially bureaucratic entity automatically seeking greater power. Linked to this is a tendency not to adopt a bureaucratic notion of the nature of decisionmaking and the rationale of power and good. Instead, the ambitions of the rulers, and sometimes of their people, were the key element, and these ambitions frequently focused on dynastic honour and personal glory, each of which were goals in their own right, as well as characteristics that greatly affected the interpretation and pursuit of other goals. Antiquity helped to set patterns for subsequent behaviour, while there was frequently a key theme of the ruler as the intermediary of divine action. Both gods and kings were to bring victory, each justifying the other by these means.[3] This pattern was true of much of human history. At the same time, the roles of gods and kings varied. Some, such as being merciful, were not bellicose. However, the cultural imperative of being merciful without being effeminate underlined the more powerful need to be seen as manly.

Prestige, ambition and function were all linked through success in conflict, as in the triumphs of Republican and Imperial Rome.[4] To take the seventeenth century, a period for which records are better than for earlier periods, this situation was true of monarchs in China, India and Persia as much as Europe, but, similarly, the Iroquois tribal confederation in North America was concerned with glory, honour and revenge, rather than economic issues.[5] The sense that monarchs had of their own reputation played a major role in the choices they made, not least in resolving conflicting priorities. Although war was defended in terms of justice, it served to win prestige and glory, and to assert and affirm rank and privilege, and notably those of rulers struggling to establish their own position and those of new dynasties, such as the Tudors in early sixteenth-century England, the Bourbons and Romanovs in early seventeenth-century France and Russia respectively, the Braganzas in Portugal and Manchus in China later in the century, and the Bourbons and Hanoverians in Spain and Britain in the early eighteenth century.

Many rulers led their forces on campaign and into battle, Henry VIII being particularly proud of his victorious service against the French at the Battle of the Spurs in 1513, Tsar Alexei taking a major role at the successful siege of Polish-held Smolensk in 1654, and the Kangzi Emperor leading the victorious Manchu/Chinese forces against the Zunghars in 1696. This number included those not noted as warleaders, such as Philip IV of Spain who, in 1642, joined the forces that unsuccessfully sought to suppress the Catalan rising.

War as a means of winning prestige and glory, of avenging injuries and redressing wrongs, and of affirming rank and privilege, was also true for social élites, whether or not their position was expressed, as in Europe, as an hereditary aristocracy. Indeed, these factors helped explain both the attitudes of ministers and generals in the service of their own rulers as well as their concern for their personal *gloire* or, in Spanish, *reputacion*. These goals were important for the readiness of members of the aristocracy to turn to violence.[6]

The quest for fame and fortune also explained the willingness to serve 'foreign' rulers, service which was common, not least as its ties were largely personal, with personal honour proving a key concept in such circumstances. Moreover, this personal relationship worked both ways, leading to rulers, such as the Austrian Habsburgs and Russian Romanovs, being happy to have many commanders and officers who were not, at least by birth, subjects. In turn, the reward of service created mutual obligations that helped to make these individuals subjects, notably if they received land, which was the case for many who served the Austrian Habsburgs, especially as the suppression of the Bohemian revolt in 1620 was followed by the expropriation of much of the Protestant aristocracy. Lands confiscated from Protestant nobles who resisted Ferdinand II in the Bohemian revolt, which began in 1618, were conferred on Ferdinand's generals, creating the basis for a political system that lasted until the First World War.[7]

The Pursuit of Prestige

A key concept here is the pursuit of prestige, which for the France of Louis XIV (r. 1643–1715) was discussed in terms of *gloire*, which can be loosely translated as glory. Prestige can be treated, in a reductionist fashion, in functional terms by pointing out that success in war brought a prestige that acted as a lubricant for obedience, as well as a platform for kingship and divinely sanctioned rule. Furthermore, this process was enhanced because part of the adult male social élite was employed in the military, and thus their reputation and self-esteem were bound up with the prestige of victory. These points are indeed pertinent and will be returned to; but it is important to realize that such a reductionist use of prestige should not be pushed to the extent of denying an inherent reality for the latter. That, indeed, is the tendency when presenting prestige in simple functional terms, as making it serve a utilitarian purpose reduces it to a form of political cost-benefit embedded in material culture. Instead, it is necessary to see *gloire* not simply as the means of power, but also as its aim. In particular, the key players were given purpose and cohesion by a shared commitment to fame. The latter brought weight alike to individuals and to the continuities that they represented and which gave them meaning, notably dynasties.

Dynastic Rivalry

Dynastic competition was a crucial element in international relations, and warfare was in part an adjunct of this competition, helping to translate tensions and disputes over other points into both acute rivalry and providing fresh causes of serious dissension. Prestige was not separate to other factors, but an aspect of them.

For example, the Ottoman and Safavid dynasties, which ruled the Turkish and Persian (Iranian) empires respectively, clashed in the early sixteenth century over territorial interests, notably in eastern Anatolia (Turkey), Iraq and the Caucasus; but there was also an ideological rivalry that was closely linked to prestige. The struggle between the Sunni and Shi'a branches of Islam was taken to a new level of intensity when the Shi'a Safavids conquered Iran and Iraq in the

1500s. This struggle was personalized because Isma'il, the founder of Safavid power, was seen as a prophet. Conversely the Sunni Ottomans enhanced their prestige in 1517 by conquering Mamluk-ruled Egypt. This conquest also entailed taking over the Egyptian position in the Hejaz (western Arabia), an overlordship that brought with it the guardianship of the sacred sites of Medina and Mecca, to add to Jerusalem (already conquered from the Mamluks in 1516). This guardianship was important to the process by which the Ottomans, by background a minor tribal dynasty, established themselves as deservedly a great world power. Their conquest, in 1453, of Byzantium (Istanbul), the capital of the Eastern Roman empire, was also important to this process as it had defied previous attacks by Islamic powers.

The Ottoman attempt to seize prestige was matched by other Islamic dynasties keen to demonstrate their claim to eminence. Thus, across much of Eurasia, it was important to show descent from the Chinggisid dynasty of Chinggis Khan that had brought the Mongols to power in the thirteenth century. For example, Babur, the founder of Mughal power in India in the early sixteenth century, emphasized this descent. This stress on background helped create standards of behaviour, while also establishing a background against which achievements could be assessed. A sense of responsibility to forbears and posterity, a sense of values enshrined in the tale-based culture of the period, was significant. Moreover, legitimacy in moral and religious terms was perceived to be sanctioned by divinely granted military victories.

The Chinese equivalent was the emphasis on dynastic records and histories, for achievement and time itself were noted in terms of dynastic building blocks, and the relationship between these dynasties and, more particularly, the legitimacy of the process of succession from one to the next, became key issues.

Gloire was thus a duty as well as a pleasure, a task for the individual that represented his responsibility to forbears, family and posterity. This bundle of obligations was not expressed in some seminal text, but it constituted a key element in the strategic geographies of dynastic monarchies and would-be dynastic rulers. In part, this key element arose because the drive for *gloire* was both internal: the product of aspirations within polities; and external: one generated by rivalries between them. For *gloire* was topic, affect and tone in competition between monarchs. Süleyman the Magnificent (r. 1520–66), the Ottoman ruler under whom the empire greatly expanded, actively competed in developing imperial symbolism with his contemporary rival, the Habsburg Emperor Charles V (r. 1519–56). This competition for prestige was also one that was waged actively on the battlefield, in Hungary and the Mediterranean, with performance on the latter deliberately designed to further this competition. Charles frequently suggested an attack on Constantinople, the Ottoman centre, but did not do so, in large part because of the enmity of France, which allied with Süleyman. Charles often took personal command of his troops, which he saw as necessary to his honour and reputation.[8]

In competing with each other, rulers were also competing with their predecessors, as they fought to cope with the psychological burden imposed on them by past success, in what in some respects was therefore a strategic geography of the past. For Süleyman, this meant doing better than his famed great-grandfather Mehmed II, the conqueror of Byzantium, who, however, had failed in his attacks on Belgrade in 1456 and Rhodes in 1480, helping to create an impression that the Ottomans had been stopped, which, in turn, helped set assumptions about relative power. Süleyman, in contrast, captured both positions in successive campaigns at the beginning of his reign in 1521 and 1522. Similarly, Henry VIII of England saw himself as in the shadow of Henry V, notably in relations with France, and Louis XIV of France in that of his grandfather, Henry IV.

Monarchs were encouraged to think in these terms by the ambience of kingship. They tended to live in palaces built and embellished by predecessors and decorated with celebrations of their triumphs. Philip V of Spain (r. 1700–46) favoured the royal palace in Seville, in which there was a series of celebrated tapestries depicting Charles V's successful expedition against Tunis in 1535. This, obviously, was not why Philip launched an expedition in 1732 against Oran, also in North Africa, but the climate of impression in the palace was favourable. So also with the orders of knighthood that monarchs headed, such as the Golden Fleece for the Habsburgs and the Garter for the kings of England. These orders encouraged an emphasis on personal prowess, namely skill in the martial arts, such as fencing and jousting, and bravery in combat, continuing earlier chivalric conduct.

Hunting was presented as a form of bravery in combat, with the emphasis very much on the risks, rather than on hunting as a carefully managed activity in which animals were driven to the slaughter. Instead, the tales of hunting, ones repeated on canvas, were of fierce beasts, such as wild boars that slew dogs and horses of the hunt, and threatened the noble hunters. At the end, often with an echo of Classical themes, the beasts and monarchs of the animal kingdom were dispatched by the monarchs of the human world, the latter displaying not only bravery but also the exemplary nerve and leadership that led to victory. Such accounts provided a background to war, and the latter also had a potent visual message with monarchs depicted, on canvas and in fresco and stone, on horseback. Again, this depiction brought prominence and one that focused all attention on the monarch.

This stress can be seen as anachronistic in terms of the development of war if the latter is presented for the fifteenth century on in terms of the rise of gunpowder weaponry. There is, indeed, a standard narrative that emphasizes the latter on the world scale and continues by presenting both cavalry and personal prowess as anachronistic or, at best, still significant in areas where gunpowder weaponry lacked impact. This narrative is used, for example, to explain Ottoman victory over the Mamluks in 1516–17 and over the Hungarians in 1526, and to discuss changing styles of warfare, whether in Europe or Japan. Personal prowess appears particularly redundant as, however brave, or socially exalted, all were subject to the bullet or the cannonball.

This account provides one way of looking at a strategic geography focused on *gloire*. It can appear redundant as well as backward-looking and, in particular, a strategic geography waiting to be swept aside by one more suited to an age of rising powers successfully articulated through bureaucratic means and politically increasingly reliant on a notion of state and/or nation that was separate from that of the dynasty or at least not dependent on it. Linked to this comes the question of whether there was a process of baton-exchange in strategic geography comparable to that allegedly in means of waging war effectively. In short, the culture of war is presented as defined in terms of a modernity and process of modernization in which technology played a major role.

Modern notions of politics might seem to challenge dynastic *gloire*. The idea of a distinction between dynasty and nation, ruler and state, was clearly valid in some cases, notably where there was hostility to what was seen as a foreign rulership, as in Hungary under the Polish-born Wladyslaw II (r. 1490–1516).[9] Yet, as in Hungary or in France in the 1590s and Russia in the 1600s, the call was usually for a different monarch, not for republicanism, and this situation ensured that the image and focus of national effort remained that of service under a good king. The ethos of the aristocracy contributed directly to this. In the Dutch Revolt against Philip II of Spain that began in the 1560s, the rebels focused for several decades on finding a monarch, such as a French prince, or a monarch-substitute.

A definition of aristocratic honour with reference to military service was encouraged by the emphasis on honour, service and glory on the part of rulers. Their peacetime courts and wartime campaigns provided opportunities for dramatizing patronage through displays of prowess and munificence, as with the central role of hunting in court life and also the use of tournaments and other forms of mock combat.[10] As a child, the future King Sebastian of Portugal, like many heirs, was encouraged to show a penchant for war games. He was to die in battle in 1578. Wargaming continues to be an important part of the military world,[11] encompassing conflict simulation for the military as well as popular leisure activity.

In both peace and war, troop reviews proved part of the process of linking honour and renown with military activity. Thus, in 1580, Philip II reviewed the Spanish army near Badajoz before it successfully invaded Portugal. Some operations, moreover, took on the characteristics of an aristocratic review, such as Charles V's campaign against Tunis in 1535, which was accompanied by large numbers of Spanish and Italian nobles. Yet, campaigning was also dangerous for aristocrats. In 1512, Gaston of Foix, French commander in Italy and the nephew of Louis XII, was killed at the battle of Ravenna, while in 1544, René Prince of Orange, stadtholder (governor) of Holland, was killed by a cannon ball while besieging a position in France.

Many rulers fought as part of the process of command. In 1501, Babur, the Mughal leader, fired a crossbow while defending the city of Samarqand from Uzbek assault, and he subsequently fired a more conventional Central Asian bow.[12] In contrast, his grandson Akbar fired a musket, as at the siege of the Rajput stronghold of Chitor. Shah Tahmasp I of Iran (r. 1524–76) was helped in asserting his authority in the face of conflict over control of the regime until 1533 by victories, notably at Jam over the Uzbeks in 1528. In 1537, he gained prestige when he recovered the city of Herat from the Uzbeks and captured that of Kandahar.

Princes were also expected to show prowess, as Edward, the 'Black Prince' did against the French at Poitiers in 1356. Such displays were particularly important in monarchical systems that lacked primogeniture, as merit was displayed by these means. At the battle of Başkent in 1473, the forces on both the Aqquyunlu and the Ottoman flanks were commanded by the sons of the rulers.

In turn, the image and results of battles were displayed in order to secure glory for participants and, in doing so, sustained the way in which such glory was gained. This was true of rulers and of other commanders. Bravery in the field was seen as an important attribute of command. Thus, in 1496, the Spanish commander Gonzalo de Córdoba gained great renown by being one of the first into the breach in the walls of French-held Ostia. The ceremonial entries of French monarchs, and other rulers, celebrated royal valour and success,[13] while Francesco II Gonzaga, Marquess of Mantua presented his performance at the battle of Fornovo in 1495, where he had fought bravely and captured many prisoners (albeit failing to block the French march north), as a victory; and Andrea Mantegna's painting the *Madonna della Vittoria* was produced accordingly. Similarly, Francesco's additions to his ancestral seat at Gonzaga were decorated with scenes from family military history, while the palace of San Sebastiano he built provided an opportunity for the display of what he saw as an apt comparison, Mantegna's series the *Triumphs of Caesar*, painted from 1482 to 1492.[14] Francis I of France fought at Marignano and Pavia, being captured at the latter in 1525, while Titian painted a splendid equestrian portrait of Emperor Charles V to celebrate his victory over the Schmalkaldic League of German Protestants at Mühlberg in 1547. Apparently, the emperor was not actually on a horse at the time.

The depiction of rulers often bore no reference to their activities and potential. Charles I of England (r. 1625–49) was depicted in marvellous equestrian poses of command, but was a poor war leader. Louis XIII of France (r. 1610–43), not in fact an impressive leader, was portrayed as a great heroic figure, and depicted as Jupiter, Apollo, Neptune, Alexander the Great, and 'the new Hannibal'. Engravings were matched by pamphlets that emphasized royal successes.[15] Although European theorists such as Francisco de Vitoria and Justus Lipsius insisted that neither honour nor glory should play any role in decisionmaking linked to warfare, and neither factor played a major role in wars conducted by the Dutch with their republican culture in the seventeenth century, the values of the period involved a struggle of will and for prestige. The ends sought were, first, a retention of domestic and international backing that rested on the gaining of *gloire*, and, secondly, persuading other rulers to accept a new configuration of relative *gloire*.

This focus led to a concentration of forces on campaigns and sieges made important largely by the presence of the king as commander. In addition to an emphasis on campaigning, as seeking stages in the defeat of opposing forces, it is necessary to adopt a broader approach to victory and to underline the extent to which success had a symbolic value. From this perspective, decisiveness has to be reconceptualized, away from an emphasis on total victory, understood in modern terms as the destruction of opposing armies and the capture of their territory, and towards a notion that may have had more meaning in terms of the values of the period.

Like other rulers, Louis XIV (r. 1643–1715) enjoyed both commanding and reviewing troops. His triumphs, such as the crossing of the Rhine in 1672, and the successful sieges of Maastricht (1673), Ghent (1678), Luxembourg (1684), and Mons (1691), were celebrated with religious services and commemorative displays. His successor,

Louis XV, was to repeat this process. In the *Salon de la Guerre* at the royal palace of Versailles, finished and opened to the public in 1686, Antoine Coysevox presented Louis XIV as a stuccoed Mars, the God of War.[16] Louis also appeared as a warrior in works of art that had a different theme, for example Charles Le Brun's painting *The Resurrection of Christ* (1674), which was painted while France was at war. By the 1690s, over 20,000 French nobles were serving in the army and navy, a bond that testified to aristocratic confidence in Louis and that underlined the political value of his position as warleader.

Louis was scarcely alone. Similarly, Frederick William, the Great Elector of Brandenburg-Prussia (r. 1640–88), commissioned Andreas Schlüter to design an equestrian statue depicting him as a military commander: in armour and holding a field marshal's baton.[17] His victory over the Swedes at Fehrbellin in 1675, actually a relatively minor clash, was to be important to both dynastic prestige and its identification with war. Rulers were conspicuous in martial activities, as a reputation for resolution was of great significance, both to them and to their subjects, as well as proving important in operations. Thus, during the Dutch siege of French-held Maastricht in 1676, William III of spent much time in the trenches and was shot in the arm. Two years later, he was described at the battle of St Denis as armoured with breastplate and helmet 'with thousands of bullets about his ears'.[18]

The references to gods and heroes of the past were also seen in non-Western societies. China is frequently presented as a largely pacific culture, in large part because of a strong anti-military bias among the official and unofficial historians of the Ming dynasty (r. 1368–1644). This account, however, underplays the extent to which the emperors were committed to maintain the military primacy of their dynasty, and devoted time to military decisions. Their image as Sons of Heaven hindered any stress on compromise and conciliation.[19] In the sixteenth century, nevertheless, bellicose values were more strongly affirmed in India, in large part because the rulers there had to fight for their position. Aurangzeb, who was a general as well as a prince, notably in Afghanistan, won the throne by defeating his three brothers, and then, as emperor, was an active war-leader.

Establishing the importance of a set of values does not demonstrate that they necessarily took the key part in particular decisions. It is also unclear how best to align the context and decisions for individual rulers and for rulers as a whole. At the same time, it is likely that, by being an important component of the context within which decisions were taken, these values played a major role in these decisions.

There are particular problems arising from the nature of the sources, first because these tend to relate to policies, rather than the motivation for policies, and, secondly, because they vary by rulers. So does secondary work. There is some important scholarship, notably Geoffrey Parker's major study *The Grand Strategy of Philip II* (1998);[20] but most rulers lack such attention. Strategy comes to the fore in two issues: the discussion of the allocation of resources and energies between different commitments, as well as decisions for war and peace. However, the cultural issue relates largely to the atmosphere within which decisions were taken.

In comparison with the present situation, there was a willingness to fight, even an eagerness to do so; and, however it is described, the change from the former situation to the present one was a fundamental development in the culture of war. Indeed, doubts about the value of cultural interpretations have to address the significance of this development. Moreover, however the pre-modern is defined and dissected, it was far from constant. For example, the Byzantine empire put a greater emphasis on negotiation, bribery and persuasion than its Roman predecessor had done.[21]

The Nature of Political Systems

The willingness to fight can be explained not only in terms of the interests and ambitions of rulers, but also of the nature of sociopolitical systems that focused on these rulers. In many respects, there was a commonality of purpose. For example, the pursuit of land and reputation linked monarchs, nobles and peasants. As wealth was primarily held in land and transmitted through blood inheritance, it was natural at all levels of society for conflict to centre on succession disputes. Although peaceful successions of new dynasties did take place, as in England in 1603, war and inheritance were often two sides of the same coin, a problem exacerbated by varying and disputed succession laws.

Far from being made anachronistic by the rise of more modern government forms, notably states, bureaucracy and representative politics, there was a strong linkage between these processes and the more traditional culture of war. Indeed, state-building generally required, and led to, war. The prime purpose of new governmental agencies was largely that of raising resources for war, while domestic politics owed much to the problems created by this process as well as those caused by failure in war. Moreover, the nature of the state was not incompatible with monarchical power. An idea of political community, headed by the ruler, but to which he could be held accountable, offered a significant challenge, although monarchical *gloire* helped integrate groups into the gradually emergent 'states'. Moreover, the martial configuration of new states remained under monarchical or quasi-monarchical control and direction. A major instance was provided by the Dutch revolt against the rule of Philip II of Spain in the late sixteenth century. The creation of a republic led to the establishment of a military system under a quasi-monarchical figure, Maurice of Nassau, from 1585 the stadtholder (governor) of a number of provinces as well as Captain General and Admiral General of the forces of these provinces. Maurice was in effect commander-in-chief and played a major role, both in organizational terms and with command in the field. Oliver Cromwell played a similar role in Interregnum England (1649–58), becoming Lord Protector in 1653.

These republican figures also subscribed to dynasticism, Cromwell being succeeded by his lacklustre son Richard who, however, was unable to retain the position, while the house of Orange–Nassau provided the monarchical component of Dutch politics thereafter, including, in the person of William III of Orange, another leading general. Although he did not become a king until after he conquered England in 1688 and also adopted a Calvinist attitude to some of the trappings of rulership, William shared in the bellicose values of European princely society. Moreover, he exemplified the value of dynasticism because his position in England was that of a co-ruler with his wife, Mary II, the daughter of the excluded monarch, James II, who was William's uncle as well as his father-in-law.

An emphasis on monarchs, glory and dynasticism as key constituents of a culture of war has the advantage that it matches contemporary views. In contrast, the idea of the origins of the modern impersonal state in Europe in this period rests on relatively little beyond the arguments of a small group of, arguably, unrepresentative thinkers, arguments that tended only to come to the fore when resistance to the monarch had to be justified. Instead, religious factors were more important. These factors fused with those of monarchical interest in a number of respects, most obviously that of contested successions. In the case of the civil wars in France and Sweden in the 1590s or the overthrow of James II by William of Orange in 1688–91, there was a strong religious dimension, and this factor was also important for the motivation of the actual combatants: each soldier was fighting for his individual as well as national salvation.

The political practice of the age was still essentially monarchical, and in a traditional fashion, whether it is China, India, the Ottoman empire, or Christian Europe, as considered in the sixteenth and seventeenth centuries. As a result, both the goals and the practices of rulership and foreign policy contributed to the frequency of confrontation and war, while the latter, in turn, helped continue the norms of rulership and policy. The role of ministers might appear an important qualification of any argument centred on rulers, but the position of ministers generally depended on royal favour. Dynastic considerations, and those focused on the prestige of individual rulers, clearly played an important role in ministerial discussions.

Cross-Cultural Conflict

As a reminder of the plasticity of the term culture, it can be used for the early modern period (as for other periods), not only in this sense as an explanation of the motive forces leading to war and affecting how conflict was waged. The term can also be employed not only for elements in warfare between polities that claimed the sanction of the same culture, but, more particularly, for war between polities that saw themselves, or can be seen, as derived from different cultures. However, the use of culture in this context also faces problems. Continuing distinctions between cultures may appear in different contexts and be used for different purposes. Thus, cultural distinctions can be employed for purposes, and analyses, of integration or segregation, explaining why politics cohered or fought each other. Although cultures can be variably defined, it is apparent that contemporaries had a strong sense of such differences, and conflict played a major role in shaping cultural identities.

Wars across cultures did not arise as a simple consequence of difference, but it was far harder to solve difficulties in such cases. A key instance was provided by the contrast between settled agrarian societies and their nomadic pastoral counterparts. Fear of the horseman, of the raiders from the steppe, played a major role in the consciousness of settled societies, especially those of Christian Europe, northern India, and China. This fear looked back to centuries of repeated attacks, and was a testimony to the military potency of mounted archers. Indeed, to advance another use for the term culture, the period until the eighteenth century can be seen as that of the onslaught of the horse-people, and fears of their likely attack presented as an aspect of their threat. In 1526, the Mughals brought down the Lodi Sultanate of Delhi, in the 1640s to 1650s the Manchu conquered China, in the 1720s the Afghans overthrew Safavid Persia and, from 1752 until 1761, they successfully invaded northern India.

Many wars may thus seem an inevitable product of clashing systems, but, alongside violence, frontiers were more varied zones of interaction. Trade and other aspects of mutually beneficial or symbiotic behaviour were also very important. Furthermore, rather than being a matter of clashing cultures, nomadic attacks frequently arose because the commercial and other relationships had been disturbed or the terms were no longer acceptable to one party. Thus, from this perspective, conflict was not the natural characteristic of the relationship, but a product of its failure. One consequence was that 'barbarians' or 'outsiders' no longer seem a product and part of the inchoate 'other' against which civilization must defend itself, but, instead, were part of a world of civilization, albeit on unequal terms. Ascribing a rationality and motivation, other than those of the most basic, to 'barbarians' can be linked to a re-evaluation in which they enter into wars, rather than being in a permanent state of war.

A similar re-evaluation is possible in the case of cross-cultural conflict between, for example, Christendom and Islam, or the Mughal empire and the Hindu polities of southern India, notably the Marathas in the late seventeenth century. Alongside long-term antagonisms, there were periods in which conflict was localized and essentially limited to frontier differences and groups, while there were often alliances across cultural divides. How far such a situation is compatible with the use of cultural terms is unclear, but it throws instructive light on the concept of a clash of civilizations.

Co-operation across cultural divides was common, and often motivated by the need for alliance against shared enemies, as when Uzum Hasan, the Muslim ruler of the Aqquyunlu state of Iran and Iraq, sought Venetian support against the Ottoman Turks in the 1470s, albeit to only limited effect; or when the Ottomans co-operated with France against the Emperor Charles V in the second quarter of the sixteenth century. The resulting pattern of French co-operation led to Louis XIV being termed 'The Most Christian Turk'.

Yet, such co-operation was not the ideological message of either side. In 1495, Charles VIII, one of Louis' predecessors, announced a crusade against the Ottomans, which linked Charles to the prestige of an earlier king, Louis IX, St Louis, who had led the Seventh Crusade in 1248 and died on a new crusade in 1270, and also enabled him to claim prestige as a leader of Christendom. In Islam, the notion of *jihad*, war with the infidel, was actively propagated, and the shedding of Muslim blood was discouraged, while, in Christendom, there was a continual sense of an Islamic threat and a continuation of crusading ideology and practice. In China, some officials opposed any conciliation of Mongols and Manchu as capitulation to barbarians.

The perception of cultural menace led to military and diplomatic measures, and could also lead to domestic counterparts, as with the Spanish expulsion, first, of Muslims and, later, of *moriscos*, converts to Christendom, who were regarded as a potential fifth column. More generally, identities were challenged by persecution and forcible conversion. Sacred sites were seized and converted or desecrated.

However, although neither Christendom nor Islam in this period readily lent themselves to syncretic practices in their zone of contact, it is also striking how it was possible to move from war to wars, from the perpetual attack on the infidel to specific quarrels fought for particular causes or as a result of events, attitudes and, yes, cultural norms, at a distinct conjuncture. This was also true of the domestic situation. When the Safavids occupied Baghdad in 1508, they destroyed its Christian community, which is instructive, and also highlights the extent to which the previous Muslim rulers had not done so.

Thus, any sense of continual cross-cultural conflict had to be tempered by the need for rulers to choose between different options and the possibility of their doing so. Indeed, culture as an explanation is valuable if it leaves space for agency, but not otherwise. To use cultural interpretations in a determinist fashion is unhelpful, but, conversely, culture takes on added value if it can be used to analyse as well as describe aspects of this agency. In leaving space for agency, there is also the opportunity of leaving space for change and variation.

For example, trans-cultural wars were not necessarily caused by differences in culture. Yet such differences might be responsible for hostility and for affecting the conduct of war, for example by encouraging or facilitating slaughter, enslavement or expropriation, as with the Portuguese in Brazil or the Russians in Siberia. In New England in the seventeenth century, the clash of native and European military cultures encouraged a high level of violence.[22] There were also crossovers between these cultures, notably scalping, which was pursued prior to the European arrival, and then used by the Europeans and native allies to develop relations.[23]

However, cultural differences could encourage conflict for a number of related reasons. Major cultural contrasts could be perceived as a serious violation of order, most usually divine order, that encouraged ideological pressure for war. In such a situation, the defiance of heavenly, or other, order could be seen as an act of violence that required correction. Thus, the very presence of infidels apparently necessitated purging them from the community and polity. In such a situation, the 'aggressor', therefore, was not the persecutor, but rather the individuals, groups or polities that defied order, attitudes that looked towards twentieth-century genocide.

Secondly, such cultural contrasts could make it more difficult to negotiate differences and to arrive at compromises, or even to define what might be meant by compromise. Thirdly, such contrasts could lead powers to define their actions as if they were not dealing with comparable polities, or even people with any rights. Moreover, it was possible to regard violence in this context not as war but as policing actions that were not governed by the conventions or assumptions that more normally affected its conduct.

The concluding theme in this section, however, is of possibilism, not determinism. Religious hostility might help lead Babur, the founder of Mughal rule in India, to erect a pyramid of skulls after his major victory over the Hindu Rajputs at Kanua in 1527, an act presented as an appropriate treatment of infidels; but the Mughals soon came to depend in part on Rajput political and military co-operation, and his grandson Akbar married Rajput princesses. Similarly, to return to *gloire*, the search for prestige and the benefits gained from it were both real and important. They helped ensure that military resources were focused on operations likely to yield *gloire*, notably sieges conducted by armies under royal command. Yet, when Ivan IV of Russia (the Terrible) sought a Baltic coastline or other rulers pursued similar territorial benefits, they were motivated by material considerations that cannot be largely explained in terms of *gloire*, even though successes *en route* were celebrated in these terms.

Outlining separate categories for classification creates a number of problems, not least determining both relative importance and the question of what is to be seen as progressive. The discussion of war tends to focus on battles, more particularly between specialized military units, and far too little attention has been devoted to the 'small war' or 'little war' of raids, skirmishes, and small-scale clashes. As yet, there has been no systematic study of this level of conflict, although it was one in which distinctions between the regular forces of the state engaged in such fighting and irregulars were often far from clear. Moreover, irregular forces could be very substantial and several represented bodies with some of the attributes of independent statehood, for example the Cossacks. The range of such forces and conflict requires emphasis, and they should not be seen as necessarily less effective than the 'high end' of warfare, represented by large-scale battles on land and sea and by the regular sieges of well-prepared fortresses.

Linked to these tensions over the relative significance of different types of conflict comes those over the description of warfare. For example, in the scholarship on Central Asian and pre-colonial sub-Saharan African conflict, there is a contrast between the argument that much, probably most, conflict was, as raiding war, qualitatively different from Western warfare, and, on the other hand, the claim that 'real' warfare, similar to that practised in the West, can be seen, and not simply what is dismissed as raids. Looked at differently and challenging the use of Western terminology that downgraded warfare in other parts of the world, raiding can also be seen as real warfare. This issue is further confused by the extent to which military cultures have been constructed and simplified by misleading external categorization in terms of militarism or passivity.[24]

The Culture of Military Assessment

The issue of subsequent academic construction is indeed pertinent when discussing the inherent military cultures of particular societies, although, at the same time, war-making was in fact culturally specific in particular societies.[25] Moreover, the culture of war could change in its characteristics and/or manifestations, as when Japan in the early seventeenth century essentially gave up war while maintaining many of the social and cultural attributes of bellicosity.

These factors all played a role in the pull and push dynamics of military activity, the dynamics arising from the demands placed upon the military and, on the other hand, the possibilities that it could offer; with military capability and action framed in accordance both with the tasks or goals that political and military contexts gave rise to, and with the possibilities they created. These pull and push dynamics could be seen in terms of strategies, operations and tactics, each of which reflected tasks and possibilities. The dynamics could also be seen in force structures, notably the varied emphases on numbers of troops as opposed to experience, infantry as opposed to cavalry, and firepower as opposed to mobility.

The Mamluk élite, who controlled Egypt from 1250 to 1517, put a premium on cavalry who did not associate the use of firearms with acceptable warrior conduct. Firearms were regarded as socially subversive, as was also to be the case with samurai aversion to firearms in seventeenth to nineteenth-century Japan, although, as Japan then was a group of islands at peace, the comparison should not be pushed too hard: it relates mostly to the emphasis on élite warriors. Hostility to the use of musketeers obliged successive Mamluk sultans in 1498 and 1514 to disband musketeer units they had raised. Sultan al-Nāsir Muhammad (r. 1496–8), who sought to form a unit of black slaves armed with firearms, was overthrown. Like the Aztecs in Mexico and aristocratic officers in England,[26] the Mamluks stressed individual prowess and hand-to-hand, one-to-one, combat with a matched opponent. These values sapped discipline and made those who adopted them vulnerable to forces that put an emphasis on more concerted manoeuvres and on anonymous combat, particularly employing firepower.

However, recent work has suggested a need for the re-evaluation of these views as part of a more positive approach to the Mamluk willingness to reform.[27] It is clear that Mamluk élite soldiers were passionate horse riders, while the infantry was reserved for other strata of society. Horse riders could not use firearms at the beginning of the sixteenth century, and there seemed scant reason why the highly trained Mamluk cavalry élite should dismount when the training required for firearms was not so intensive. Yet, at the same time, the Mamluks turned to firearms, using cannon from the 1360s. Moreover, in their conflict of 1465–71 with Shah Suwār, who had deposed his brother as emir of Dhu'l-Kadr (in eastern Anatolia/Turkey) and renounced the emirate's ties of vassalage to Egypt, and who the Ottomans secretly backed, the Mamluks employed cannon in their successful captures of 'Ayntāb (1471), Adana (1471) and Zamanti (1472). In their war with the Ottomans in 1485–91, the Mamluks cast cannon at their camp at Ayas and used them, alongside ballistas and mangonels, more traditional, non-gunpowder, pieces of ordnance, at the siege of Adana. The Ottomans were also able to cast cannon in the field. In this war, the Mamluks encountered firearms in large numbers for the first time, and they immediately started their military reforms. In 1490, the Mamluks used handgunners successfully against the Ottomans, advancing to Kayseri. Under capable leaders, the Mamluks could still check, if not defeat, the Ottomans.

Other factors also played a role, which undermines any attempt to provide a monocausal cultural interpretation. Mamluk reforms faced strong disadvantages from the outset compared to the Ottomans; notably lack of resources, such as iron, and of skilled manpower. The Mamluks tried, but could not cope, while the Ottomans were stronger. Moreover, the sultan's overthrow in 1498 was linked to the fact that he was a son of a reigning sultan, that generally in the fifteenth century the dynastic principle had been abolished, and that the old companions of his father resented his staying on the throne as usually the new ruler had to be chosen from among them. In addition, the opposition to the black slaves armed with handguns may have been more of a problem of ethnicity than arms. Moreover, in contradiction to the 'cultural' assumption of most modern scholars that cavalry was functionally anachronistic and thus its use a product of inappropriate cultural preferences, cavalry remained effective. The key Mamluk victory over Suwār, that at the Jayhūn river in November 1471, was preponderantly a cavalry struggle.

Rather than discussing such factors, Egyptian literary sources from the seventeenth century had to explain the downfall of the Mamluks and chose to do so with the topic of firearms and the luxurious, indeed decadent, life that had allegedly estranged the élite from their people. Thus, as with modern assessments, cultural preferences played a role in the problematic character of the evidence from which different cultural factors are deduced. At the same time, the impact on force structure of social preferences can be seen as another aspect of cultural pressures. Thus, the prominence, in French society and politics, of the nobility was linked in the sixteenth century to a force structure and doctrine dominated by heavy cavalry.

Emphasizing individual prowess and élite warriors provided a significant part of the culture and mythos of warfare, but did not always describe the reality of conflict. For example, in sixteenth-century Japan, individual prowess and élite warriors were not as important as sometimes suggested because the emphasis had long since shifted to generalship, large-scale troop movements, and the manipulation of logistics. In addition the mystique of bladed weapons and hand-to-hand fighting on medieval battlefields was an invention of the late nineteenth century, when Japanese military planners were considering how to defeat Western technology. Thus, as with Mamluk Egypt, the standard approach, with its emphasis on particular cultural elements, reflected, at least in part, subsequent assessments that, in turn, were an expression of cultural preferences. Their use in order to support a standard narrative of military history is troubling.

Gloire and Organization

Linking the subject to organizational issues, any emphasis on the individual warrior underlined and risked undermining the often complex pattern of order in military systems, as concepts of subordination meant relatively little when the stress was on individual prowess. Yet, this stress was not necessarily incompatible with organized systems of warfare. For example, sixteenth-century galley fighting in part served to display the merit of the prominent warriors who commanded the galleys and who led boarding parties. The same was true with fortifications in that those who led storming parties into breaches, or who resisted attack in these breaches, acquired great renown. Such renown both served as a reminder of the extent which forms of warfare, whether old or new, served to display valour and other traditional knightly skills, and also recognized the extent to which such skills were still pertinent for the leadership required from officers in military units whatever the form of warfare. Gunpowder weaponry and discipline were not incompatible with traditional military skills, but the latter required adaptation for new environments.

Conclusions

Gloire therefore emerges not as a flawed, even redundant, ethos and practice but, repeatedly, as both dynamic and functional. What can be termed the culture of *gloire* linked the military to both politics and the social élite, and also provided a vital organizational tool as *gloire* proved a lubricant of obedience. Indeed, *gloire* and prestige helped deal with the problems of reconciling the imperatives of pride and social status to the exigencies of command, control and co-operation.

Gloire did not become redundant with the changes in the ethos, practice and, indeed, culture of war that stemmed from the bureaucratization and industrialization of the nineteenth and twentieth centuries, nor with the spread of this Western model across the world. Instead, *gloire* as a set of assumptions and factors changed its meaning and application, being seen for example in the culture of valorous self-sacrifice advocated before and during the First World War.

This after-history of the culture of *gloire* requires study. That is not the purpose of this chapter, but the after-history is important as it helps challenge the view that because *gloire* was to become unimportant so it was essentially redundant earlier or, at best, *en route* for redundancy. Such a teleology does not provide a way to understand what is in chronological terms the bulk of military history.

3

Strategic Culture: The Case of Britain, 1688–1815

The present imposes on the past in many ways and strategy is no exception, as emerges in the discussion of British strategic culture and strategy in the 'long eighteenth century', a discussion focused on the key struggles, the Seven Years (1756–63), American Independence (1775–83), French Revolutionary (1793–9) and Napoleonic (1799–1815) wars, each of which was of great importance for global history. Not only is there the question of the impact of employing the concepts of strategic culture and strategy, for which the language then was different or absent, but there is also the danger of shaping, notably into a false coherence, the often disparate discussion, limited planning, and bitty points of evidence, that exist.

The present can also be instructive. In Britain, in 2010, the general election was followed by a Strategic Defence Review and by pressure for a discussion not only of military planning, doctrine and structures, but also of foreign policy, energy security, security policing and related issues, the whole being described as a National Security Review.[1] In short, whatever the view of theorists who might like to separate strategy from policy, that is not a distinction that recommends itself to politicians. This is an insight from the present that is pertinent when looking to the past understanding of strategy. Clearly, the situation varied by state and period, but a key element for most of the past was the lack of any unpacking of strategy and policy, a lack that reflected the absence of any institutional body specifically for strategic planning and execution, and also the tendency to see strategy and policy as one, and necessarily so. Tami Davis Biddle has recently defined grand strategy as 'a plan for the intelligent application of national resources to achieve national aims'.[2] Aims, plan and resources, however, are not neatly segregated facets.

Definitions

Turning to a different aspect of the conceptual dimension, the very existence of strategy, strategic culture and strategic policy in the eighteenth century is highly problematic as far as some well-informed scholars are concerned.[3] This delay in the development of the idea of strategy is held to have reflected conceptual and institutional limitations. Certainly, compared to the formal, institutional processes of strategic discussion and planning in recent decades, strategy was, at best, limited and *ad hoc*, lacking both structure and doctrine. This limited character can be seen as lessening the possibility of moving on from strategy to strategic culture but, conversely, the absence of a mechanism may well have ensured that the body of assumptions and norms referred to as strategic culture were, instead, more effective, indeed 'more normative'.

Despite repeated experience of war by Britain, especially for most of the years between 1689 and 1720, 1739 and 1763, and 1775 and 1815, and continued concerns that it might recur, there were serious deficiencies in the administration of the war effort (for example, the separate administration of the Ordnance), let alone planning.[4] These deficiencies focused on structures, not least the lack of a General Staff, although it is worth noting that the most significant structural problem in the period, that of army–navy co-ordination,[5] remained the case as recently as the Falklands War of 1982. Moreover, whatever the theory, modern joint structures and doctrines face the reality of continued hostility between the services, a rivalry that comes clearly to the fore when, as in Britain in 2010, procurement issues are linked to key questions of tasking and organization. The degree to which this hostility can be seen as having a cultural dimension relates not just to the politics of organizational rivalry but also to the sentiment that encourages a continued commitment to historical identities.

Alongside these flaws in the eighteenth century, it is worth underlining the issue of comparative capability. If British war-making had deficiencies, not least in strategic planning, so also did that of other powers. Indeed, the greater emphasis in most Continental states on the role of the sovereign created serious problems, because monarchy was no guarantee of competence, as Spain under Charles IV clearly demonstrated in the 1800s. Moreover, the delegation of royal powers within a ministerial system still provided opportunities for factionalism, as in France under Louis XIV (r. 1643–1715), Louis XV (r. 1715–74), and Louis XVI (r. 1774–92), and Austria under Charles VI (r. 1711–40). This factionalism may have lacked the public contention seen in Britain, but was none the less serious as a consequence.

However, treating the existence of strategy as highly problematic mistakes the absence of an articulated school of strategic thinking for the lack of strategic awareness, a key point throughout the history of strategy. The claim, for example, that, as there was no term for strategy, so Imperial Rome lacked strategic thinking, fails to give sufficient weight to the lasting need to prioritize possibilities and threats and, in response, to allocate resources.[6] The earlier, Punic Wars between Carthage and Republican Rome have been discussed in terms of what are presented as contemporary views of grand strategy, with the latter seen to depend on long-term planning and a good perception of geographical relationships.[7]

In the eighteenth century, strategic awareness was bound up in the long-standing question of how best to bend the will of opponents.[8] As far as the British navy, the key external arm of the state in the eighteenth and nineteenth centuries, was concerned, there was considerable experience of balancing between tasks. This need and experience can be seen with the detachment of squadrons from home waters for the Baltic and the Mediterranean, an issue that remained a recurrent feature in naval planning and, with a different geographical span, is still pertinent today. Forward deployment can limit as well as enhance flexibility. Moreover, a strategy of naval commercial interdiction played a role in operations against the Dutch in the late seventeenth century and, including a powerful trans-oceanic dimension, in the Anglo-Spanish crisis of 1725–7. Furthermore, the planned use of British naval power in international crises, as in 1730, 1731, 1735, 1770–1, 1787, 1790 and 1791, can be seen as wide-ranging and reasonably sophisticated given limitations with communications and institutional support.

The same is true for Britain in 1689–1815 of planned operations on land, although, here, there is a degree of greater complexity because such operations involved coalition warfare, as was also clearly the case in the twentieth-century world wars. Therefore, there was an intertwining of military planning and diplomatic exigencies; and whatever is meant by strategy cannot be separated from coalition diplomacy. Each, indeed, were aspects of the other. This intertwining can be seen with the War of the Spanish Succession, in which Britain was involved from 1702 to 1713, and again in the War of the Austrian Succession, in which Britain was involved from 1743 to 1748. Strategy existed as a concept, even if the word was not used in English until about 1800, when it was borrowed from the French. The earliest citation in the second edition of the *Oxford English Dictionary* is from 1810. Moreover, as much of the scholarly discussion of the eighteenth century relates to terms not employed by contemporaries, such as Enlightenment, it is difficult to see why this approach should not be employed in the military history of the period,[9] and of earlier centuries.

A second context is provided by an understanding of strategy in the widest sense, namely to relate to the health and strength of the country as a whole. From this perspective, the British role in the Seven Years War (1756–63) was a symptom, albeit a very significant one, of a wider anxiety about the state and future of both country and people, an anxiety similar in some respect to that seen in Britain in the 1900s after the Boer War of 1899–1902. The latter anxiety encouraged the Liberal and Liberal Unionist social welfarism of the period, as well as the development of the Territorial Army movement. The contours of contemporary public political concern helped drive the politics of the conflict. The anxiety referred to in the mid eighteenth century reflected the extent to which organic theories of the state were important. There is a tendency, in contrast, when considering the century, to emphasize mechanistic themes, not least because of the intellectual thrall of Newtonian physics, and the extent to which notions of balancing power were regarded as of importance both for international relations and for domestic constitutional issues. As far as the former were concerned, states were seen as sovereign but linked in a system treated as self-contained, and as part of a static and well-ordered world. The concept was based on the model of the machine which, in turn, was regarded as well ordered and as enabling its parts to conduct activities only in accordance with its own construction. The mechanistic concept of the system of states was well suited to the wider currents of thought, specifically Cartesian rationalism, as well as its successors.

These currents of thought, which represented a rationalizing culture of a particular type, provided not only an analytical framework, but also a moral context for international relations. For example, to take balance-of-power politics, which, as generally presented, appear as selfishly pragmatic, bereft of any overarching rules, and lacking any ethical theoretical foundations, in practice, however, the situation was somewhat different. There was a widely expressed theory of the balance of power, and rules for its politics, outlined in tracts, pamphlets, doctoral dissertations, and explanations of the reasons for the resort to war. The relationship between such theoretization and rules, on the one hand, and decisionmaking processes, on the other, is obscure, and clearly varied by ruler and minister, but such discussion set normative standards that helped shape policies and responses.[10] Strategy, in short, drew on widely diffused concepts of how power should operate, and this element of political placing and cultural conditioning is crucial.

Without denying a central role for notions bound up in the balance of power, it is necessary to complement them with an awareness of organic assumptions. These were important not so much at the level of the international system (until the nineteenth century), but at that of individual states. Moreover, these assumptions helped provide a dynamic component that is generally lacking with the more structural nature of the mechanistic themes. This dynamic component was vitalist in intention. In particular, there was a sense of a state as the expression of a nation, of the latter as linked in a national character, and of this character as capable of change and as prone to decay. The latter looked in part to cyclical accounts of the rise and fall of empires which drew much of their authority from the commanding role of Classical Rome in the historicized political thought of the period, but there was also a strong input from ideas of health. A traditional sense of the nation as akin to a person remained important, and helped focus attention on embodiments such as Britannia and John Bull. This idea translated into the international sphere with a sense of nations, as also in the early twentieth century, as inherently competitive, and as under threat from challenges that were foreign as well as domestic in their causation and mechanism.

Strategy and Limits

Turning to strategy, notions of balance both encouraged action on the part of a Britain opposed to the hegemonic power, France, for most of the period; and yet also acted as a restraint, not least because of anxieties about the possible consequences for British politics and society of such action in terms of developing an over-mighty government and becoming an over-expanded state. Yet, such restraint only guided strategy up to a point. In particular, in normative as well as prudential terms, in so far as the two were possible, war and imperial expansion appeared possible, successful and necessary for most of the period up to 1945, and Winston Churchill pursued colonial gains for Britain as late as the Second World War: at the expense of the Italian colony of Libya and also the Kra isthmus in Thailand. Within Europe, states until the twentieth century sought simultaneously to consolidate authority and to gain territory, each goals that involved normative and prudential valuations; and to opt out would not have appeared sensible. With its stress on honour and dynastic responsibility and its concern with *gloire* and the normative values of combat, the dominant political culture of Continental Europe was scarcely cautious or pacific. This situation helped compose the strategic culture of individual states.

Due to domestic circumstances, particularly parliamentary power and the small size of the army,[11] as well as its island position, Britain was different as far as European expansion was concerned; but this difference has to be handled with care. At one extreme, for Britain not to have resisted the American Revolution (1775–83) would have appeared as bizarre as for Philip II of Spain not to oppose the Dutch Revolt two centuries earlier. More generally, as far as expansion was involved, a prudent defence of interest, and not overreach, was at issue in activity, and this was true whether the case was advancing Spanish goals in Italy (from the 1490s to the 1740s), or pursuing British objectives in the Ohio Valley Region in the early 1750s, or *arguably* the USA in the Middle East today.

For either Spain under Philip II or Britain in the long eighteenth century (1689–1815), to respond to rivals by trying to avoid conflict and instead by defining mutually acceptable spheres of influence was difficult, if not impracticable, and, again, the parallel with the modern USA may be considered. Such a policy would have been politically and ideologically problematic. It would also have been a serious signalling of weakness. Lastly, for Spain, as far as the Ottomans, France or the Dutch were concerned, as for Britain in 1689–1815, as far as France was the case, there seems little reason to believe that compromise could have been reached and sustained short of large-scale conflict, which was the prelude to peace treaties; and, in a very different context, the same case can be made for the 'war on terror'.

Thus, strategic reach could only be defined as part of, and yet also in response to, what others might see as overreach. Indeed, far from being alternatives, reach and overreach were part of the same process. Moreover, the very success of both Spain and Britain makes it clear that overreach is a difficult, although still useful, concept. The conquest, by relatively small forces, of large areas, and the successful laying of claim to others, did not demonstrate the value of limits. A desire to avoid risk would have prevented Britain from responding to French moves in 1754–5 and 1792–3, or have kept the Spaniards in the Caribbean offshore from the American mainland in the early sixteenth century; neither of which would have appeared prudent in hindsight; and, in the British case, such a course would have been impossible. Risk itself is an aspect of the culture of decisionmaking, and notably so in military matters.

Furthermore, the element of external (as well as domestic) perception central to the apparently objective notion of strategic overreach also reflects the ideological and cultural assumptions of the perceiver both at the time and subsequently, assumptions that are frequently subliminal, but nonetheless very significant. This situation is the case for both Britain and Spain. For Spain, there is a long-standing external perception which can be described as Whiggish or liberal. This perception reflects critical views on Catholicism and, correspondingly, the customary association of progress with Protestantism. Aside from being anachronistic, the Spanish empire emerges in this teleological account as something that had to be defeated in order to usher in the future. Given this perception, it is not surprising that the idea of overreach is applied to Spain, and that its strategy is judged accordingly.

Strategy and Dynasticism

Comparison with Britain then comes to the fore.[12] First, it is important to stress the role of contingency, and thus apparently imminent limits, on Britain during the period 1689–1815, a contingency that helped ensure that Britain had a 'hybrid' strategy, one that combined different elements and varied by time and space.[13] If Spain suffered rebellions during the period 1560–1660, so also did Britain in 1689–1815. Moreover, in Britain there was a rival (Jacobite/Stuart) dynasty, with all the issues that posed for stability and loyalty, a situation that did not occur in Spain until the 1700s and, then again, in 1808–13.

Britain, furthermore, faced a threat that Spain did not confront in 1560–1660, that of foreign invasion. Indeed, in 1688–9, the male line of the Stuart dynasty was overthrown. Subsequently, invasion attempts on behalf of the Stuarts were mounted on a number of occasions, including in 1692, 1708, 1719, 1744, 1745 and 1759. Each was backed by France, apart from the 1719 attempt, which was supported by Spain. Thereafter, invasion attempts were mounted by France in its wars with Britain, including in 1779, 1798 and 1805. Nothing comparable could be launched by Britain against France. The frequency of the attempts, and the even more insistent level of threat, brings forward the question of appropriate strategy, both for the state and, more problematically, for the dynasty.

The latter is not the perspective that attracts more commentators. It has little to offer structural discussions of empires or empire-like states and their strategic position, and does not fit with the need or drive in much of the literature, that of finding historical resonance for America's modern position and problems. The understandable tendency to write the past from the perspective of the present, not least in terms of its vocabulary and analytical concepts, therefore creates problems. In particular, the role of dynasticism in the past is downplayed.

However, the question of strategic grasp and overreach can be reconceptualized to ask whether gaining rule over Britain represented overreach for the Orange and Hanoverian dynasties, and was also an aspect of the culture of *gloire* considered in the last chapter. In the case of the Orange dynasty, the reign of William III was short (1689–1702), he had no children, and he was already in opposition to Louis XIV of France. If becoming ruler of Britain opened up another military front for William, and tied up Dutch and allied troops that might otherwise have been deployed against France on the Continent in 1688–90, it did so in a way that also weakened France. The British war became a major source of military and naval commitment for Louis XIV and, after that situation had ceased, William III benefited greatly from British resources, both in the war that continued until 1697 and in the subsequent post-war negotiations. Indeed, there was an instructive contrast between William's failure to sustain a strong European alliance able to limit Louis XIV after the Dutch War ended in 1678 and the greater success shown after 1697, both in negotiating a European settlement with France, the Partition Treaties of 1698 and 1700, and, after the partition of the Spanish Empire was rejected by Louis in 1700, in William preparing a Grand Alliance for the forthcoming war.

The question of shared strategic interests is more problematic as far as the Hanoverian dynasty was concerned. Initially, the British connection, which began with the accession of George I in 1714, appeared a way to advance Hanoverian dynastic claims to territory and status, not least in the partition of the Swedish empire as a result of the Great Northern War (1700–21). George II (r. 1727–60) continued this policy, with hopes of gains for Hanover in Germany. Yet, these hopes were not realized until the Congress of Vienna in 1814–15 adjusted Europe after the Napoleonic Wars. Instead, the vulnerability of Hanover was repeatedly demonstrated, whether by the threat of Prussian (1726, 1729, 1753, 1801 and 1805), or of French (1741, 1757, 1803 and 1806) attack. The electorate of Hanover was seriously devastated by the occupying French forces in 1757, and its participation in the Seven Years War proved very costly, and indeed for Britain, because troops were deployed in Germany from 1758, in part to assist Hanover, although also to assist Britain's ally, Frederick II, the Great, of Prussia. The difficult consequences led Hanoverian ministers to speculate about ending the dynastic link with Britain,[14] a situation that, indirectly, looked towards Hanoverian neutrality in 1795–1804.[15] The British commitment to the dynasty could be regarded as the cause of Hanover's plight in 1757, not least as George II, under strong pressure from his British ministers, notably William Pitt the Elder, rejected the option of neutrality for the electorate.

Conversely, strategic limits can be seen in another aspect of the relationship, because the attempt to pursue what could be presented as shared Anglo-Hanoverian interests in Europe ran up against such hindrances as the dynastic rivalry of the ruling houses of Hanover and Prussia; secondly, the Austrian defence of the authority of the Holy Roman Emperor and the interests of the Catholic Church against Protestant rulers such as Hanover; and, thirdly, the expansionist schemes of Russia.[16] The result was repeated Anglo-Hanoverian failure, as well as problems for Britain, albeit a failure overshadowed by trans-oceanic British expansion.

Strategy and the Limits of Imperial Power

This point opens up the question of where emphasis should be placed in strategic analysis, and again whose emphasis. It might be suggested that this is a simple question of contrasting contemporary with modern values, but neither is that clear cut. For example, there is an important debate about the extent to which eighteenth-century Britons were committed to trans-oceanic goals,[17] the dominant view in the literature of the 1990s, or, rather, European ones, an argument increasingly prominent in more recent years.[18] Similar debate attaches to Britain at the present moment, while there is likely to be a strengthening of debate in the USA, not least as the Republicans seek to define a new policy in response both to the Bush legacy and to the Obama presidency.

Such debate underlines the problematic nature of the thesis that interests are clear, and in some ways differentiated from culture, a point that needs stressing when there is discussion of strategy. Indeed, this very discussion about strategy is largely a matter of the debate over interests, however defined: national, state, dynastic, class, and so on. This point makes the debate more, not less, important.

Returning again to eighteenth-century Britain, there is the parallel between the American Revolution and that against Philip II in the Netherlands, and the question of how far the two indicate limits of strategic capability. Here, limits can be seen as much, if not more, in terms of policy as of the geography of strategy, the where of campaigning. Indeed, a focus on the latter may seem to represent a militarization of strategy and the question of limits that is disproportionately important in the literature. In contrast to this militarization of issues of policy and strategy, other (political) policies would certainly have led to very different situations, affecting the possibility of rebellion, the likelihood of support within the areas that rebelled, and the prospect for a reconciliation short of revolution. This issue cuts to the quick of the discussion about strategic effectiveness because it removes this question from the realm of mechanistic theories of the state/empire – of the form of thus far is appropriate, but more ambition and activity causes a reaction, rather like a machine cutting out, or a rubber band losing its stretch.

Instead, it is the very drive of the system that is at question when policies and the pressures for obedience and order are considered, an approach that puts the accent on the culture of power understood in terms of both goals and means. Partly for this reason, there is a need to include domestic policy as a key aspect of strategy. Indeed, as earlier with limits, the value of a flexible definition for strategy emerges. It is conventional to restrict the term to the military, but this practice is not terribly helpful from the perspective of the pursuit and limits of power, as strategy emerges as primarily political in background, goal and indeed means, with the use of force simply an aspect of the means, and frequently one that is only to be employed as a substitute. Thus, strategy should be understood in terms of a process of policy formation, execution and evaluation, all involving cultural elements, a process to which military purposes are frequently secondary.

In part, the definition and discussion, in recent decades, of an operational dimension to war provides a key opportunity for reconceptualizing strategy, away from its usual military location, and, instead, towards an understanding of the concept that is more centrally political and cultural. In any event, even at the operational and tactical levels, political considerations played, and play, a key role. They can be seen as aspects of the political character of warfare, notably again the sense of limits in means as well as goals, each of which are an aspect of strategic culture. This point is not a semantic play on the notion of limited war, instructive as that is in this context, but, instead, an emphasis on the extent to which war-making in the eighteenth century involved limits or their absence, for example in the treatment of prisoners and civilians, or the extent of scorched earth policies; while there were differences between conflict designed to retain and/or incorporate territory and warfare more focused on battle with, even the destruction of, opposing forces.

The Tone of Strategy

As far as Britain was concerned, limits can also be debated in such terms as the extent to which territorial expansion was pursued from the centre, or largely by colonial lobbies and proconsular generals and officials, for this contentious political question is directly germane to the question of the appropriateness of the use of armed force at particular junctures and, indeed, the extent to which limits were a matter of debate and nuance, and certainly not clear cut. This was also the case with such 'ethnic violence' as the contentious expulsion of the Acadians from Nova Scotia or indeed the contested policies followed towards native Americans. Limits in tone thus overlap with limits in policy, the two influencing and also expressing each other.

   Variations and limits in tone bring up key cultural elements that act as a qualification to the ready ahistorical transference of imperial examples for analytical purpose, for example from ancient Rome to the modern United States. Thus, although religion was important to the various aspects of the character of British imperialism,[19] it can be suggested that it did not have an equivalent impact to that of Catholicism under Philip II of Spain and, indeed, his two successors. This view can be qualified and debated, but that very process underlines the extent to which the cultural or ideological dimension, and everything it entailed for an understanding and telling of strategic culture, interests and limits, has to be understood in terms of a specific historical context and cannot be readily reduced to, or by, any form of structuralism and determinism.

Seven Years War, 1756–63

For example, as far as the Seven Years War was concerned, anti-Catholicism was crucial in affecting British attitudes,[20] and this point is worth underlining because it encouraged a sense that the struggle should be persisted in even in the face of news that was very negative, which was the case in the early days of the war.[21] Anti-Catholicism led to a sense of existentialist and meta-historical struggle. Policy and strategy rested on a clear ideological commitment, which for the troops provided a much more immediate one than dynasticism or national interests.

At a different strategic level, British war-making in this conflict was greatly affected by the possibilities and exigencies of alliance politics, as indeed had been the case throughout the years of war with France from 1689, and many, but not all, earlier conflicts, for example the Third Anglo-Dutch War of 1672–4. Britain alone could hold off attack but, in spite of the hopes of 'Blue Water' power exponents focusing on naval and amphibious operations, could not overthrow its opponent, which was a lasting problem in British strategic culture. In the Seven Years War, despite the, often bombastic, subsequent commemoration of the conflict, Britain's ally, Frederick II, the Great, of Prussia, possessed the resources (just) and skill solely to put up a good resistance to Austria, France and Russia, while Britain had only been able to defeat France (and Spain in 1762) in the sense of capturing colonies and sinking warships (and blocking the Spanish invasion of Portugal). Coastal raids on France accomplished little, and Britain's loss of the Austrian and Dutch alliances in 1756 ensured that there was no war in the Low Countries.

The strategy of the war was a complex mixture of taking initiatives and responding to those of Britain's enemies, their relationship framed in the contexts of domestic and international politics. Key questions arose from the impact of the entry into senior office of William Pitt the Elder (as Secretary of State) and the alliance with Frederick II. The former led to an emphasis on trans-oceanic operations as a result of his linkage with Patriot and Tory political groupings and themes. As such, the policies advocated in 1757 by William, Duke of Cumberland, George II's son and the head of the army protecting Hanover, were pushed to one side. Pitt had had military experience, but only as a peacetime cavalry cornet, and he had no real view on the conduct of war other than that he wanted it to be vigorous.

In driving an aggressive strategy in North America, Pitt pressed for the defence of the British colonies and the conquest of Canada from France, but the extent to which this entailed battles or sieges was up to the commanders on the ground and to circumstances. The same was true of naval operations. Britain, British trade, and British overseas operations had to be protected from attack, but it was difficult to force battle on opponents unless they left harbour, and therefore the blockade of France's ports came foremost. As far as British policy-makers were concerned, the war had resulted from French aggression in the Ohio Valley region, and the extent to which the conflict was intended to yield additional gains was only clear with the hindsight of success, demonstrating the dependence of strategic culture on contingencies. Prior to that, it was likely that the war would end, as the War of the Austrian Succession had done in 1748 with the exchange of gains. The latter outcome was the norm, and was not the basis for any strategy focused on conquest other than to acquire gains that could be exchanged.

War of American Independence, 1775–83

In contrast to the Seven Years War, the political context was very different in the War of American Independence, which underlines the extent to which the key to strategy is the political purposes that are pursued. In short, strategy is a process of understanding problems and determining goals, and not the details of the plans by which these goals are implemented by military means. Strategic culture provides the general assumptions and context for this process. Strategy in the War of Independence has to be understood in this light because this strategy was very different in type to that during the Seven Years War. In the latter case, the British focus had been on conquest in North America from France and not on pacification there. The latter was very much subservient to the former, although different policies were pursued for the purpose of pacification. These included an eighteenth-century equivalent of ethnic cleansing in the expulsion of the Acadians from Nova Scotia, as well as the very different post-conquest accommodation of the Catholics of Québec, which looked towards the Quebec Act of 1774.

In the War of Independence, in contrast, pacification, not defeat, was the British strategy, and the question was how best to secure it. As a civil war, the purpose of the conflict was clear, the return of the Americans to their loyalty, and the method chosen was different from that taken in response to the Jacobite risings in Scotland and northern England in 1715–16 and 1745–6. In the latter cases, as later in the face of the Irish rebellion in 1798, the remedy had been more clearly military, although, in making that argument, it is necessary to note post-war policies for stability through reorganization, most obviously in the introduction of new governmental systems for the Scottish Highlands and Ireland.

In the case of America, there was not this sequencing but, instead, a willingness to consider, not only pacification alongside conflict, but also new systems as an aspect of this pacification. In one sense, pacification began at the outset, with the misconceived and mishandled attempt by the British army to seize arms in New England in 1775. The most prominent instances of pacification were the instructions to the Howe Brothers in 1776 to negotiate as well as fight, and, even more clearly, the dispatch of the Carlisle Commission in 1778. Moreover, the restoration of colonial government in the South was a concrete step indicating, during the war, what the British were seeking to achieve.

Alongside that, and more insistently, were the practices of British commanders. Although the American Patriots (rebels) were traitors, they were treated with leniency, and suggestions of harsher treatment were generally ignored. This point underlines the extent to which conduct in the field both reflects strategy and also affects the development of strategic culture. The cultural norms of war are created through usage, as well as vice versa.

Britain's fundamental strategy rested on a policy cohesion that had military consequences; passivity in Europe combined with the preservation of status in America. Britain acted as a satisfied (or as later critics such as the nineteenth-century German Chancellor Bismarck would have seen it, satiated) power, keen obviously to retain and safeguard its position, but not interested in gaining fresh territory. Representing a satisfied power, British ministers were wary of becoming involved in European power politics. Here the American war fitted into a pattern that had begun with George III's rejection of the Prussian alliance in 1761–2. There was to be no recurrence for Britain of the situation during the Seven Years War, namely war in alliance with a Continental power, no alliance with Prussia (nor anyone else) to distract France, and, as a result, in military terms, no commitment of the British army to the Continent, as had occurred in 1758. However unintentional, that situation had proved particularly potent, or had been shaped thus by William Pitt the Elder with his presentation of British policy in terms of conquering Canada in Europe. It was initially far from clear, however, that Britain's involvement on the Continent would work out as favourably as, in the event, happened. Given the use made of this example, that point provides an instance of the nature of strategic thought and culture as recovered memory.

There was also no significant domestic constituency in the 1770s for an interventionist strategy in Europe, and notably none for any particular interventionist course of action. Aside from the practicalities of British power, and the nature of British politics, the Western Question, the fate of Western Europe, more particularly the Low Countries, the Rhineland and Italy, had been settled diplomatically in the

1750s, by the Austrian alliances with Spain and then France; removing both need and opportunity for British intervention. This shift in power politics was crucial, for in Britain the public support for interventionism on the Continent was fragile, if not weak, unless the Bourbons (the rulers of France and Spain) were the target. The domestic coalition of interests and ideas upon which public backing for foreign policy rested was heavily reliant on the consistency offered by the resonance of the anti-Bourbon beat. British military strategy in the war cannot be separated from wider currents of political preference and engagement. This point underlines the issues created for British strategy in the 'war on terror' in the 2000s to 2010s by problems with the extent of public engagement.

What British strategy appeared to entail in North America varied greatly during the conflict. The initial British impression was of opposition largely only in Massachusetts, and this suggested that a vigorous defence of imperial interests there would save the situation. This view led to British legislation in 1774 specific to this colony and to a concentration of Britain's forces in North America there. The initial military operationalization of strategy continued after the clashes at Concord and Lexington in 1775, both because the stress on Massachusetts appeared vindicated and because there were not enough troops for action elsewhere, a key failure in British preparedness and one that underlined the preference for prudential war that the officers took from the literature they read.[22]

In the event, British policy failed, both in Massachusetts and elsewhere. In the former, the military presence was unable to prevent rebellion or to contain it, and eventually, in March 1776, the British had to evacuate Boston when the harbour was threatened by American cannon. Elsewhere in North America, the lack of troops stemming from the concentration on Boston ensured that British authority was overthrown in the other colonies involved in the revolution; while the Americans were able to mount an invasion of Canada that achieved initial success, bottling up the British in Québec.

As a result of the events of 1775–6, the second stage of the war, a stage expected and planned neither by most of the Patriots nor by the British government, led to a major British effort to regain control, a policy that entailed both a formidable military effort and peacemaking proposals. Here, again, it is necessary to look at the military options in terms of the political situation. The end of the rebellion/revolution could not be achieved by reconquering the Thirteen Colonies (and driving the Americans from Canada). The task was too great, which underlines the question of how strategic culture is affected by the possibilities of conflict. Instead, it was necessary to secure military results that achieved the political outcome of an end to rebellion, an outcome that was likely to require both a negotiated settlement, and acquiescence in the return to loyalty and in subsequently maintaining obedience. This outcome rested on a different politics to that of the conquest of New France (Canada) during the Seven Years War.

What was unclear was which military results would best secure this outcome. Was the priority the defeat, indeed destruction, of the Continental Army, as it represented the American Revolution, not least its unity; or was it the capture of key American centres? Each goal appeared possible, and there was a mutual dependence between them. The British would not be able to defeat the Americans unless they could land and support troops, and, for this capability to be maintained, it was necessary to secure port cities. Conversely, these port cities could best be held if American forces were defeated, as the British abandonment of Boston in March 1776 in the absence of such a victory made clear. The equations of troop numbers underlined the situation, not least the problems posed for finite British military resources by maintaining large garrison forces. Indeed, the latter point lent further military point to the political strategy of pacification, as such a strategy would reduce the need for garrisons and produce local Loyalist forces, as well as diminishing the number of Patriots. Any decision that prioritizes goals can be presented as cultural in character.

In an instance of a long-standing issue in both strategy and operational planning, the British emphasis possibly should have been on destroying the Continental Army, which was definitely a prospect in 1776–7. Instead, the stress was on regaining key centres, not least as this policy was seen as a way of demonstrating the return of royal authority, particularly by ensuring that large numbers of Americans again came under the Crown. Indeed, from the period when the empire struck back, the summer of 1776, the British gained control of most of the key American points, either for much of the war (New York from 1776, Savannah from 1778, Charleston from 1780), or, as it turned out, temporarily (Newport from 1776, Philadelphia from 1777).

This policy still left important centres, most obviously Boston from March 1776, that were not under British control, which indicated the fundamental political problem facing the British and, more generally true of strategic planning as a whole, especially in civil wars: whatever they won in the field, it would still be necessary to achieve a political settlement, at least in the form of a return to loyalty. The understanding of this issue was an achievement for the British, but also posed a problem, while, correspondingly, this understanding was also both achievement and problem for the Patriots.

This point helps explain the attention devoted by American Patriot leaders throughout the war to politics, as political outcomes were needed to secure the persistence and coherence of the war effort. The British, in turn, could try, by political approaches and military efforts, to alter these political equations within the Thirteen Colonies. At times, they succeeded in doing so, as in the new political prospectus offered in South Carolina after the successful British siege of Charleston in 1780. Indeed, in tidewater South Carolina, British authority was swiftly recognized. This success appeared to be a vindication of the British strategy of combining military force with a conciliatory political policy, offering a new imperial relationship that granted most of the American demands made at the outbreak of the war. It was scarcely surprising that northern politicians, such as Ezekiel Cornell of Rhode Island, came to doubt the determination of their southern counterparts.

To treat this conflict, on either side, therefore simply as a military struggle is to underplay the role of political goals and related preferences in political culture. Indeed, these goals affected not only the moves of armies (a conventional, but overly limited, understanding of strategy), but even the nature of the forces deployed by both sides. The American focus on a standing army that reflected the social composition both of European counterparts and of colonial society was very important to the character and internal dynamics of the American force and to the longer term development of American society.[23] More significantly for the war itself, the British use of German 'mercenaries' and, even more, native Americans and African Americans, provided opportunities for political mobilization on the part of the hostile (American) Patriots. Correspondingly, American reliance on France increased domestic support for war in Britain and hit sympathy for the Patriots, who could now be presented as hypocrites, willing to ally with a Catholic autocracy (two, when Spain joined in in 1779), and with Britain's national enemy as well.

These alliances brought the war to a new stage, as there was no inherent clarity regarding the allocation of British resources between the conflict with the Bourbons and that with the Americans. Whereas it was relatively easy for the Patriots to abandon the Greater American plan of conquering Canada, after failure in 1776 was followed by British military efforts in the Thirteen Colonies that had to be countered, there was no such agreement over policy in Britain. Partisan politics came into play, not least the politics of justification, with the Opposition pressing for a focus on the Bourbons and the ministry unwilling to follow to the same extent, not least because it neither wished, nor thought it appropriate, to abandon hopes of America. This rift underlined the extent to which strategic culture rests on contested political assumptions, and the latter challenged a fixed approach to the former.

This debate was not settled until Yorktown, not so much, crucially, the battle in October 1781 as, rather, the political consequences in Britain, specifically the fall of the Lord North ministry the following March, and the fact that it was not succeeded by a similar one following royal views (as would, for example, have been a ministry under Edward, Lord Thurlow, the Lord Chancellor, a close ally of George III) but, instead, the Opposition, under Charles, 2nd Marquess of Rockingham, came to power.

As a result of the central role of politics in strategy, 1782 was a key year of the war. It was a year, ironically, in which the Patriots had singularly little military success, George Washington, in particular, getting nowhere with his plan to capture New York. Moreover, this failure was more generally significant as it marked the decline in the Franco-American alliance, a decline that reflected both the problems of pursuing very different military priorities and, far more significantly, a war weariness on the part of the French government that was also linked to the priorities of European power politics. Furthermore, in 1782, the French fleet in the West Indies was defeated by Admiral Rodney at the battle of the Saintes; a key instance of the role of battle in determining strategic options. Thus, militarily, the war was going Britain's way. New warships were being launched, public finances were robust, fears of rebellion in Ireland and of disaffection in Britain were largely assuaged, the Bourbons were increasingly unable to attempt another invasion of Britain, Gibraltar had been held, and the British position in both India and Canada was more resilient than had been feared.

However, the politics was now of peace and settlement that were not focused on a return of America to its loyalty; and strategy was framed accordingly. Instead, the priority was the disruption, if not destruction, of the coalition of powers fighting Britain and, hopefully, better relations with an independent United States (as it later became). Paradoxically, this strategy was to be successful in both the short and the long term, which simply underlines the conceptual problems of conceiving of strategy in terms of its military operationalization.

French Revolutionary and Napoleonic Wars, 1793–1815

This point also emerges where the French Revolutionary and Napoleonic Wars are concerned. These conflicts proved a key episode in

British strategy, not only because they were important in their own right for developments in the period, but also because they served as the crucial frame of reference for British public discussion about strategy until the next 'Great War', that with Germany in 1914–18. This continuity, moreover, was maintained because France was Britain's leading rival until the *Entente* of 1904 between them, a situation underlined as late as 1898 when the two powers came close to war in the Fashoda Crisis. Indeed, Russia, which challenged British interests and views from the Balkans to the Far East in the nineteenth century, with a particular emphasis on the threat to the British position in India, could be subsumed into this Anglo-French enmity as a result of the Franco-Russian alliance that developed in the late-nineteenth century in reaction to their joint antagonism to that between Germany and Austria.

The French Revolutionary and Napoleonic Wars underlined a lesson seen with the challenge, variously from Spain and France, from the 1530s to the 1740s, namely that the threat from a foreign power, the key element in re-active strategy, was linked to domestic issues, in the former case Catholicism and, from 1689 in addition, Jacobitism. In contrast, the ideological challenge from the French Revolution abated after Napoleon's seizure of power in France in 1799, and this situation looked towards that throughout the nineteenth century, and, indeed, until intervention in the Russian Civil War at the end of the First World War; namely a disassociation between international and domestic strategic threats.

This dissociation has played too prominent a role in the literature, as nineteenth-century strategy and policy have generally been seen in terms of realist power politics, but the suggestion here is that this analysis is misplaced. Indeed, the British governing élite fostered a strategic imagination that was set by domestic, rather than international, paradigms. Moreover, the dissociation also enabled the British people between 1815 and 1914 to perceive wars as foreign and largely inconsequential to Britain and its way of life. In turn, this attitude affected the strategic imagination; as indeed it continues to do. For modern Britain, a key factor is that, despite talk of the country needing to be on a war footing, for example against terrorism, no policy choices should entail conscription, as conscription is no longer acceptable either to public culture nor to the views of government. The contrary view argues that threats drive domestic considerations, as in 1916, when Britain adopted conscription despite its clashing with the liberal and libertarian tendencies in British thought. Yet, the French Revolutionary and Napoleonic Wars saw serious threats without the introduction of conscription, although press gangs were employed to increase the number of sailors.

Comparative capability is an issue in strategy that has to be addressed with reference to the tasks that militaries were expected to execute; and here there were particular problems for Britain as a consequence of its island status and trans-oceanic interests. The British military was expected to dominate and ensure the security of the British Isles, to operate on the European continent, and to defeat European, and a wide range of non-European, opponents across the oceans. These tasks entailed not only strategic commitments but also the problem of prioritization that was the key issue in the public and governmental politics of strategy, for example colonies versus Europe in the 1790s.[24]

These politics were crucial to strategic formulation because it was not partly insulated from political pressures by the institutionalization and secrecy that characterized strategic planning in the twentieth century and today. Furthermore, the politics of strategy helped provide a considerable measure of continuity, with issues and problems interpreted and debated in terms of what was by 1793, when Britain entered the French Revolutionary War, over a century of experience of conflict with France and also with a long-standing background of conflict with Spain. In each case, experience was perceived through the perspective of collective (and contentious) public myths, such as the hopes invested in 'blue water' strategy: naval mastery and the consequent trans-oceanic conquests through amphibious operations.

The established treatment of strategy and strategic culture for the period is operational or combat-orientated,[25] but this approach underplays the central role of the Home Front. Strategy, as before, related to two aspects of domestic politics: first, potential supporters of the foreign power and, secondly, conventional high politics. These overlapped, with George III very concerned about the loyalty of the Whig opposition and the extent to which their attitudes encouraged the French Revolutionaries and Napoleon. Furthermore, George was worried that if the opposition gained power, as they were to do in 1806, Britain's war goals would be jeopardized, if not the war abandoned, as it had been in 1782, although he was to be proved wrong in 1806.

A key element of the war strategy was therefore the exclusion of the opposition from power and this was very important to George III in his negotiations with politicians, as in 1804 when William Pitt the Younger returned to office. If the issue was not quite as central to George as that of preventing Catholic emancipation (the extension of equal civil rights to Catholics), it was nevertheless of great importance to him. A continuity in strategy can indeed be seen between wartime planning and discussion over the terms to be offered in peace negotiations, both those in the 1790s and those in 1806.

This was not the limit of the domestic dimension. There was also a concern about popular radicalism and the potential it enjoyed to recruit support. As a result, two major strands of wartime strategy were action against radicals, particularly the trials and changes in the law of the 1790s, and the sponsoring of loyalism. The latter was a spontaneous public movement, arising in particular in the case of the navy from the fruitful combination of patriotism and success,[26] but was also sponsored and sustained by government action. Loyalism had a direct military consequence in the shape of the massive increase in militia and volunteer forces. These provided a key force for domestic security, not least against any action by radicals (matching the role of the American militia against loyalists during the American War of Independence), and also were intended to strengthen the country against invasion.[27] The militia and volunteer forces made it possible to increase the number of regulars who could be sent on expeditions, anticipating the role of the Home Guard in the Second World War. Loyalism therefore illustrated the multiple overlaps of the domestic and foreign spheres of wartime strategy, overlaps of which contemporaries were well aware. There was a marked emphasis on winning public support.[28]

At the same time, this military need indicated the extent to which strategy was in part a matter of reinterpreting the nuances of domestic power relations. Raising militia and volunteer forces underlined the need for the state to co-operate with local interests in obtaining resources, an aspect of the long-standing balance between the Crown and local interests. Militia colonels regarded their regiments as patronage fiefs, immensely valuable to them as county magnates and public men for both patronage and prestige. As a result, important changes in the militia laws had to be negotiated with the colonels, and even the practice of regular drafts into the army was carefully conducted to protect their interests.

The domestic dimension was most acute in Ireland, which had been seen in, and after, the War of American Independence as a potential site of rebellion. There was one in 1798, which was followed by a French invasion. Another, far more minor, rising took place in 1803. Their failure should not direct attention away from the key role of defence in British strategy. This lay behind many military activities, including the construction of fortifications on the south coast of England in the 1790s and 1800s.

Domestic strategy and strategic culture were a matter also of national reform, which was similar to the position abroad, for example in Prussia after her defeat by France in 1806, and was not unprecedented in British history. Aspects of the 'Revolution Settlement', or governmental and political changes that followed the 'Glorious Revolution' of 1688–9, owed much to the pressures of war with France in 1689–97 and 1702–13, not least the establishment of the Bank of England in 1694 and Union with Scotland in 1707. The same was true in 1793–1815, just as the Liberal Unionists of the 1900s also pushed domestic regeneration as an aspect of a strategy of international confrontation. In each case, specific changes, as well as the process of change as a whole, were seen as strengthening Britain, and as key elements of the strategy for keeping the country resilient and competitive, and of directing the energies of society. As far as naval power was concerned, national strength was clearly important to an economic strategy of protecting trade and harming that of opponents, because this ensured the financial clout necessary to support operations abroad, both British deployments and the actions of allied forces.

Important reforms included the introduction of income tax (1799), which helped make possible a shift from financing war by borrowing to financing it through taxation. This shift, from 1798, was a response to the liquidity crisis of 1797, and made it easier to endure setbacks, as borrowing was very dependent on confidence. A focus on taxation also fulfilled the vital strategic goal of making public finances far less dependent on the inflow of foreign capital which had been a key feature of the borrowing regime. The French occupation of Amsterdam in 1795 had threatened this flow. Moreover, parliamentary union with Ireland (1800–1) was regarded as a way of reducing the vulnerability represented by Ireland, as it was regarded as making the link with Britain acceptable to Irish opinion. Catholic relief was an important aspect of the same policy, one more specifically designed to ensure Irish manpower for the army. There was also a stress on the acquisition of information as a way to strengthen government. The first national census (1801) was important, but more immediate value was gained by detailed mapping by the Board of Ordnance designed to help operationally in the event of a French invasion.[29]

The focus of major reform initiatives in the late 1790s and early 1800s underlines the value of providing a chronological perspective. The sense of a domestic challenge, and the need for a corresponding strategy, was strongest in the 1790s and, in contrast, less pronounced after victory at Trafalgar over the combined Franco-Spanish fleet in 1805. The radicalism of the late 1800s and early 1810s did not seem revolutionary: although there was some admiration for Napoleon in the British Isles, his abandonment of republicanism greatly tarnished his appeal and that of French political models. Napoleon also lost interest in the cause of Irish independence, which had always been peripheral to his concerns. Robert Emmet had received a promise of support when he visited Napoleon in 1802, but his preparations for an ultimately unsuccessful rising in Ireland in 1803 were correctly made without any anticipation of French backing.

If the chronological dimension provides an important perspective for the strategy of domestic preparedness, it also offers a crucial one for the very different issue of tasking. The latter might appear readily set: France had to be defeated. In practice, however, there were two separate, but related, strands that repay attention. First, there was the issue of what was the goal of the war with France, and, secondly, that of the range of opponents and allies, and how this range inter-acted with the first strand. As far as France was concerned, there was a crucial tension, one fundamental to strategy, between the argu-ment that France had to be defeated in order to contain it, and the far more ambitious approach that containment could only be secured if its political system was transformed, most clearly by a restoration of Bourbon rule. Even before serious hostilities began there was a sense that this was to be a different conflict because of the ideological gulf separating the two sides, and that this would require new military measures.

Yet, developments also played a key part in the changing assump-tions of strategic culture. As a reminder of the variety of factors involved in the strategic learning curve, George, like his ministers, became more dissatisfied with the allies from 1794,[30] and this dissatis-faction greatly affected the debate over where best to deploy forces. The collapse of the Allied position on the Continent in 1795, with military defeat exacerbated by what was seen as Prussia's disgrace-ful abandonment of the struggle (Spain did likewise), left George, nevertheless, both resolute and also convinced that peace negotia-tions would be foolish as likely to save the French political system. His attitude proved an important element in the strategy of possible peace, although the ministry's willingness, both in 1796 and in 1797, to negotiate with France could have led to an end to the war, with all the implications for the contemporary and subsequent judgement of strategic tasking that this would have entailed. However, the negotia-tions failed.

Success won France allies and dependants from 1795. This process reflected the failure of British policy in Europe, but both greatly enlarged the opportunities for British offensive action overseas (par-ticularly after the United Provinces, through conquest, entered the

French sphere in 1795 and as a result of Spain allying with France in 1796), and also created fresh issues of prioritization. The situation provided another instance of the extent to which circumstances helped affect strategic culture. In part, these issues were reactive, as the ability of France to win allies created problems for Britain. For example, British naval power was strained after the Franco-Spanish alliance of 1796 and again when the two powers co-operated from 1804. In addition to the immediate threat to the home islands, this alliance affected British global strategy by making it necessary to keep more warships in European waters. Furthermore, Spanish ports became a potential target for British amphibious operations.

Prioritization was also an issue in relations with Russia. Britain had not hitherto fought Russia, but had come close in 1719–20, 1723, 1726–7 and 1791, and tensions had also been serious in the early 1780s during the Armed Neutrality. After the collapse of the Second Coalition (against France), in which Britain and Russia had co-operated in 1799, Paul I (1796–1801) became very interested in the idea of joining with Napoleon against Britain. He was assassinated in an internal coup before this policy could be developed, but his talk in 1800–1 of invading India helped encourage British interest in the defence of the latter, underlining the impact of the French invasion of Egypt in 1798 and encouraging Britain to reconquer the latter in 1801.

Under Paul's successor, Alexander I, Russia took a major part in the War of the Third Coalition against France (1805–7), indeed the leading role on land in 1806–7. However, Alexander's Treaty of Tilsit with Napoleon in 1807, a treaty that reflected the limitations of Britain's navalist priorities and, conversely, the failure of the attempt to pursue an interventionist alternative, was followed in 1808 by Napoleon planning joint action with Russia in Asia against Britain.[31] This threat helped lead to a more active British policy towards Persia, and also encouraged the British occupation of Alexandria in 1807, which was successful; but the subsequent failure of an inland advance on Rosetta led to the evacuation of Egypt. This failure demonstrated the folly of bold claims about British superiority, claims that encouraged a number of rash extra-European operations, notably attacks that failed at Buenos Aires in 1807 and New Orleans in 1815.

The possibility of war with Russia underlined the range of goals and means that British policymakers and commentators had to consider. The range of possibilities was further demonstrated by the unwanted war with the United States in 1812–15, and was underlined by uncertainty over Russia. Once war with the United States had started, there was the question of how far it should be defensive (the protection of Canada), and how far offensive. This was a question not only of goals, crucially whether there should be an effort to make permanent territorial gains, but also of the methods designed to secure them, for example the encouragement of dissident slaves in the American South. Furthermore, the issue of prioritization between the United States and the war with France was important. If the identity of opponents was, with the exception of the constant dark star of France, unfixed, this was also true of allies. The ability of Napoleon to obtain alliances[32] greatly affected the nexus of British goals, objectives and means.

Despite the Trafalgar glow of national self-sufficiency, which was to be very important to subsequent British assumptions, it was not possible to defeat France in Europe and thereby to consider the overthrow of its government without the support of a continental alliance system, and British strategic culture had to adapt to such a situation. Through such an alliance, Napoleon eventually was twice defeated and overthrown: in 1814 and 1815. After the Napoleonic wars, this co-operation was made to seem inevitable, but, as a reminder of the problem of gauging the viability of strategic culture, it was not; and it was only in March 1814, at Chaumont, that the allies agreed not to conclude any separate peace with Napoleon but, instead, to continue the war and then join in maintaining the peace. This agreement was only possible because Napoleon's excessive demands made the Austrians no longer willing to negotiate and to leave him in power. Concern about allies also greatly affected the nature of possible peace terms, on behalf of Britain, Hanover and Britain's dependent allies.

British war-making was therefore much influenced by the possibilities and exigencies of alliance politics, which was one of the many aspects of continuity across the supposed divide of the French Revolution. Allies brought advantages, but they also posed the problem of making goals appear attainable, and therefore of encouraging a failure to set feasible objectives. Indeed, a war of this length and strain invites the question about the feasibility of goals. As in 1940, Britain could hold off attack, but could not overthrow its opponent, which is a reminder of lasting problems in British strategic culture. The French Revolution and Napoleon created a strategic opportunity and need for a very different war with France to those of 1756–63 and 1778–83; instead a return to those of 1689–97, 1702–13, and 1743–8, when a powerful alliance system had provided opportunities for launching attacks on France, as in 1707 and 1747, when there were advances on Toulon, or in 1709 and 1744, when there were advances on Lille. The First and Second Coalitions (of the 1790s), however, were no more successful than the earlier alliances in delivering a serious blow to the French home base; the Third and Fourth Coalitions (of the 1800s) posed no real prospect of such a blow, and that only happened in 1814 as a result of unprecedented efforts and an unusual degree of international co-operation.

Until then, British strategy and strategic culture, and whatever is meant by the British way of war, were affected by the presence or absence of the key resource, that of alliance partners.[33] This issue is not eccentric to British (and other) military history, but central to it: not only was tasking involved, and the political strategy crucial in terms of the dynamic and cohesion of coalitions, but also military strategy.

There was a parallel in India, where the mastery won by Britain between 1790 and 1817 depended at least as much on the ability to benefit from the mutual enmities of the leading regional powers – Mysore, the Marathas, Hyderabad, Nepal and the Sikhs – as from success in more conventional 'point of conflict' military history. This was also to be crucial in seeing off the challenge of the Indian Mutiny in 1857–8: Britain then benefited greatly from Indian assistance, not least from Hyderabad, Nepal and the Sikhs.

In Europe, alliance with Austria and/or Prussia made it possible for Britain to intervene in the Low Countries and Germany, and led to pressure for such action, in particular to sustain the alliance. Strategy was as one with policy. Conversely, prefiguring the contrast between 1914 and 1940, the collapse of such an alliance, as in 1795, 1797, 1801, 1806, and 1809, removed this option, cutting short, for example, plans for British operations in north Germany in 1806, or ensured that action was restricted to amphibious operations that, even if successful, could only achieve so much. The tradition of the amphibious operation was one of seizing particular points, not of engaging an army and defeating it. It was only against a weak power, such as Denmark in 1807, and in pursuit of limited objectives, that a different outcome could be secured.

The Peninsular War offered an alternative from 1808. Britain had campaigned extensively in Iberia in the past, both during the War of the Spanish Succession (1702–13) and in 1762. However, there was no real institutional memory, while those campaigns had been waged in order to achieve goals particular to the region (the victory of 'Charles III' in the struggle for the Spanish throne, and the defence of Portugal respectively), and not as part of a strategy of overthrowing French power; although France was a party against Britain in each struggle. However, the problem of hitting France fatally captured the mismatch between British operational success in Iberia and British strategic capability as a whole: the latter was indirect as best. As such, prefiguring conflict with Italy in North and East Africa in 1940–1, the indirect capability was more significant politically, in showing real and potential allies that Britain could, and would, challenge France on land, than militarily, in the shape of distracting French forces from fighting the allies. However, such a distraction was important to the equations of military strength for Britain's allies (Russia, Prussia, Austria) in Germany in 1813. Furthermore, conflict in the peninsula kept an important part of the British army battle-hardened.

Conclusions

The burgeoning economy of Britain and of the oceanic trading system, and the strength of its public finances, were crucial to the war effort (as in the earlier conflicts), not least in enabling Britain both to survive Napoleon's attempt to blockade Britain through his Continental System, and to set the parameters of strategy. Yet these parameters had to be understood by politicians, while, more generally, parameters did not settle the issue of prioritization. As a result, the politics (both domestic and international) of strategy arise throughout as the key issue. A similar point can be made for other states. Strategy as politics does not exhaust the subject, but it makes sense of a context in which political debate was more potent than institutional continuity. Furthermore, the absence of an equivalent, in terms of policy or royal power, to the messianic imperialism and authority of Philip II of Spain resulted in a strategic debate in eighteenth-century Britain that was more open to political cross-currents.

4

Organizational Cultures: Western Warfare, 1815–1950

The widespread applicability of the concept of culture and of related terms and vocabulary is amply demonstrated by the discussion of military organizations. As with other uses of the concept, its application is not without problems, while there are also questions about how best to relate organizational culture to changes in the nature of modern war. The period from the end of the Napoleonic wars in 1815 to the end of the Second World War in 1945 saw major changes, but the fundamental character of conflict does not change. Killing and risking being killed, for the sake of forcing others to accept one's will, remains the fundamental condition of warfare, and also poses the lasting problem of the contrast between output, in the shape of military activity, and outcome, in the form of an accepted political solution. The theme of continuity was also pushed hard by combatants in some of the conflicts, whether Nazis pursuing a supposed German destiny in terms of European living space, Russians seeking warm-water ports, or, far more recently, al-Qaeda arguing that Islam should regain control of lands once under Muslim sway, notably southern Spain and Israel.

Yet, there have also been fundamental discontinuities in the context and nature of warfare. The shift from nineteenth-century imperialism to the concept of sovereign rights seen with the rise of international law in the 1900s and the establishment of the League of Nations in 1919 after the First World War (1914–18), was significant as affecting the context. Then and on other occasions, this international context was more than a matter of legality and organizations. Attitudes towards the international system and its very operation owed much to cultural factors, and these attitudes were important both as a cause of conflict and as a means of military activity. Cultural affinities and differences affected the processes of transmitting ideas and technology within the international system. Indeed, culture played an important role in gaining access to the networks and institutions that were important to this transmission. For example, it was necessary to be regarded as acceptable in order to be allowed to participate in the system of foreign military observers, which became significant in the second half of the nineteenth century. The same was true of the system of military attachés.[1]

Responding to New Technologies

Technology also led to significant discontinuities. A section on sea power in a book on seventeenth-century warfare would scarcely discuss submarines or aircraft carriers, while aerial capability in the nineteenth century was restricted to balloons without engines and also primitive rockets. These spheres of conflict were to be very different in the twentieth century, a difference which underlined the extent and rate of change in the period 1815–1945 and, more particularly, the challenges posed by change in the last half century of that period. For example, by 1909, American battleships were being designed with larger coal bunkers, allowing a steaming radius with 10,000 nautical miles, which was a major increase on the situation in the 1890s. In addition, leading naval powers were responding to the transforming potential offered by radio, while aircraft were of increased interest to armies and navies. In 1900, the American navy commissioned the USS *Holland*, its first submarine, in 1912, the American Eugene Ely piloted the first plane off a ship, while the British army integrated air power into manoeuvres in the early 1910s.

As a marked instance of a culture of war, interest in the future of warfare gripped the literary imagination, public debate and government discussion and planning. Air power very much suggested new possibilities, and a sense of unlimited boundaries was revealed in the novelist H. G. Wells' 1897 serial *The War of the Worlds*, in which Martian missiles convey war machines that overrun England and destroy London, only to fall victim to bacteria. Wells captured an awareness that war might not conform to rules or limits, and this anxiety was to be fully vindicated in the two human world wars of the twentieth century. Responses to technological possibilities also owed much to the different political cultures of particular states. In Britain, where, whatever the reality for the subjects of empire, the emphasis was on defensive considerations, technological developments, such as changes in battleships, were pursued accordingly; whereas in Germany the stress in the first half of the twentieth century was on using technology to permit a major change in the international system. In turn, as a reminder of the problem of using the state or nation as a unit without qualification, this stress was very much that of the German political Right.[2]

Tested in the First World War, these new technologies became more potent in the Second World War (1939–45), so that air power by the time of the Combined [Anglo-American] Bomber Offensive against Germany in 1942–5 was seen as a strategic tool, a capability that was to be amply demonstrated with the dropping of the American atomic bombs on Japan in 1945. The nature of naval conflict was also transformed by air power, in large part because of the experience of conflict and the issue of how lessons were learned and presented. Although Britain, the USA and Japan developed a significant aircraft carrier capability in the 1930s, they also emphasized battleship construction, while Hitler and Stalin also sought to acquire battleships. This emphasis on battleships reflected a reluctance to embrace change, but there was also a concern about the vulnerability of carriers and a lack of experience of the effectiveness of air power.

The situation was transformed during the Second World War. Air power not only proved highly effective in the struggle by Britain, Canada and the USA against German submarines in the Battle of the Atlantic, helping turn the tide against them in 1943; but also played the key role in the struggle between Japan and the USA for dominance of the Western Pacific. In the battle of the Coral Sea in 1942, surface units did not see each other and the fighting was a matter of air attacks, and this pattern was the dominant, although not sole one, thereafter. American aircraft destroyed much of the Japanese fleet in 1942–5.

On land, the technology by 1945 was also very different to that of 1914. Large-scale advances, such as that of the Americans across southern Germany in 1945 and of Soviet forces into Manchuria, also in 1945, were highly mechanized, and rapid-moving as a result. Tanks were supported by mechanized infantry and artillery.

War and Social Change

Alongside changes in the nature of conflict came significant changes as a result of conflict. Two, in particular, stand out for attention. First, war played a key role in forcing social change. This was particularly the case with the emancipation of women, as the needs of the vastly expanded war economies of the two world wars led both to a massive expansion in labour demands and also ensured that men were removed from the labour market to serve in armed forces. The major expansion of the female labour force led directly to a questioning of gender roles, and to a pressure on established social mores. Thus, in Britain and the USA, there was more freedom for women, because far more were employed, frequently away from home; because of an absence of partners, and, in many cases, fathers; and, in part, because of different attitudes. Divorce rates rose, as did illegitimacy. Racial politics also changed in many societies, not least with a challenge to established hierarchies of labour. In India, in the Second World War, the dominance of the 'martial races' in recruitment to the army ended as recruitment patterns became more wide-ranging, while in the USA there was a large-scale movement of African Americans to the growing industrial zones of the Mid-West and the West Coast.

War and Politics

Secondly, war led to the fall of the great empires. The First World War led to the overthrow of the Austro-Hungarian and Ottoman (Turkish) empires, which had each lasted for over half a millennium. Moreover, the strains of war and defeat resulted in the overthrow of the Romanov dynasty in Russia, the first stage of the Russian Revolution, a key event in world history as it launched Communism into political power. In turn, the Second World War greatly weakened the Western colonial empires, both as a consequence of the Japanese conquest of Asian colonies, which weakened the crucial prestige of Western rule, and due to the strains of war in imperial homelands. This process was repeated during the Cold War, with the Dutch, French, British and Portuguese empires greatly strained by a failure to defeat colonial insurrections.

Yet, the stress on change has also to take note of important continuities. The prime killer of men in the Second World War was neither aircraft nor tanks but, as in the First World War, artillery. The large numbers of troops were deployed in different formations to those of Napoleonic warfare at the start of the nineteenth century, but there were important similarities between the conscript armies in both periods, not least in terms of tactics and operations based on the availability of large numbers of troops. Indeed, the organizational centrality of mass armies was a characteristic that was as important as technological change.

Conscription and Nationalism

Conscription was the key aspect of the organizational culture of many armies in the nineteenth century, and for much of the twentieth century. As such, conscription demonstrated the central importance of political factors to military organization, and certainly the extent to which the latter could not be separated from the political context. The operative element in the latter was as much that of the general assumptions of a political culture as the specifics of particular political conjunctures. The former ensured that conscription was unacceptable in Britain and the USA other than when faced by a struggle for survival as in the world wars, and, even then, conscription was only introduced in Britain in 1916 with considerable difficulty.

Armies, therefore, were an expression of politics, with changes in these politics being important to developments in the strength of militaries as well as to the taskings or goals which helped to direct military doctrine, strategy and force structure. The essential shift in the nineteenth century was from professional militaries heavily based on voluntary service to larger, mass systems in which conscription played a central role. The former system had been adopted in part in reaction to the previous bout of mass warfare, that of the French Revolutionary and Napoleonic wars (1792–1815). The French reliance on the massive force produced by a conscription that was justified by the Revolutionaries in terms of alleged nationwide unity and enthusiasm, the *levée en masse*, created a crisis for other states. Commentators struggled to understand French success so that they could devise responses, with Clausewitz trying to develop a national strategy for Prussia.[3] Under the pressure of defeat by France, rulers turned to the French remedy. In March 1813, when Frederick William III summoned the Prussian people to fight for their king, fatherland, freedom and honour, this step was essentially due to a need for numbers in the war with Napoleon. Bourgeois (middle-class) officers came to play a greater role in the Prussian army.[4]

Large-scale warfare was troubling to conservative commentators for political reasons, but it also undermined the war effort. The drive for numbers could create social pressures that wrecked support for the war, as in France and northern Italy in 1813–14. As a consequence, governments in the years from 1815, a period of reaction against what was presented as 'Bonapartism', favoured a military politics of limited struggles swiftly won by professional armies, as seen with the Austrian intervention in Italy in 1821 and the French intervention in Spain in 1823. The organizational culture focused on a professionalism understood in terms of long service and of a military establishment that in many respects was separate from society. In the USA, for example, this separation was seen with the high percentage of troops who were recent immigrants, notably Germans.

Social, political, cultural and economic changes altered this situation. The last is the easiest to split off, although the growth of large-scale industrial production of course had consequences in terms of social, political and cultural developments and can lead to a focus on what has been termed a warfare state.[5] If the term culture is to be widely applied, not least as the dominant noun, for example with the phrase political culture, then culture can sum up much of the social and political change as well. The leading cultural development here was the basis for, and consequences, of, the ascendant nationalism of the late nineteenth century; and the military consequence was conscription.

Conscription had specific military consequences, for example encouraging the long-term imprisonment of prisoners of war, and, more generally, increasing the power of the state while also replicating social patterns of hierarchy and élite control. The latter underlined the political aspect of organizational issues. At the same time as hierarchy and élite control, military service also offered up possibilities for mobility, within the military, within society, and geographically. This was the case not only in the West but also more generally. Thus, the army in Korea, including its examination system, provided opportunities for social mobility.[6]

As a term implying a socially comprehensive and insistent mass movement, nationalism developed most clearly in the second half of the century. Stronger states, improved communications, national systems of education, mass literacy, industrialization, urbanization, democratization, and ideological and intellectual changes, all focused on the idea of nation. Due to these changes, national consciousness became nationalism across Europe, the latter more politically potent and energizing than the former. There was a symbolic weight to nationalism as it channelled and fulfilled the ritual aspects of community. Furthermore, more than simply accommodating the rise of the universal male franchise, nationalism could also welcome and benefit from it. Nationalism also provided a new basis for the group dynamic for, and in, conflict; a dynamic captured by the German philosopher Hegel in 1821, when he argued that the characteristic of modern warfare was that it was 'the act not of this particular person, but of a member of a whole. Moreover, it seems to be turned not against single persons, but against a hostile group, and hence personal bravery appears impersonal'.[7]

Conscription became normative, even though it was not necessarily popular. This was scarcely surprising given the very poor circumstances of military service, including very low pay, inadequate accommodation, and, frequently, a lack of food and uniforms. Again pushing political culture, or at least long-term issues of politics to the fore, conscription frequently became an issue in debates over political identity. Thus, in Brazil, where conscription was not introduced until 1916, the army was essentially a penal institution, and issues of class and race were significant. In France, where political and social divisions were potent, there was vociferous opposition to the army and to the military demands of the state in the late nineteenth century. In France, the military and the conservatives wanted a longer term of service for conscripts, whereas the Left wanted broader, but short-term, military service. In July 1913, when military service was increased from two to three years, there were riots in the garrison towns of eastern France. Moreover, conscription had a serious military cost, in that it did not guarantee a high level of tactical preparedness or fighting ability. Indeed, this lack of preparedness helped to account for the frontal-attack tactics of the First World War.

Despite these limitations, conscription proved to be a key military resource, enabling Paraguay to deploy a large army when it attacked the relatively small standing armies of Argentina and Brazil in 1865. Conscription also helped to frame the military culture of many states in the late nineteenth century. As a result of conscription, young men at an impressionable age and in patriarchal societies, where it was easier for authority figures to impose discipline, were exposed to state-directed military organization and discipline. The individualism potentially offered by rising literacy and education, and the development of the photography of soldiers, was more than countered by the pressures of conformity and control. Moreover, this state direction was centralized, with an important change from earlier organizational ideas and related patterns. In particular, both the sub-contracting of military functions to entrepreneurs and the autonomy of aristocratic officers were ended, or at least greatly eroded; although elements of both played a significant role in the ostensibly state-directed new model armies.

Traditional concepts about the essential suitability of the landed orders to act as officers and commanders remained strong, as did their converse, the view that peasants and workers inherently lacked the necessary characteristics and values. In functional terms, such ideas represented a limitation on efficiency and excellence, although one that was different in kind to that arising from the exclusion of women from the military process other than as providers and supporters. In ideological terms, there was an emphasis on professionalism, but, despite the rise of formal military education, this professionalism was constructed in part in social terms. There was a heavy emphasis on the landed orders in entry to military colleges and subsequent promotion.

Austria, France, Germany and Russia all developed large reserve armies: conscripts served for about two or three years and then entered the reserves, ensuring that substantial forces of trained men could be mobilized in the event of war, and that the state did not have to pay them during peace. Combined with demographic and economic growth, this system increased the potential size of armies. More generally, whereas liberal states and circles, as in Britain and the USA, tended to support a strong navy, conscription for the army helped in the militarization of society, being both a means and a cause by which competitive governing élites were able to draw on greater economic resources and on patterns of organized and obedient social behaviour.

Moreover, aside from military service serving as a rite of passage that boys accepted in their quest to become men, military organization served to integrate the nation. For example, troops were frequently stationed away from their localities. This practice, found for example in France and Italy, delayed mobilization, but it helped to break down the local identity of soldiers and to encourage an awareness of the nation. This system was greatly assisted by the spread of the rail network. The military also served to help suppress, or at least police, popular protest and opposition.[8]

Attitudes to War

Military display and music played a comparable role of symbolic and cultural integration. The prestige of military service rose; although, as a reminder of the role of conjuncture and the contingent nature of culture, the situation varied. In particular, success in war played a part as did political circumstances. For example, in the 1870s, as a result of success in the Wars of German Unification (1864, 1866, 1870–1), military service became more prestigious in Germany, where cities came to vie for garrisons. The situation in Britain was very different.

Due to nationalism, and the attendant increases in the scale of mobilization of resources, it became more apparent to contemporaries that war was a struggle between societies rather than simply between military forces. Depending on the terms to be used, this awareness helped frame strategy or, at least, the strategic culture affecting planning. The context within which decisions were taken for war was certainly influenced by the degree to which, in a nationalist age, the expression and manipulation of public opinion came to play a greater role in political culture. Public debate was encouraged by social change, particularly urbanization, the decline of deference, and the rise of literacy; by organizational developments, especially the growth of the press and the spread of the franchise; and by political pressures. Failure or the perception of failure thus led to public demands for action.

That war became an expression of nationalism, rather than of dynasticism, was obviously the case with the republican states of the western hemisphere from the USA to Chile; but it was also increasingly true in Europe as monarchs adapted to the mass politics and to the increasingly urbanized and articulate societies of the states they ruled. Napoleon I, a monarch with his origins and career very much in the army, helped to make the transition. His military dictatorship of France from 1799 to 1815, emphasized the honour of dedication and professionalism (both focused on Napoleon) that the army sought to inculcate in its members and in the empire as a whole. In 1802, he created the *Legion d'honneur* for service to state and country, and over 30,000 soldiers received the medal, which bore Napoleon's image. He called on soldiers to defend their reputation and the honour of the French name. More generally, the creation of national armies encouraged and reflected the concept of a national community, the 'nation in arms', a concept that left only a limited role for any dynastic dynamics of identity and interest.

Cultural attitudes to conflict were significant, as conflict was seen as the normal consequence of serious disputes, and cultural restraints on the decision to fight were minimal. The cultural symbols and historical memories that shaped the political imagination of the age had a particularly military cast. The sense that international war was normal, combined with the monopolization of the decision to fight, and the control of organized force by governments, provided a basic norm and continuity across much of the West, albeit being challenged by rebellions such as that in Russia in 1905.

However, the use of the term the West begs the question whether this description of the position in the West arose from a cultural difference to the non-West, or whether it was simply a description of a global situation in which key variations owed more to circumstances than to culture, notably the pressure on states and societies in the non-West caused by Western (and non-Western) imperialism and global economic competition. For example, China faced serious rebellions, notably, but not only, in the 1850s–60s, 1910s and 1930s, but that was not because the political culture was inherently against a government monopolization of organized force. Instead, in each case, there was a determination to wrest control of government.

Returning to the nineteenth-century West, war was commemorated in the arts and in urban spaces. Streets, bridges, buildings and pubs took their names from episodes of war. In Britain, military leaders such as Napier, Wolseley and Roberts, joined sites of martial glory: the Almas, Inkermans and Omdurmans, which survive as street names to this day commemorating victories in 1854, 1854 and 1898 respectively. After the victories of 1805 and 1815 over France, London gained Trafalgar Square and a Waterloo Bridge, Place and Station. Pub names also recorded victories and generals. Empire Day, 24 May, which was introduced in British schools in 1904, proved an opportunity for jingoist imperialism. Similarly, Parisian avenues and railway stations recorded victories such as Austerlitz, Jena, Wagram and Solferino. After the victory of 1870, Germany celebrated Sedan Day.

More generally, battlefields became the site of monuments and the destination of travellers. The publication of battle accounts and maps reflected popular interest, as did the range of visual display, including panoramas, dioramas, history painting, engravings, the illustrated press and photographs. Moreover, illustrated magazines provided dramatic and heroic engravings which offered an exemplary account of military life, furthering nationalism.[9] The same happened in the world of the stage. Piper George Findlater VC who, shot in both feet, had sat up and played the regimental march to encourage his colleagues in the Tirah Expedition Force in storming a hostile position, had a second career re-enacting the episode on British music-hall stages.

Defeats were also celebrated if they could be presented as the basis of national renewal, as with the Prussian defeat by the French at Jena in 1806, and as glorious national sacrifices, as in Rodin's sculpture *The Call to Arms* (1879), which commemorated the defence of Paris against the Germans in the war of 1870–1.[10] Founded in 1882 as part of a widespread process of volunteer bellicosity,[11] the French *Ligue des patriotes* staged regular pilgrimages to battle sites from the siege of Paris, while the novelist and politician Maurice Barrès (1862–1923) did the same for 1870 battlefields in Alsace from the 1890s. In the 1900s, his novels emphasized the place in the French soul of Alsace-

Lorraine, which had been lost to the Germans as a result of defeat in the war. He became president of the *Ligue* in 1914.

At the same time, glory linked with politics to encourage a new iteration of the cult of decisive victory, one suitable for an age of nationalist mass politics. Commentators claimed that war was also appropriate for this kind of politics, as the resulting patriotism and unity would ease the burden of domestic tensions. Such ideas looked towards the First World War, and raise the issue of the role of the culture of politics in its outbreak. If specific events led to crises, the assumptions that helped to condition responses were affected by this culture of politics.

In turn, the new, more ideological politics that stemmed from the First World War affected the culture of conflict. In December 1917, Felix Dzerzhinskii (1877–1926), the head of the Cheka or Soviet secret policy, declared 'we are not in need of justice. It is war now – face to face, a fight to the finish'.[12] Lenin, the Communist leader, followed up in January 1918 by demanding extra-judicial executions against speculators and bandits causing food shortages. That September, the Cheka was ordered to shoot opponents summarily. The disruptive aftermath of the First World War, combined with the rise of ideological alignments and totalitarian states, ensured that political violence became more pronounced in Europe,[13] as (differently) in China, which created a more challenging context for regular militaries, in terms both of tasks and of control. Sectarian and ethnic violence[14] looked towards more recent conflict.

The Military as Organization

It is also instructive to consider the nature of the organizational culture of the military. If, as argued here, a key element was provided by the wider political context in the shape of conscription, then that still left the organizational nature of the military open for debate. The potential for debate was accentuated because the period saw major changes in weapons systems, and it was unclear how best to organize the response. In terms of weaponry, the changes from 1800 to 1950 were unprecedented, not least because of the development of aerial and submarine capability, as well as the impact on land warfare of greatly enhanced mobility and firepower.

The pace of change reflected its normative character, both within individual militaries and on the world scale. As far as the latter was concerned, the world was increasingly under the sway of the West, directly or indirectly, from the mid nineteenth century. The organization of the Japanese army towards the close of the century, in response first to French and then to German models, and of the navy, under the inspiration of the British navy, was a key example of this impact. Other non-Western navies, notably those of China and Turkey, also imported Western weaponry, organization and concepts. 'Top-down' modernization was important to military development.[15]

Moreover, at the level of individual armies, notably in the West, it proved relatively easy to introduce innovations and to respond to the pace of technological advance. The latter was seen, for example, in the rapid and almost continued adoption of new types of warship, naval armament and naval tactics in the period 1840–1960 in response to fundamental changes in ship power and design, and in naval potential at sea. To extend the use of culture, this situation owed much to an industrial culture focused on the positive response to technological innovation, and a strategic culture in which armaments were closely linked to policy.[16]

Innovation was helped by control and discipline, and there was an obvious contrast with the introduction of new weaponry and tactics in the period 1450–1650, as the dominance then of military entrepreneurs and mercenaries made it difficult to push through change that was unwelcome to them in the West. The same was true of the *sipahis* (feudal cavalry) in the Ottoman forces. In contrast, those elements of the military that were far more under governmental control in 1450–1650, such as the *janissaries* (slave soldiers) of the Ottoman empire, the *ghulams* (slave soldiers) of the Safavid empire of Persia (Iran), and the militia-type forces of the United Provinces (Dutch Republic) and Sweden, were more amenable to change. Partly as a result, they could also be more effective, although it is misleading to draw a simple, causal line from change to effectiveness.

Control and discipline were certainly much in evidence in the militaries of the nineteenth century and the first half of the twentieth. There was an often harsh treatment of ordinary rankers, which was the case whether they were volunteers or conscripts. Thus, the social politics of the military interacted with institutional structures and practices, which reflected and sustained systems of control. Such discipline was seen as a necessary means not only for battlefield success but also to enable the military to be employed for social control. The military also faced a volatile social environment within their ranks, one in which the large-scale movement of people from countryside to towns was accompanied by growing individual autonomy, not least as a consequence of increased literacy. The social factors which had made commanders after 1815 wary of mass forces, and feel, instead, more favourably inclined towards trusted units of long-service regulars, were still pertinent at a time when such massed forces were regarded as essential. Under the strain of prolonged war and defeat, there were to be military mutinies, notably in Russia in 1917 and in Germany in 1918, or collapses in discipline as in France and Italy in 1917.

The social politics of the military was not one which, by modern Western standards, sought to encourage initiative at the level of individual soldiers. Observers at the time, however, commented favourably, frequently using the language of industrial production and method. In 1896, Captain Birkbeck, a British observer at the German military manoeuvres wrote: 'It is impossible not to be deeply impressed by the smoothness and ease with which the German military machine works...a well-trained and thoroughly practical staff....The German army corps is no collection of units hurriedly collected for a time.' Two years later, Captain Holland added: 'a system by which losses of smaller units are ignored, provided the main object is gained, the great aim being to train the soldier to carry out his orders regardless of consequences'.[17] The mechinization of war gripped the imagination of many commentators as a consequence of, and for, modernity and modernization.

Discipline was linked to the capacity for introducing change as well as ensuring steadiness. Already, in the eighteenth century, British military observers had been impressed by Prussian manoeuvres. In this case, notably during the reign of Frederick II, the Great (1740–86), there was the appeal of success alongside the impressive show of discipline which helped enable Frederick both to use his novel technique of the oblique attack and, as at Leuthen in 1757, to regroup and manoeuvre afresh on the battlefield. But new technology had not played a role in this appeal of discipline and success, unlike in the late nineteenth century. If the appeal of discipline is seen in cultural terms, or as an aspect of cultural factors, then the cause and character of it are instructive.

By the 1860s there was, in successful armies, such as that of Prussia/ Germany which, thanks to victory in 1864–71 became a trendsetter, an emphasis on training as a changing process which had to reflect developments in weaponry. Combined with the expanded officer corps, which was necessary in order to direct and control the greater number of soldiers and to ensure their effectiveness, appropriate training was an essential adjunct to these enhanced weapons. Thus, in 1900, observers noted that volley firing was being abandoned in favour of individual fire.[18] That year, Belgian manoeuvres displayed the defensive strength of trenches and the lessons learned from the Anglo-Afrikaaner Boer War then being waged in South Africa.[19] It was not clear what lessons to draw from conflict, how far, for example for 1861–71, to put the focus on the American Civil War, as opposed to the Wars of German Unification which, instead, dominated attention; or the same for 1899–1905 for the Boer War (1899–1902) as opposed to the Russo-Japanese War (1904–5). Nevertheless, in each case, the emphasis was on learning lessons in a disciplined fashion. The Russo-Japanese War encouraged a stress on railways as the key means of sustaining force and underlined the need to overcome the tactical strength of defensive positions.[20]

The emphasis that enhanced weaponry put on training was accentuated in the twentieth century by the growing specialization that came from the development of new forms of fighting. The latter led to a process of specialization, and thus distinction, within the military, and to more specialized training. The British army committee that in 1938 recommended the merger of the Royal Tank Corps and the newly mechanized cavalry regiments, noted that, in the past, troops had been trained within their own regiments, but that 'this system is impracticable for a corps equipped with armoured fighting vehicles, and it is clear that in future training will be necessary at a depot equipped with suitable vehicles and staffed by technically qualified instructors'.[21] In the USA, tanks were prohibited to the cavalry under the National Defense Act of 1920, although still being purchased and called 'combat cars'.[22] Similarly, at sea, the development of submarine warfare and naval aviation encouraged a process of specialization. This process also involved issues of institutional allocation and organizational politics.

The amount of scholarship devoted to military reform in the interwar period (1919–38) enables us to see not only the attempt to learn the lessons of the recent conflict,[23] but also the role of faction and personality.[24] Moreover, these were affected by, and expressed in terms of, beliefs, arguments and tendencies of the period, such as the drive of a new generation to correct the failings of their elders.[25] Although there were significant variations between individual states, the political culture of the period was also significant as it permitted public debate. In Britain, Basil Liddell Hart, a protagonist for reform, was military correspondent first of the *Telegraph* (1925–35) and then of the *Times* (1935–9).[26]

Air Power

National variations also played a key role with air power as each state used their experience of the First World War to interpret it in a different fashion.[27] There was also a major institutional dimension. It was unclear how far air power would be developed and preserved as a separate entity and how far subordinated, instead, to the existing services of army and navy. Linked to this choice, which is of great consequence because of debates about the role and capability of air power today, came fundamental issues of strategic, operational and tactical capability and conduct. The creation of air forces was a major institutional change in the organization of war because it institutionalized a commitment to air power. In turn, this commitment was a cause of heavy expenditure which led to pressure from the other services to limit the independence of air forces. Whereas, in Britain, the Royal Air Force became a separate service, in America the National Defence Act of 1920 placed air power under the Army Air Service, while naval aviation was kept separate.[28] British airmen developed bold claims for the potential of air power in order to justify its independence, although the Air Ministry was more moderate in its claims than independent air enthusiasts. It was argued that bombers would be able to destroy opposing economies, and thus that they could win any great power war.

The British played the key role in developing the concept of strategic bombing, and this was based on a range of cultural factors, indicating the variety offered by the latter terminology. British assumptions were based on optimism, institutional need (in the shape of the requirements of the Royal Air Force), and the wish to have a Great Power capability in European warfare without having to introduce conscription or to incur the grievous casualties seen in the First World War. Although there have been attempts to offer a less critical reading,[29] it is apparent that the British assessment of strategic bombing was not based on a sufficiently informed analysis of the impact of bombing in the First World War nor of subsequent developments in capability.[30] It was argued that large bombers would be able to fight off fighter attack, and thus not require fighter escorts. As a consequence, the RAF had twice as many bombers as fighters for most of the inter-war period. These bombers were seen not only as likely to be effective in war but also as a deterrent against attack, and priorities were not changed until 1938. That year, fear about the effectiveness of German air attacks affected British thinking at the time of the Munich crisis.

Similarly, the American Air Corps Tactical School developed a policy of high-flying daylight precision bombing designed to damage an opponent's industrial system. This policy greatly influenced American strategy in the Second World War, but, in practice, precision was to be difficult to achieve and the deficiencies of the 'self-defending bomber' ensured that bombing's strategic effect was bought at a heavy cost.[31]

In contrast, France, Italy and the Soviet Union put a heavier emphasis on tactical air power. It would be overly simplistic to argue that strategic and institutional cultures interacted in some automatic fashion, or that one led to the other. Nevertheless, it is instructive to consider differences between national developments, not least because air power was relatively new, as practice and concept, and thus the legacy of former arrangements, in terms of the sediment of previous organizations and doctrines, was not at issue.

In the case of Germany, it is necessary to explain the failure to develop a strategic bomber capability. In contradiction to the tendency to focus on only one cause, a variety of factors can be emphasized. One is posed by 'realist' factors in the form of capability, rather as the Soviet Union had an insufficient industrial base for its aviation industry.[32] The Germans prioritized their air force (*Luftwaffe*) once Hitler came to power in 1933, and accordingly spent about forty per cent of the defence budget on it in 1933–6, but the air industry did not develop sufficiently to support an air force for a major conflict. The Spanish Civil War (1936–9), in which they intervened on the side of Franco's Nationalists, also suggested to the Germans that large long-range bombers were not necessary: they used dive-bombers, instead, in Spain, and developed dive-bombing tactics. Seeking a strategic bombing force that could act as a deterrent, Germany had initially led in the development of the four-engine bomber – the 'Ural' or 'Amerika' bomber, but had only built prototypes. The capability to produce the engines necessary for the planned heavy bombers was lacking. More generally, there were problems with the availability of aviation fuel for the air force. Deficiencies notwithstanding, by 1945 Germany was producing new aircraft with impressive capabilities.

There were also factors that could be seen as 'idealist' rather than 'realist'. Hermann Goering, Air Minister and Commander-in-Chief of the *Luftwaffe*, was not interested in what he saw as the less glamorous side of air power, and this harmed the *Luftwaffe* in the subsequent war. There was a preference for numbers of planes, as opposed to a balanced expenditure that would include investment in infrastructure, for example logistical provision, especially spares. This preference owed much to the poor quality of leadership. Goering was also less than careful in his appointments. Ernst Udet, whom he made Technical Director, was overly interested in dive-bombing. Goering's concern for plane numbers helped to lead, in 1937, to the abandonment of the four-engined bomber programme, as it was easier to produce large numbers of twin-engined bombers.

Furthermore, again bridging strategic culture and organizational culture, the search for a force structure that would make *blitzkrieg* a success, a search made necessary by Hitler's preference for quick wars and his planning for rapid success, led to a lack of support for strategic bombing, which was seen, instead, as a long-term solution. *Blitzkrieg* entailed no obvious requirement for a strategic bombing force. Instead, the *Luftwaffe* focused on gaining air superiority and launching big 'terror' bombing raids (rather than sustained strategic bombing), and saw little merit in battlefield air support, and certainly not in close air-support. Most of the *Luftwaffe* was not designed to act as a tactical close support force.

The relationship between strategic bombing and other uses of air power can therefore be discussed within a context in which cultural elements play a big role, while, at the same time, accepting that these elements are frequently used in so broadbrush a fashion that they apparently cover, if not everything, then at least a large number of factors. The variety of assumptions in the 1930s about air power certainly reflected strategic cultures that drew also on views about the best way to conduct military operations. Thus, in France and the Soviet Union, the stress was on tactical doctrine and force structure, and operational doctrine developed accordingly. The Soviet air force was largely an extension of the army. In Britain, in contrast, there was resistance to the possibilities of ground-support operations on the part of those committed to strategic bombing.

Moreover, in a parallel to attitudes towards the inappropriate reliance on tanks alone in mobile warfare, rather than on mixed-armed forces, the need to provide fighter escorts for bombers was not appreciated by the British or the Americans until they suffered heavy casualties in the Second Word War. At the same time, the American ability to rethink the situation, and to plan and produce accordingly, led to the development of a long-range escort fighter capability so as to support the bombing. This flexibility was an important attribute that gave force to American strategic culture.

Events thereafter interacted with the development of strategic culture. The American use against Japan in 1945, first of large-scale firebombing[33] and then of the atom bomb, in order to lead to the surrender of Japan without it being invaded, provided a new thrust to air power. Moreover, its value was subsequently seen as rectifying the weakness of Western forces on land compared to the numerical preponderance of their Communist rivals. This strategy was linked to institutional change, with the creation, in 1947, of an independent air service, the United States Air Force (USAF). In order to fulfil its independent role, and to take the leading part in the Cold War with the Soviet Union, American air force thinking was dominated by its capability for strategic nuclear bombing. The ability to strike at Soviet centres was seen as both an effective deterrent against Soviet attack and as the essential purpose of American air power. This emphasis was given force by the role of officers from Strategic Air Command in the senior ranks of the Air Staff, an element that can be described in terms of organizational culture, as well as by a fascination with aerial self-sufficiency and big planes, which can be described as a culture of power, and by the absence of a powerful drive for integrated warfare, which would have encouraged the development of doctrines for co-operation with the army and navy. Strategic nuclear bombing also played a major role in British air planning.

In the Korean (1950–3) and Vietnam (1965–73) wars, frustration with the limited opportunities for, and success of, ground-support and interdiction bombing encouraged the Americans to an emphasis on strategic bombing which drew on the experience of the Second World War and on the force structure and doctrine of the USAF. This bombing was affirmed as likely to affect political will and to damage economic resources, but it certainly did not destroy the North Vietnamese will to fight, nor their war machine. As a consequence of the long-term emphasis on strategic bombing in air power culture, doctrine, organization and procurement, the USAF was perhaps not sufficiently flexible in trying alternatives. However, again as an instance of the difficulty of judging culture, not least knowing how best to assess experience, which is the presumed alternative to, and constraint on, culture, Anglo-Australian bombing in the 1950s also achieved very little in counter-insurgency operations in Malaya.

The role of circumstance arises in terms of affecting the parameters within which decisions were made. Thus, prior to the mid 1930s, despite the bold claims made by the protagonists of air power, its effectiveness was very limited. In contrast, from then to the early 1950s, aero-technology was relatively inexpensive, but potent enough to produce an age of mass industrial air power. However, from the early 1950s, the provision of a mass of air power resources was increasingly expensive. Such points establish a chronology within which the cultural elements can be assessed. At the same time, it is also pertinent to look to longer-term lessons. In the case of air power, as indeed of other military elements, a key point is the value of jointness. Thus, the history of air power shows that much of its capability rested (and rests) on being part of an integrated fighting system with an operational doctrine that relied on co-operation between arms and sought to implement realizable political goals. The same was true of the impact of mechanization on land warfare.

Conclusions

These points about the value of jointness, however, cut across the stronger cultural appeal of distinctive services and weapon types, an appeal that is a matter not only of the public but also of the (self-) identification of the military. Again, however, the play of contingency in the use of culture comes into focus, for these factors both vary by state and chronologically. In some countries, such as Singapore, there is not the rivalry between services, over goals and manning equipment as well as resources, seen in others such as Pakistan and Britain. Secondly, this rivalry can change, and other alignments and identities can arise. Many militaries do not have the conservatism and institutional continuity seen with the regimental system of the British army; although, conversely, this system has been important to morale and cohesion.

The period 1800–1950, particularly the first half of the twentieth century, saw the development of new organizations to handle radically new weapon systems, but there was also a considerable degree of continuity. The latter reflected a characteristic of military organizations, namely the desire to produce the system that helps ensure predictability and fighting quality. At the same time, the drive to defend existing practices and assumptions played an important role in the response to the new.

At the level of individual militaries, there were also contrasts in command style. These contrasts can be seen in terms of organizational culture, notably by comparing the militaries of totalitarian and democratic states, as in the Second World War. Yet, there are also important contrasts within each category. Thus, on the Eastern Front, although both had very serious failings, there were qualitative differences between Hitler and Stalin, with the former proving more the prisoner of his own propaganda. Such specificities challenge categories and theories, and encourage their use in a flexible rather than a deterministic fashion.

5

Strategic Culture: The Cold War

The Cold War, the struggle between the Communist and non-Communist blocs from the Second World War to 1989, offers over-lapping instances of cultural elements in motivation, conduct and rationale. To provide an instance of the looseness of the cultural category, the ideological struggle between Communism and its opponents, variously liberal, capitalist, and fascist, can be seen as cultural. However, the contrary emphasis on 'realist' considerations as being the key factors in dispute can also be seen as a cultural element, because the desire to make the ideological appear rational, and/or to express it in these terms, reflected cultural norms, as well as serving political strategies. Moreover, the degree to which the Cold War led to the mobilization of whole societies ensured that the term has been used to analyse everything, from comics to pro-natalist policies, from science fiction to gender politics. This range has great value, not least in capturing a potent sense of cultural challenge and the varied dimensions of ideological conflict during the Cold War, but also poses problems.

Fundamental Divides

On 14 March 1946, the British embassy in Moscow asked if the world was now 'faced with the danger of the modern equivalent of the religious wars of the sixteenth century', with Soviet Communism battling against Western social democracy and American capitalism or 'domination of the world'. Concern about public opinion was an important aspect of the Cold War and provides a new aspect to strategic culture, linking it more closely to the political culture of particular states. Thanks to the importance of public opinion, Communist states controlled information and made major efforts to block radio transmissions from the West, providing another aspect of conflict, for anti-Communist radio stations were sponsored by Western governments.

There was also the propagation of Soviet propaganda by every means. Frank Roberts, a British diplomat in Moscow, forwarded details of a Soviet election campaign lecture he had heard on Christmas Day 1945 – 'Reference was made to American economic imperialism and to the disastrous economic situation likely to arise in USA as the result of mass unemployment', which did not in fact occur. Moreover, the lecturer expressed the view that no international question could be decided without Soviet participation. The summary of the reports in London by Christopher Warren of the Foreign Office noted that 'by resurrecting the bogey of foreign aggression, and by completely distorting the information about the outside world which reaches the Soviet peoples and also by their intensive measures to indoctrinate them with the Marxist-Leninist religion' the Soviet government could affect popular views.[1]

Attempts to influence opinion and mould domestic developments were less forceful in the USA and Western Europe, but were also insistent. In the USA, anti-Communism reached its spectacular apogee in the claims about Communist influence in Hollywood and government made by Senator Joseph McCarthy who gave his name to a process of public legislative inquisition known as McCarthyism. In practice, although McCarthy overreached himself with his criticism of the American army, a focus for patriotic values, and was discredited by his methods and extremism, anti-Communism was far more wide-ranging and insistent in the USA, and it contributed to the conservative ethos of the 1950s, which was reflected in the Republican Eisenhower presidency of 1953–61, as well as to the victory in the 1960 election of John Kennedy, a Democrat who had warned about the development of a 'missile gap' in favour of the Soviet Union.

The Domestic Dimension

In Western Europe, there was also a vitalist concern about the health of society, with anti-Communism playing a role in the discussion of a wide range of social problems and policies, notably employment, but also housing, education and health. A central goal was that of preventing a disaffected working class from turning to the Communists, and this concern contributed greatly to full-employment policies and Keynesianism, which can therefore be seen as part of the strategic culture.

There was a linked determination to limit Communist infiltration of the trade unions, and the Americans took an active role against Communist trade unions in France and Italy. In 1947, 'Wild Bill' Donovan, the former head of the OSS, the American Office of Strategic Services, the forerunner of the CIA, helped persuade the American government to fund anti-Communists in the French trade unions that, he claimed, were a Communist fifth column. This theme was to be the basis of Ian Fleming's first James Bond novel, *Casino Royale* (1953), as the villain was paymaster of the Communist-controlled trade union in the heavy and transport industries of Alsace, the most vulnerable part of France to Soviet attack. This trade union was presented as an important fifth column in the event of war with the Soviet Union. The early novels depicted SMERSH, Soviet foreign intelligence, as the prime threat to the West.

There was considerable sensitivity in Britain about the extent of Communist influence in the trade unions. In 1949, the Labour government sent in troops to deal with a London dock strike that it blamed on Communists. The following year, Hugh Gaitskell, the Minister for Fuel and Power, and leader of the Labour Party from 1955 to 1962, claimed that a strike in the power stations was instigated by Communist shop stewards and served for them as a rehearsal for future confrontation. Critics argued that these views reflected Cold War paranoia, but the belief that Communists were encouraging agitation in the trade unions and the British empire was widespread and well grounded. Fleming both contributed to such attitudes and derived benefit from their popularity.

On 13 April 1948, the British Cabinet had discussed the need for propaganda against Communism, specifically activity by the Labour Party, the Co-operative and trade union movements, and the churches, to help anti-Communist Socialist tendencies. British achievements were to be emphasized to give confidence to Social Democratic parties in Europe. The Cabinet also decided that the BBC should be pressed about the speakers it asked to appear on the Brains Trust and the Friday Forum, leading radio programmes. On 1 June, the Cabinet returned to these themes, and it was argued 'that the BBC should not afford facilities to enable sectional interests to continue to express their opposition to an Act which had been passed'.[2] Propaganda was an important aspect of the intersection of culture and war.

The pro-Western policies of Clement Attlee's Labour government (1945–51) were supported by the vast majority of the Labour Party and trade union movement. Communist and Soviet sympathizers within both were isolated, and the Communist Party was kept at a distance. This situation helped prevent the development of a radical Left and was linked to the alliance between labour and capital that was to be important in the post-war mixed economy, although the emphasis on state control and regulation was damaging to entrepreneurial ethos. The Attlee government decided to develop the British nuclear bomb.

Thus, ideology and popular mobilization operated in particular political contexts, and it was in these contexts that the strategy of external confrontation was pursued. The latter was not separate to domestic policy, for, as in chapter 3, strength at home was linked to strength abroad, and there was also belief in a common ideological struggle. Indeed, the purges of supposed domestic opponents pushed hard by Communist regimes reflected a conviction that the interior was the prime site for activity, strategy and conflict. This belief was a matter not simply of ideology, but also of economics. Heavy industry and collectivized agriculture were developed in order to transform economies, consolidate Socialist societies and win the economic struggle with the West. In many respects, what conventionally passes as strategy and conflict, namely military planning and martial acts, instead played a secondary role to these domestic concerns, and the armed forces were policed ideologically and managed socially accordingly.

This prioritization was particularly notable in the case of China, certainly after the Korean War ended in 1953. Mao Zedong, the Chinese Communist dictator, put the modernization of China first and devoted relatively limited effort to the military. Modernization was very much presented in existential terms. He rejected the traditional Chinese notion of 'Harmony between the Heavens and Humankind' and, instead, proclaimed 'Man Must Conquer Nature.' In 1958, Mao declared 'Make the high mountain bow its head; make the river yield the way', and, soon after, in a critique of an essay by Stalin stating that men could not affect natural processes such as geology, Mao claimed, 'This argument is incorrect. Man's ability to know and change Nature is unlimited.' Indeed, for Mao, nature, like humankind, was there to be forcibly mobilized in pursuit of an idea.

Here, however, we hit a problem with the use of the term strategic culture. It can be seen as a substitute for ideology, or as a way to discuss the manner in which ideology was advanced: for example, was Soviet caution in the post-Khrushchev era from 1964 a matter of the impact on policymakers of the Second World War and/or of advanced age in instilling a degree of caution in pursuit of the ideology of Communism?

There is also the question of the use of language and symbolization; an aspect of the ideological struggle and a cultural element. In the 1 April 1946 issue of *Time*, the leading American news magazine, R. M. Chapin produced a map entitled 'Communist Contagion', which emphasized the nature of the threat and the strength of the Soviet Union. The latter was enhanced by a split-spherical presentation of Europe and Asia, making the Soviet Union more potent as a result of the break in the centre of the map. Communist expansion was emphasized in the map by presenting the Soviet Union as a vivid red, the colour of danger, and by categorizing neighbouring states with regard to the risk of contagion, employing the language of disease: states were referred to as quarantined, infected or exposed.

As battlefields in what became the Cold War, these states were greatly affected by their presentation in terms of the strategic culture of the major powers. However, the level of strategic assumption and planning of these powers did not mean that other levels were dependent or unimportant. Instead, the attempt to shape world politics in terms of a geopolitical and ideological competition directed by the great powers was challenged by independent initiatives. In many states, notably those in Latin America, the Middle East and Africa, the military played a crucial role as a political force, in some states resisting change and in others seeking to bring it about. As a result, the strategic culture of individual militaries combined with the organizational culture of their role in the state. For example, in Egypt, Syria and Iraq, the army staged what were presented as 'progressive' coups, while, in Indonesia and Turkey, the army turned against the Left in the 1960s and 1970s respectively.[3]

Cold War 'Realism'

Strategists and those who discuss strategy like to see their *métier* as a rational, realist activity, very much based on the world as it is. This approach was much encouraged during the Cold War, not least because the availability of nuclear weapons and the risk of nuclear war producing MAD, mutually assured destruction, led to an emphasis on restraint, caution, and sobriety in judgement. Furthermore, the very idea of a Cold War presupposed restraint as both sides avoided direct and large-scale conflict that might have apocalyptic consequences. On the American side, there was an emphasis on restraint, as with the refusal to intervene against the Communists in China in support of the Nationalists during the Civil War of 1946–9, and in Vietnam in support of the French against the Viet Minh in 1953–4. The idea of a 'roll-back' of Communism in Eastern Europe was discarded in favour of defensive policies focused on protecting Western Europe, notably in the response to anti-Communist risings in Eastern Europe in the 1950s. Preventive air-strikes against Soviet nuclear capabilities had been seriously considered, only to be discarded.[4] Soviet forces, moreover, were able to suppress nationalist insurrections in the regions annexed by the Soviet Union.[5]

A measured, restrained policy was very much advocated by Henry Kissinger, a historian of nineteenth-century international relations who became an American 'defence intellectual', publishing *Nuclear Weapons and Foreign Policy* (1957). He was to become National Security Adviser in 1969 and then Secretary of State from 1973 to 1977. Kissinger's theme was *Realpolitik* and his language that of realism. Far more intellectually self-conscious than most politicians, Kissinger naturally looked for similarities between past and present, and found them in the concepts and language of national interests, the balance of power, geopolitics, and the pressure of Russian expansionism. In contrast, the tendency of ideologies to treat the world in terms of a gradient of ideological congruence or rivalry was regarded by Kissinger as naïve.

Kissinger's strategic culture was based on defining and using mutual interests. During the Vietnam War, he sought to employ Sino (Chinese)-American co-operation to isolate and put pressure on the Soviet Union, in order to get the latter to persuade Communist North Vietnam, which was already seen as a Soviet client, to reach an accommodation with anti-Communist South Vietnam, and thus end the war. In turn, President Richard Nixon and Kissinger reminded China that the American alliance with Japan would enable the USA to restrain Japan if its growing economy was to lead it back to expansionism. To Kissinger, national interests were essentially variable, but the pursuit of interest was fixed, so that he advised Nixon in 1972: 'I think in 20 years your successor, if he's as wise as you, will wind up leaning towards the Russians against the Chinese. For the next fifteen years we have to lean towards the Chinese against the Russians. We have to play the balance of power game totally unemotionally. Right now, we need the Chinese to correct the Russians and to discipline the Russians'.[6]

Realism is usually presented as the opposite and antidote to idealism. Kissinger very much saw himself as a realist, with his emphasis being on national interests, rather than ideological drive, and the former traced to long-term geographical commitments within a multi-polar and competitive international system. These produced a strategy, the culture of which was rational and realistic. A refugee from the anti-Semitism of Nazi Germany, Kissinger associated ideology, emotionalism and ostentatious moralizing in foreign policy with the destructive Germany he had fled. Instead, Kissinger favoured a statesmanship based on rational calculations of national self-interest in which the stress was on order and security.[7] Kissinger also appealed beyond ideological rivalries when trying to ease relations between Israel and its Arab neighbours, notably after the Yom Kippur War of 1973.

Beyond inherently having a cultural dimension that can be rooted in a particular psychology and set of experiences, it is scarcely surprising, however, that Kissinger's realism, like that of other politicians and powers, was also located in a political context that created a particular dynamic in which 'realism' and 'idealism' interacted. What can be termed a cultural dimension can also be found in this interaction. In the case of Kissinger, it was necessary to ensure and defend American disengagement from South-East Asia, which now appeared militarily necessary as a result of failure in the Vietnam War, but within a context of continued adherence to a robust containment of the Soviet Union. This defence was made more difficult in light of pressures on American interests elsewhere, particularly the Middle East and South Korea, as well as of the consequences of serious economic and fiscal problems.

Alongside these realist pressures came the crucial matter of political location, a long-standing factor. The Republican charge in the late 1940s, one then stated vociferously by Nixon as an opposition politician, had been that the Democratic Truman administration had 'lost' China to Communism, and this charge had proved a way subsequently to berate the Democrats. Similarly, Kennedy had run for President in 1960 in part on the claim that the Republican Eisenhower administration, in which Nixon was Vice-President for both terms, had failed to be sufficiently robust, not least in maintaining American defences.

Although, as President from 1969 to 1974, Nixon was helped by divisions in the Democratic Party, and its leftward move, he also had to consider potential criticism from within the Republican Party. As a consequence, Kissinger's rationalization of American diplomatic strategy has to be understood at least in part as a political defence, a point more generally true of other rationalizations of policy. Such rationalizations link 'realist' issues, in that they comment on the current situation, with cultural ones in terms of the language and ideas deployed, as well as with regard to their need to be effective in a given political culture in a particular conjuncture. In producing this defence of his diplomacy, Kissinger had to argue against powerful assumptions in American political culture in the period, in claiming not only that the USA could align with a Communist power, but also that such an alignment could be regarded as worthwhile because China and the Soviet Union had clashing interests, and therefore that the alignment should not be seen as a form of Communist deception of a duped USA.

The role of contrasting assumptions within American political culture were shown later in the decade, as Kissinger, Jimmy Carter, Democratic President from 1977 to 1981, and the process of *détente* with the Soviet Union, were criticized as weakening the West by a group of conservative Democrats, led by Senator Henry (Scoop) Jackson, as well as by key Republicans who were influential in the Ford administration (1974–7), notably his Chief of Staff, Dick Cheney, and the Secretary of Defense, Donald Rumsfeld, each of whom was to have senior appointment in the administrations of George W. Bush from 2001 to 2009.

These contrasting assumptions within political culture make very apparent the extent to which the idea of political culture has to be used with care. Rather than treating culture as a hegemonic concept, a form of *zeitgeist* (spirit of the age), that readily explains policy, via the medium of strategic culture, it is more pertinent to note that political culture is not a unity, but rather a sphere of debate; and that this point is true in autocracies as well as democratic societies. Debate may be over goals or may only be over implementation, but the latter can also be important and divisive.

There are efforts to segregate strategic culture from debate, largely by means of institutional specialization and the related secrecy of decisionmaking, and by arguing that both patriotism and the national interest requires such segregation. Nevertheless, strategic culture is affected by the process of debate. The segregation just referred to is an aspect of this debate as it represents an attempt to contain it.

Contention existed, moreover, not only within states but also within alliances, with a two-way process linking the two. Alliance dynamics, indeed, helped not only direct strategic culture but also provided key episodes in the Cold War, notably the Sino-American *rapprochement*. The extent to which cultural factors, in the sense of assumptions about other societies, played a role in these alliance dynamics is instructive. For example, under Stalin, there was a reluctance on the part of the Soviet Union to see other Communist powers as more than clients, and notably in the case of Asian states. Mao's China was a key recipient of this patronage and attempted direction. For example, the Soviet Union was reluctant to return the Chinese ports of Port Arthur and Dalian, which it had taken from Japan in 1945, and, despite Mao wanting the ports returned, did not do so while Stalin remained in power. The extent to which racist, quasi-colonial, or imperial attitudes played a role in American policy towards South-East Asia is open to debate. So also, more generally, with the relationship between American (and other) military and political commitments in Europe, where the Cold War did not lead to conflict, and those elsewhere, notably in Africa and Latin America where bloody and destructive conflict was common, albeit largely waged by surrogates, such as Cuba in the case of the Soviet Union.

Discussion about the nature of political realism had a military corollary in the shape of American strategic debate between massive retaliation and more limited warfare, which was linked to greater mobility. The latter approach came to the fore in the late 1970s in the aftermath of the Vietnam War and the Israeli success in the Yom Kippur War of 1973.[8]

Competing Societies

Alongside strategic planning, the Cold War also saw a competition of societies and ideologies in which attitudes to goals bulked large. These attitudes can be presented in terms of ideology and/or political culture, the latter often being a diffused and implemented version of the former. In the event, the Americans could deliver rockets and consumerism, while the Soviets found the latter a harder goal in large part because of the serious deficiencies of a Communist controlled economy.[9] In July 1959, Nixon, the Vice-President, and Nikita Khrushchev, the Soviet leader, significantly squared off in a kitchen in the American National Exhibition in Sololniki Park, Moscow, to debate the virtues of the two systems, Nixon boasting about colour television. Khrushchev criticized the 'gadgets' of the capitalist American home, but, as leader, set out to ensure consumer satisfaction; although the Socialist consumerism that was to be on offer in the East, for example sensible 'Socialist fashions', suffered from a serious lack of understanding of the populism and market mechanism of consumerism. In addition, television and film helped make American consumerism notable and attractive. When I visited Dresden in 1980, I noticed that Hollywood films were on show.

Moreover, the West adjusted to economic challenges in the 1970s and 1980s with less difficulty than did the Communist states, and shaped the resulting opportunities more successfully. In the 1930s, the crisis of the capitalist model had helped produce a new authoritarianism, notably in Germany, but also elsewhere, characterized by autarky, populism and corporatism. In contrast, in the 1970s and 1980s, widespread fiscal and economic difficulties, many linked to globalist pressures, led either to the panacea of social welfare or to democratic conservative governments, especially in the USA and Britain, that sought to 'roll back the state' and that pursued liberal economic policies, opening their markets and freeing currency movements and credit from most restrictions. The economic crises did not lead either to authoritarian regimes or to governmental direction of national resources.

The Soviet bloc was in a very different situation, with both ideology and political culture being at issue. Economic downturns interacted with already pronounced systemic faults. In particular, there was a failure to ensure adequate mechanisms for incentive, which reflected the lack of entrepreneurship and capitalism. With bright people unable to follow the Western pattern of raising money for investment and, moreover, generally excluded from state monopolies governed by timeserving and unimaginative bureaucrats, it was not surprising that the Soviet system could not engage adequately with change.

The command economy, with its micromanagement in planning and execution from the centre, was failing. Limited growth, moreover, intensified competition for resources, and the state lacked an adequate mechanism to cope with this competition which, anyway, it did not fully understand. The nostrums of Marxist–Leninism offered no help and decreasingly little inspiration. Economic rationality was not possible due to the political structure and ideology of Communist states. This lack of rationality was particularly true of the ideological commitment to heavy industry, especially steel, a commitment that was important to their political culture.

Conclusions

The Cold War therefore provides a key instance of the process by which military capability was related to socio-economic development, with priorities and success in the latter related to suppositions that were ideological and cultural. To that extent, war is 'total', in that it is the product of a society and its norms and assumptions.

The largely unexpected fall of the Communist regimes in Eastern Europe and of the Soviet Union also vindicated the views of those, on both sides of the Iron Curtain, who saw popular attitudes as highly significant. The inability of the Communist states to elicit widespread enthusiasm and large-scale popular support was significant to the crises of their leadership in 1989–91. The failure to counter the image of progress offered by the West was highly significant. In military terms, there was no real battle: the Communist governments fell with little violence, despite the strength of their armed forces. The extent to which this process also challenged the viability of Western militaries was not grasped by Western military commentators.

A discussion of the Cold War reveals again that the looseness of the cultural interpretation can bring different uses of culture into contact. This discussion also shows that exploiting the concept of strategic culture successfully entails addressing the nature of the society in question: while social structure is pertinent, the key element is the set of assumptions and beliefs that can be referred to as political culture. These assumptions and beliefs lack the clarity and systematic character of an ideology, but ideology is not as analytically helpful as political culture because the latter refers to the whole of society, whereas ideologies tend to be the choice of a minority.

6

From the Cold War into the Future

War from 1990

For long, the world wars were seen as the definition of modern warfare: large-scale, industrial, total and deadly were key adjectives. The arithmetic of threatened nuclear destruction during the Cold War between the USA-led West and the Soviet-led Communist bloc from 1946 and 1989 appeared to keep this description valid. Indeed, there was sufficient nuclear potential to destroy human life, and the catastrophe of nuclear conflict appeared imminent on a number of occasions including 1962 (the Cuban Missile Crisis) and 1983, when the Soviet Union considered launching an attack. Moreover, it was clear which side had won the world wars, and which lost.

Yet, the experience of conflict for the major powers after 1945 was in practice very different to the idea of total war. Wars for survival were replaced by expeditionary warfare, such as the Americans in Vietnam from the early 1960s to 1973, and the Soviets in Afghanistan from 1979 to 1988. Moreover, conscription ceased – in the USA in the early 1970s; and there was no total mobilization of the resources of society. Indeed, spending on the military as a percentage of total national expenditure fell in most major states, and notably with an increase in the share devoted to social welfare.

At the same time, war was devastating in many parts of the Third World, notably, but not only, because it was linked to famine and disease, as well as to more deliberate policies of attack on civilian society. This warfare was frequently in pursuit of ethnic or social warfare strategies aimed at the reduction, if not extirpation, of groups that were judged a threat, most graphically with the massacres in

Rwanda in 1994, but also, for example, in Congo, Sudan, Nigeria and the Ivory Coast. Much of the resulting conflict lacked the regularity sought by the professional forces of the major powers, and this absence served to underline the diversity of the nature of warfare. There was often a pronounced overlap with political struggles for control within states, notably in Africa, the continent where conflict was most insistent from the 1980s.

In turn, when such irregular Third World forces came into conflict with the regular militaries of major states, for example Afghans against Soviet units in the 1980s and against NATO units in the 2000s, there was an asymmetrical warfare that raised major, and continuing, questions about the nature of military capability and the pursuit of effectiveness in war. This situation is not a new one. Across the twentieth century, despite technological prowess, Western military superiority on land was more conditional and less secure than is generally implied. This was especially so in the Middle East, for example in Egypt and Iraq after the First World War, when the Western forces found it difficult to do better than their Ottoman predecessors. Yet, despite the limitations, it was a case of Western troops in Beijing (1900) and Baghdad (1917); and not vice versa.

The serious problems faced by the Americans in stabilizing Iraq, having conquered it in 2003, and by NATO in Afghanistan from the mid 2000s have forced the leading powers to rethink tactics and doctrine, notably leading to a greater emphasis on counter-insurgency. These problems have also raised questions about the ability of military planners to think strategically concerning the nature of domestic support for long-term military commitments. The last indicates a major shift from the situation in 1900. Imperialism no longer enjoys public support, while militarist values are publicly displayed in very few societies. There has been a revolution in attitudes to the military that represents a profound change in the context of conflict.

Considering the early years of the twenty-first century, but with no necessary guidance to the future, it was readily apparent that the central narrative of military history that had been dominant for so long, that focused on 'high-tempo' symmetrical warfare ending in victory and defeat, was inappropriate. Instead, it was clear that, alongside the continued threat of such conflict, it was necessary to devote more attention not only to 'little wars', but also to issues such as counter-insurgency, let alone civil control; with these conflicts often not won or lost but, instead, ending in a stalemate. As a result, the cultural approach had to be formulated in order to focus on such conflicts.

The early development of the USA, a state born in war, provides many points that are valid for today. First, and most significantly, the birth of a new state arose through violence. In the case of the USA, this was a matter of revolution in which there was a degree of foreign intervention. Much of this has been part of the pattern of conflict in the last sixty years. Two key points are the role of force in internal evolution and the extent of foreign intervention. The former is not quite normative, but is far more so than accounts of national history will often allow. As a result, there is a need for an account of military history in which the internal use of force plays an important role, rather than simply a focus on symmetrical conflict between regular armies, and also a need for a discussion of politics that puts an accent on force rather than ideology.

Political evolution in the shape of changes in state boundaries clearly focuses on force. Just as the American War of Independence (1775–83) began the series of wars of decolonization in the Western Hemisphere, and takes on part of its meaning in that context, so the end of the Cold War in 1989–91 ushered in another stage of the wars of decolonization. In this case, however, the colonial control that was at stake was more complex than that of the Western imperial empires of the mid twentieth century. Instead, there was an attempt to challenge the smaller-scale 'imperial' states that had developed an independent identity from the mid twentieth century, if not earlier. This process could be seen most prominently in the Slovene and Croat challenge to the Serbian imperialism that underlay the state of Yugoslavia. It was also the case with the challenge to Ethiopian rule over Eritrea, which had followed the end of the Italian empire in the Second World War, and, moreover, with opposition in Africa's largest country, Sudan, first from southern, and then from western separatists. Resistance to Israeli power in southern Lebanon and Palestine and, from 2005, to Syrian power in Lebanon, was also relevant as, thanks to the earlier conflicts of 1967–82, each power had established a quasi-imperial presence in part of the Middle East, not that that remark is intended to suggest any equivalence between Syrian autocracy and Israeli rule.

Related to this, the new wars of decolonization entailed challenges to the territorial configuration inherited from the political transformations of 1918–75, including (but not only) the end of the colonial Western empires. In essence, decolonization had not ended imperial boundaries, and these had subsequently been maintained as the frontiers of independent states. This challenge to the existing boundaries was pronounced in the Balkans and the Horn of Africa extending to Sudan, but was also seen elsewhere.

In the far-flung Indonesian archipelago, a state based on the former Dutch East Indies, there were demands, in the 1990s and 2000s, for

independence from both East Timor and Aceh (in Sumatra), demands
that were resisted by the military and linked militia groups in a crisis
that was symptomatic of the role of force in state control and of the
military in politics, for the *Tentera Nasional Indonesia* (Indonesian
National Military) continued to play a major role after the end of
the Suharto dictatorship. To turn again to culture, the military leadership has a deep contempt for civilian rule and, instead, sees itself as
above petty rivalries and self-interest. These beliefs affect its conduct,
not least opposition to accommodation with separatist tendencies.[1] In
East Timor, international pressure proved necessary to lead to an election in which the people voted for independence, a decision secured
by Australian intervention under UN auspices; while, in Aceh, a peace
agreement in 2005 brought twenty-nine years of conflict that had cost
12,000 lives to a close. Conflict between ethnic and religious groups
was also seen, notably in the Moluccas, Borneo and Sulawesi. This
conflict was linked to that over land and economic opportunity. Thus,
in Sulawesi, in the late 1990s and early 2000s, Christians in interior
areas and towns such as Tentena fought coastal Muslims, both sides
using bows and arrows, spears and home-made guns.

The challenge to existing frontiers was seen not only in separatism,
but in the habit of interventionism in other states, as with the dispatch
of the forces of Rwanda and Uganda into Congo in the late 1990s,
which helped ensure that the war there from 1998 to 2003 became the
bloodiest single conflict since the Second World War.

This interventionism reflected also an overlap between international and domestic conflict. The overlap was characteristic of many
states in Africa and South Asia. Much of the conflict of the post-1990
period was of this character, but complex issues of definition arise
in considering such conflict and, more generally, in assessing both
domestic and international struggles. In some cases, they can be seen
as an aspect of warfare, in some cases of large-scale feuding, and in
some of politics.

A key context, whatever the level of conflict, was provided by
the end of the Cold War. The collapse of the Soviet Union in 1991
destroyed the balancing element seen during the Cold War, because
China's growing economic strength did not in the 1990s and early
2000s lead it to seek to balance the USA on the global scale. The situation was different in South Asia, where, for example, America's closer
relations with India in the mid 2000s were countered by Chinese links
with Pakistan; just, as in the 1970s, Soviet links with India had been
countered by Chinese links with Pakistan, including the supply of
arms. In the 2000s, growing Chinese interest in resources, in order to
fuel and supply its economic growth, also led China into greater com-

mitments in Africa, and it is possible that a more farflung geopolitics of confrontation with the USA will develop. The growing assertiveness of the Chinese navy is indicative.

Strains in the World

As with the growing New World economies of the late eighteenth century, the global context of confrontation is far from static. In the current world, migration in search of work and other opportunities is a particular source of volatility, not least because it repeatedly crosses what have been cultural divides. The nature and rate of migration creates or accentuates both concerns about social and other changes, and a more general sense of flux that many find disorientating. However, short of the large-scale use of force combined with authoritarian policies, it is difficult to see how many states can resist these migratory pressures.

In many regions, pressure on resources is massively increased by population growth, which is more serious in the absence of equivalent economic growth and also where population issues are made more sensitive by ethnic rivalry. Thus, in Pakistan, there is rivalry between the regions as well as involving *mohajirs* descended from migrants from India. Karachi, the biggest city, had a resurgence of ethnic violence in 2010, with *mohajirs* clashing with Baluchis and Pushtuns in struggles linking criminality, politics, territorial control, and economic disputes. Over 1,100 people were killed in this violence in 2010.

Population growth, which is predicted to take the world's population from close to seven billion today to about nine billion in 2050, continues to be a particularly marked factor across the Third World, and contributes strongly to environmental degradation, not least in the shape of pressures on water supplies and on land use. At the local level, much conflict has resulted, for example between new immigrant settlers who cleared land and created farms, and longer-established peoples who used the land less intensively. This was a factor both in Indonesia, notably in Borneo and Sulawesi, in East Africa, and more generally. The resulting conflict extended to the animal world. In a drought-wracked Australia in late 2006, wild camels attacked settlements in an attempt to gain access to water. In these attacks, air-conditioning units, taps and lavatories were damaged in the search for water.

Aside from environmental pressures, civil order is also under challenge in states threatened by large-scale criminality, especially when the latter is linked to violent political movements. A good example is Colombia, where the radical guerrilla FARC movement partly funds itself by links to the large-scale drug trade.[2] Concern about both drugs and radicalism led the USA to provide aid to Colombia – over $4 billion in 2000–6, much of it to the army, with an annual level in 2006 of $600 million. As an instance, however, of the problems posed by drug wealth, some army units were, in turn, linked to drug trafficking. There were similar problems elsewhere, for example in Myanmar (Burma). Weapons trafficking is also an issue, notably with concern over nuclear proliferation.

Alongside economic issues came long-standing political and ethnic disputes. For example, in the Horn of Africa, there was a centuries-old rivalry between the Ethiopians, who lived in the mountainous interior, and the Eritreans and Somalis, who lived on the coast. The border war between Ethiopia and Eritrea in 1998–2000 led to 40,000 deaths. The struggle between Ethiopia and Somalia over the Ogaden region resulted in a large-scale war in 1976–8 and continues to be a source of tension. Indeed, this issue helped cause Ethiopian intervention in Somalia in 2006.

In the same region, but on a much smaller scale, long-standing tension between the Issas and the minority Afars in what had become French Somaliland and, from 1977, Djibouti, was accentuated when post-independence attempts to form a balanced government failed. Instead, in 1981, Djibouti became a one-party state under the Issa leader, Hassan Gouled Aptidon. In 1991, an Afar rebellion began. Many of the rebels accepted a power-sharing agreement in 1994, and those who held out finally signed a peace treaty in 2000. The Issa government had benefited greatly from the active support of the former colonial power, France, and, in turn, hosted a major French military base. Such bases were a legacy of independence from France that, in contrast, the newly independent USA was able to avoid when British rule ended, just as the Latin American states avoided hosting British naval bases.

In 2006, French aircraft continued a long pattern of French military assistance against rebellions in the Central African Republic, a former colony. Elsewhere in Africa, France had taken a major role in Congo and Chad in the 1980s, and in Ivory Coast in the 2000s. In late 2006, France had 18,000 troops abroad, mostly in Africa, including close to 3,500 in Ivory Coast and 1,200 in Chad, and close to 5,000 in permanent bases in Djibouti, Gabon and Senegal.

France's role in Africa today is different to that in North America in the late eighteenth century when the French played a major role in support of the American War of Independence against Britain; but the contrast is less marked than the forms may suggest. Indeed, the interaction of internal conflict, great power confrontation, and state evolution remains a crucial one that is worth comparative assessment. As the world's greatest power, the USA is the key dynamic force in the international context for many states. Skill in the use of American power requires an understanding of the manner in which this power interacts with tensions and divisions within these other states. This interaction provides allies and opponents for the USA, but does so in accordance with the alignments of their politics, more generally so than with reference to the purposes and goals of American power. Both the former central narrative about industrial warfare, conventional capability and symmetrical conflict, and the understanding of the current military situation across the world reflect assessments that involved preferences that can be seen as cultural alongside apparently more rational processes of obtaining and assessing information. Thus, both idealism and realism are involved in assessment.

Africa

Africa in the 2000s was indeed the continent where, as in the 1990s, warfare was most common in terms of the greatest number of conflicts and casualties. Moreover, military expenditure rose significantly in Africa. Many of the causes of conflict in Africa remained those of the late twentieth century, including ethnic violence and the chaos associated with 'failed states', a term that, again, was both objective and value-laden. In the latter, for example in Liberia and Sierra Leone, political objectives, beyond the capture of power, were hazy, and 'wars' benefited from the large-scale availability of small arms and were financed primarily by criminal operations and forced extortions. There were no chains of command, nor (often) even uniforms that distinguished 'troops' from each other, or from other fighters, and, politically, these conflicts were an instance of a more widespread process in which warlords moved from being rebels to presidents or vice versa.

Struggles over resources complicated the situation in Africa (and elsewhere), with land and water as traditional issues of dispute being joined by new resources such as government expenditure, jobs and access to raw materials, especially oil. These tensions interacted with the issue of central control over tribal groups and peripheral areas, leading to conflict for example in Sudan. Indeed, the problems there were symptomatic of wider currents in violence. Control of oil helped drive governmental determination to suppress secessionism in the south, while the government also faced a serious rebellion in the west. Militarily, the Sudanese government benefited from its control over the central point of the capital, Khartoum, from the funds gained from resource exploitation, especially of oil, which enabled it to buy Chinese and Russian arms, and from its use of air power and artillery. The conflict in Sudan spilled over into neighbouring states, especially Chad and the Central African Republic. Chad accused Sudan of backing rebels and, in response, Chad forces crossed the border into Darfur in April 2007 and fought Sudanese troops.

Dating to the 1970s, but breaking out with greater intensity in 2003, and mounted by the Sudan Peoples Liberation Army based in the Darfur region, the rebellion in the west of Sudan was directed against the oppression of non-Arabs by the government. In response, from 2004, the government used its regular forces, including aircraft and infantry moved in trucks, to support an Arab militia, the Janjaweed (much of which rode on horses and camels), in order to slaughter the Fur, Masalit and, in particular, Zaghawa native tribes in Darfur. Alongside large-scale slaughter, especially of men and boys, even very young boys, and the systematic rape and mutilation of women, natives were driven away, their cattle and therefore livelihood seized, the wells poisoned with corpses, and dams, pumps and buildings destroyed. The government was assisted by serious divisions among the opposition in Darfur, not least over negotiations and also over whether the goal was partition or a different Sudan.[3] Traditional ethnic and religious hostilities played a major role in Sudan, and helped structure antagonisms. Indeed, the separateness of the south culminated in a massive vote there for independence in a referendum conducted in January 2011.

The means of waging war in Sudan were far from those discussed by commentators, especially in America, who had discerned from the 1990s what they termed a Revolution in Military Affairs (RMA), one largely defined in terms of modern information-led weapons systems and weapons of precision and lethality. Thus, in Congo, much of the killing was with machetes, and bows and arrows and shotguns were employed, alongside the frequent use of mortars and submachine guns. The conflict also led to cannibalism, as well as to the use of child warriors[4] seen, for example, in West Africa, Uganda and Nepal and by the Taliban in Afghanistan, as well as by the Mexican crime syndicates that together deployed a level of force similar to that seen in many Third World conflicts.

Other aspects of African conflict that were distant from conventional Western warfare included the use of traditional charms and spirit mediums, although removing the term 'conventional' opens up references to parallels in the West, for example in the Balkans in the 1990s. Moreover, as in the former Yugoslavia in the 1990s, violence was often brutal and symbolic. In the Katanga region of Congo in 2004, insurgents reputedly cut off the genitals of victims and drank their blood. Similar brutality and symbolism were often seen in the conflicts between Mexican crime syndicates and by them against government forces. The use of brutality in the latter case made the symbolic point that the authority and power of the state were as nothing and that the norms on which they rested had collapsed. Over 13,000 people were killed in drug-related violence in Mexico in 2010. Extreme brutality has also been linked to a profound level of spiritual anarchy and anxiety.[5]

More generally and in Africa in particular, rivalries between states interacted with insurrections and other civil conflicts elsewhere. For example, warfare between Eritrea and Ethiopia, which involved large-scale fighting of a conventional type, spilled over into internal conflicts in Somalia. In November 2006, the Prime Minister of Ethiopia called Islamists in Somalia a 'clear and present danger' to Ethiopia, a Christian state, claiming that they were being armed by Eritrea. In turn, the Somali Islamists, the Islamic Courts Union, met at Mogadishu, the Somali capital, and declared that they would defend Somalia against a 'reckless and war-thirsty' Ethiopia. Both Eritrea and Ethiopia sent troops into Somalia.

Local struggles such as this one were interpreted by outside powers in terms of alleged wider alignments, not only regional but also global, such as the struggle between the USA and Muslim fundamentalists. In Somalia in 2006, warlord resistance to the fundamentalist attempt to capture Mogadishu was covertly supported by the USA, although, in the event, the capital fell that June to the Islamic Courts Union and the forces of the latter pressed on to attack the Somali transitional government, which had taken refuge in the town of Baidoa.

In turn, the American government encouraged the Ethiopian invasion that overthrew the Union and captured Mogadishu in the winter of 2006–7. For the USA, this was a welcome opportunity to benefit from regional animosities, and to leave the military work on the ground to local forces, although the Americans did provide some air support, a strong ground-attack capability that Ethiopians lacked. Subsequently, opposition in Somalia to the Ethiopian-backed transitional government of Abdullahi Yusuf continued and became more clearly linked to fundamentalists, notably to the *Shabab* (boys) who sought to overthrow it. The *Shabab* were a continuation of the militias that had supported the Union. Al-Qaeda also played a role. At the same time, the opposition in Somalia lacked the benefits enjoyed by the Taliban in Afghanistan, notably a largely safe haven in parts of neighbouring Pakistan and the experience gained by several years of relatively constant conflict.

From 2008, the forces of the transitional Somali government were backed by about 8,000 Ugandan and Burundian troops under an African Union 'peacemaking' mission largely financed by the USA. The fighting involved plentiful use of machine-guns, mortars, improvised explosive devices and sniping, with control over the central districts of Mogadishu being the key issue, and much of the fighting waged at close range.

A Clash of Civilizations?

The problem of relating all conflicts to a supposed clash of civilizations, an idea advanced, notably by Samuel Huntington, from the 1990s, initially in terms of Islam and Christendom, was also demonstrated in the far south of Thailand where Muslim separatists are seen as resisting a pro-Western government. There are certainly cultural elements involved in a conflict that has been ongoing since 2004, but other issues are involved. The cultural factors are more complex than allowed by the thesis of a clash of civilization. These factors included the problems of absorbing a largely Malay-speaking Muslim people annexed in 1902 by a Thai-speaking Buddhist state. Moreover, the 'cultural' issues are often made concrete by issues of military brutality, which played a major role in the upsurge of tension in late 2004 in which troops fired on demonstrators, as well as by exploitation of potential conflicts by politicians and drug barons seeking their own local advantages.

Similarly, in Uzbekistan in Central Asia, the authoritarian regime of Islam Karimov claimed that opposition was led by Muslim terrorists, a view that neglected the extent to which the long-standing dictatorship faced opposition for a number of reasons. In 2005, troops fired on a crowd in the Uzbek city of Andijan demonstrating against the poor economic situation. Yet, religion also operated as a real force providing a key lightning rod for tensions. In 2007, Pakistani forces stormed the Lal Masjd (Red Mosque), a centre of opposition by radical Muslim clergy, in the capital, Islamabad. In response, attacks on the security forces increased. The issues that led to violence might seem trivial, but the tensions were often serious, as in Kaduna in Nigeria in 2002, where Muslim anger about the planned staging of the

Miss World competition in the federal capital, Abuja, led to riots in which many were killed.

Internal Disorder and Foreign Intervention

Sectarian-linked disputes were not the only ones that were portrayed in terms of wider concerns, nor, therefore, the sole disputes to be internationalized. More widely, foreign assistance was sought, and, if necessary, hired to help resist insurrections. Thus, between 1993 and 2003, Ange-Félix Patassé, the President of the Central African Republic, survived seven coup attempts, including one in 2002 by General François Bozizé, one-time head of the army, that involved serious street fighting in the capital, Bangui. Patassé turned for support to Libya, which provided backing until 2002, and then to a Congolese rebel group, but, in March 2003, Bozizé, at the head of 1,000 men, overran Bangui. The unpaid army was unwilling to resist. Instability in the Central African Republic reflected the knock-on effects of war elsewhere, for conflict in Congo hit the Central African Republic's trade links down the Congo river.

Coups and the possibility of such action continue to play a major role in military history, underlining the central role of political concerns in a military history that is not restricted to war. In 2000, American and Brazilian pressure on Paraguayan military leaders led them to thwart an attempted coup, and that year the army eventually suppressed an attempted coup on the Pacific island of Fiji. An attempted military coup in Chad failed in 2003. There were also military coups in Fiji and Thailand in 2006, although the Thai army was unable to sustain the political order it sought to create. In Fiji, the coups reflected bitter and persistent ethnic conflict between the native Indian and Fijian population.

In Zimbabwe, in 2008, the military-dominated Joint Operations Command in effect gained control from the weakened President, Robert Mugabe, and orchestrated the use of force in order to maintain him in power against popular pressure and democratic methods. The Zimbabwe army, whose members and former members had gained assets and government posts, was linked to violent gangs in brutalizing opponents. Such violence interacted with economic problems in encouraging large numbers of refugees to flee to neighbouring states such as Botswana, South Africa and Zambia, but the economic competition they posed in a situation of high unemployment, in turn, led to violence against refugees in South Africa. Elsewhere in Africa, in September 2009, soldiers in Guinea suppressed pro-democracy demonstrators, killing and raping many. The previous December, the army had taken power in a coup. Force was used in the Ivory Coast in 2010–11 by Laurent Gbagbo in an eventually unsuccessful attempt to ignore his defeat in the 2010 election. As with Zimbabwe, this attempt underlined the extent to which the use of the military was just one aspect of the employment of force. Gbagbo also deployed civilian supporters who kidnapped and killed his opponents.[6] In 2011, power in Egypt was seized by the High Council of the Army in order to preserve stability and ensure the departure of Hosni Mubarak, the unpopular president, both of which secured the army's position. The degree to which the military elsewhere in the Arab world was willing to accept change was highly significant.

The role of the military in politics is usually considered in terms of the Third World, but that may well underplay its importance elsewhere, including the USA and Britain. If the threshold for attention is that of tanks in the street, then there is scant sign of this role, but, nevertheless, it is relevant in three respects. First, and most obviously, the military plays a role in military policy that is often greater than the constitutional situation would allow, and with civilian oversight circumvented. Secondly, an ability to rely on the military is important in giving security to government as well as an ability to implement particular policies. Thirdly, the military may well have greater political influence in specific contexts. As an example, the military has had great influence in Israel in recent decades, not only with former generals playing a major role as politicians, but also with the serving military being important in terms of policy such as attitudes towards settlements in the occupied territories and relations with other states. In some states, it is unclear how far the military is under the control of the government or how far it is in effect autonomous. This question is particularly the case in China, where the military appears far more autonomous than in Japan or India. The identification of some Chinese units with particular regions is also an aspect of the situation.

Power-Projection by the Major States

The interaction between violence within countries and external intervention provides a way to consider not only conflict across the Third World but also specific conflicts in which Western powers have committed troops, for example France in the Ivory Coast. At the same time, this context poses a difficulty for Western intervention, as it indicates the extent to which civil conflict is frequent, if not, in some countries, constant. Moreover, this approach questions the analysis that sees violence largely in terms of resistance to the Western powers. Instead, as in Afghanistan, Iraq (in which the insurgents have particularly disparate goals), and Yemen, it is appropriate to note the high levels of civil violence in many states. Moreover, this violence cannot be readily contained in the terms of Western intervention or by means of the attrition of killing insurgents.

At the same time that problems in Afghanistan and Iraq suggested that Western approaches to understanding (as well as winning) war had important limits, it is also notable that the Iraqi insurgents, like the Taliban in Afghanistan, found that their ideas and practices brought less success than they had anticipated. This failure contributed to the general inability of war-making to achieve the results desired by both sides. In Afghanistan, the problems of creating a stable political solution, and thus of making the results of military intervention durable, were fully demonstrated. The government of Hamid Karzai established as a result of the American intervention in 2001 proved very vulnerable from 2005 to a Taliban resurgence, and this vulnerability led to NATO intervention.

The fighting, however, indicated the potential of insurrectionary forces, especially when backed by a relatively secure foreign base, in this case the North West Frontier Province of Pakistan. The Taliban were not short of fighters and also benefited from the extent to which they were able to take the initiative. As far as tactics were concerned, NATO and Afghan government forces were based in settlements whose walls and orchards provided cover for Taliban assailants. Taliban ambushes of road links led to a NATO dependence on helicopters for mobility and logistics, as well as firepower, which was also provided by fixed-wing aircraft; but there was only so much air power and only so much it could achieve, especially, but not only, in bad flying conditions. As a result, the NATO and Afghan government forces frequently seemed reactive and unable to protect potential allies, which increased the political impact of the Taliban.

The Russian invasion of Georgia in 2008 underlined the problem of gauging military success. The Russians rapidly defeated the Georgian military, ending its forcible attempt to suppress secessionism in South Ossetia, but, at the same time, the invasion revealed serious deficiencies in the Russian military, not least in achieving air superiority and in night fighting, while it was unclear whether the local Russian success merited the costs of lost international support. To that extent, there was a parallel with the American invasion of Iraq in 2003, although the Russian action cost far less and could be more readily afforded, thanks to the buoyant state of the oil-rich Russian revenues. Each invasion, however, underlined the contrast between the successful operational application of greater power and the more problematic wider strategic context. As far as Georgia was concerned, this context proved to be the reassertion of Russia's idea of its own sphere of influence and power, especially in the divided region of the Caucasus, as well as America's tacit recognition that even its power does not extent militarily to Georgia, and NATO's weakness there.[7]

The significance of the Georgia conflict for the assessment of Russian power and intentions helped encourage different accounts of the conflict. This instance was an aspect of a more widespread process, that of instant military history. For example, after the Iran-Iraq war (1980–8), both governments sought to present the history of the conflict from their own, more positive perspectives, the Iraqi regime providing a revisionist view of the Karbala operations that omitted the setbacks and errors.[8]

In the case of the Americans, the key elements in the aftermath of the invasion of Iraq in 2003 proved not to be the situation in Iraq but rather the regional consequences in terms of greater relative Iranian power (as the Iraqi counterweight was removed); secondly, the terrible fiscal consequences which lessened American strength and increased its dependence on foreign capital inflows, especially from East Asia and from oil-rich states; and, thirdly, the strategic rapprochement of China and Russia which undid the major advantages the USA had gained from the Sino-Soviet rift in 1960. Military commentators were not apt to think in terms of such strategic dimensions, but they underlined the hazards posed by the unexpected consequences of going to war, as well as the extent to which the technological triumphalism of the Revolution in Military Affairs (RMA), or, as it is now discussed, transformation, was totally misplaced.[9] In part, this triumphalism was related to a more general weakness of military professionalism, one in which there was a failure to focus on strategy and to think strategically,[10] and, in particular, an inability to relate military means and political goals,[11] and a tendency to adopt a facile response to the learning of lessons and the corresponding adoption of doctrine.[12] That, in the case of America, this failure was linked to a major extension of the role, impact and cost of the military, with foreign policy frequently dominated by military interests,[13] was not coincidental.

At the same time, the problems affecting advanced militaries in part also arose from the more conventional form of the dissemination of advanced weaponry. For example, having developed heavily armoured tanks to retain force for their offensive capability, Israel

was affected in 2006 when attacking Hezbollah positions in neighbouring Lebanon by the skilful Hezbollah use of anti-tank missiles.
Hezbollah's behaviour was far from the classical guerrilla model
seen in Iraq and Afghanistan,[14] which raised major questions about
Western military planning and the agenda of transformation. Moreover, from 2010, Israel's capability vis-à-vis Hamas forces in Gaza was
affected by the deployment by Hamas of the Russian-made Kornet
anti-tank missile, which is capable of piercing 47-inch-thick armour
at a range of over three miles. The diffusion of advanced weaponry
is such that developments, for example of germ capability, are open
not only to leading states, but also to lesser competition, such as
from North Korea,from states that consider such weaponry a way of
improving their position, as well as to terrorist organizations.[15]

Thinking the Future

Consideration of the RMA looks to the future, not least to the extent
to which possible developments in military capability, for example of
genetic engineering to improve effectiveness, or of weapons systems,
such as aircraft capable of 'skipping' along on the atmosphere so
that they can fly anywhere in the world in two hours, or improve-
ments in cyber warfare[16] and space weaponry,[17] notably space-to-
earth weapons, will provide little guidance to changes in 'tasking', the
goals set for the military. These goals may well revolve around international struggles, not least for scarce resources, but it is also likely
that conflict within countries will become more prominent as systems
of social cohesion and control are placed under greater pressure, not
least as a result of population growth and its impact on resource competition.[18]

There has been, and probably will be, a significant contrast between
warfare and military capability. Some major and second-rank powers
either did not engage in war (China, Japan, Brazil), or did so with only
a fraction of their forces (India). Warfare involved some poor states,
but not all of them. Ethnic division led to serious civil conflict in some
countries, such as Sri Lanka, but not in all. Resource issues increased
tension but, as yet, competition for water and energy has not led to
the large-scale breakdowns that have been anticipated. These points
serve as a reminder of the unpredictability of war, an unpredictability
that remains a constant factor as governments and militaries seek to
plan and train for future contingencies. As far as resources are concerned, food is becoming a more pressing issue than seemed likely to
most commentators looking to the future in recent years.

Aspects of the future will be reconsidered in the concluding chapter, but several points need to be rehearsed here. First, writing about the future of war and the military serves more powerful psychological needs in Western culture than writing about the past. Again cultural assumptions and identities come into play, and it is necessary to underline that these points do not relate to some unchanging character of Western culture, but, rather, to the situation at the present. Moreover, there is room for suggesting a contrast between the USA, where interest in the future is strongest, and less confident European societies that are more likely to focus on past and present. In part, this contrast reflects demographics, notably the greater proportion of young people in the USA, but there is also a cultural dimension in terms of the standard American engagement with becoming, rather than with the point of departure. The psychological need to engage with the future rests in part on the belief that it validates the present and more particularly, provides purpose. As a result, the future has to be known and controlled.

For example, it was crucial to Americans that the RMA (or transformation) was an American military revolution and one that appeared able to meet the doctrine, politics and military strategic needs of a range of American opinions, from isolationists to interventionists, whether unilateralists or believers in American-led collective security. Similarly, it was crucial to this belief that culture was as it were understood, rather than being indeterminate, because in being understood it could be controlled.

This process of asserting intellectual control related not only to the tension between order and chaos on the battlefield,[19] but also to the political dimension. The 'clash of civilizations' proved an attractive concept because it appeared to explain the new world after the Cold War. Rebutting Fukuyama, Huntington predicted not the triumph of Western values, but, rather, the rise of 'challenger civilizations', especially China and Islam. Huntington drew on the analysis of Islam by another American scholar, Bernard Lewis, specifically his 1990 article 'The Roots of Muslim Rage'. Huntington argued that, in light of the rise of 'challenger civilizations', the established and rival concept of a global community of nation-states accepting a shared rule of international law and set of assumptions could no longer be the answer to the world's problems and, thus, satisfy demands. A global community had been the aspiration of Wilsonian and Cold War American politics and seemed achieved in the 1990s, but Huntington was less optimistic.

Terrorism was to drive this lesson home, and Huntington's book, which had been overshadowed during the triumphant (albeit also somewhat uncertain at the time) globalization of the 1990s, now appeared horribly prescient after the terrorist attacks of 11 September 2001. Indeed, Huntington's book was to be translated into thirty-three languages.

The focus was on relations with Islam, which raises the question of what would have happened had the key event of the period not been the terrorist attacks, or if the attacks had failed. Huntington was generally seen as an exponent of the likelihood of conflict between Christendom and Islam, and was praised or criticized accordingly. To some critics, Huntington, who was in fact a lifelong Democrat as well as a self-declared conservative, was a key neo-conservative who had sketched out the prospectus for the new ideological confrontation of the 2000s as well as for the assertive American policies that followed the 11 September attacks.

These policies can be seen as an aspect of a new American strategic culture. As so often, the emphasis in understanding the use of the term culture can be on the simplification of strategy for rhetorical and related purposes. At the same time, this simplification can be seen as providing a key indication of the spur to policy. Thus, when President George W. Bush, addressing a Joint Session of Congress on 20 September 2001, declared 'Either you are with us, or you are with the terrorists', he was capturing a sense of division and struggle that spoke to the American strategic assumptions stemming from the new situation created by the terrorist attacks. Some of these ideas could be presented as stemming from the prospectus outlined in the neo-conservative 'Project for a New American Century' of 1997, but the attacks generated a new political dynamic. The formulation of the last sentence captures some of the problems with the term strategic culture, as it is unclear, in this case, whether to put the emphasis on the ideas circulating prior to September 2001 or on subsequent policy. The call for a 'war on terror' was one for a universal mission in which geographical limits were regarded as an irrelevance that was to yield to will. As a result, an open-ended commitment, in both time and space, was outlined. The use of the 'war on terror' both to act as a prompt to action, and in order to structure the complexities of world affairs and to help direct alliances, can be seen as constituents of a strategic culture, but, again, capture the ambiguities of that concept.

Conversely, and without suggesting any equivalence, Osama bin Laden and his supporters can also be presented as having had a strategic culture, not least because of their presentation of Islam as a converting and controlling faith, rather than a religion limited to the devotion of the faithful. An historical imagination was important to this account, as al-Qaeda depicted Islam as having been driven back from spaces it should control, notably Israel and southern Spain, while the presence of American troops in Saudi Arabia following the Gulf War of 1990–1 was seen by them as another instance of cultural spatial violation. Al-Qaeda sought to use *jihad* as both a call for action and an organizing concept that could incorporate Islamic activism and disputes across the world, as in January 2009 when bin Laden pressed for *jihad* against Israel over Gaza. Earlier, in 1996 at Kandahar, Mullah Omar, the leader of the Taliban, was declared 'Commander of the Faithful' by a gathering of Islamic scholars and, accordingly, invested himself in Mohammed's Cloak. Alongside the emphasis on religion came a stress on social justice as a means and goal of power, which poses problems for those opposed to Muslim fundamentalists.[20] In practice, the role of *jihad* in the Islamic world has varied greatly across time.

American strategic culture also envisaged a global battlefield; as well as presenting, protecting and spreading freedom not only as the goal of war but also as an important means. Thus, the National Security Strategy, announced in September 2002, declared:

> The great struggles of the twentieth century between liberty and totalitarianism ended with a decisive victory for the forces of freedom. These values of freedom are right and true for every person, in every society – and the duty of protecting these values against their enemies is the common calling of freedom-loving people across the globe and across the ages…We will extend the peace by encouraging free and open societies on every continent.

To that end, Bush pressed for democracy, notably the American form of democracy, in the Middle East and China, which was a departure from the *Realpolitik* advanced by Kissinger and other realists, and from the priorities he had initially outlined.[21] Instead, the assumption was that a change in the values of a society, as well as of the operations of its domestic politics, would alter the country's position in international relations, and therefore the likelihood of war. Thus, the goals of conflict became the end of war, a long-standing aspect of what supporters might see as an amelioralist tendency in international relations, and critics as utopian. Building on the oft-repeated claim that democracies do not declare war on democracies, the call for democratization was an aspect of a strategy seeking to maintain stability and prevent wars, as much as to win them. Opposition to weapons' proliferation was part of the same policy. The strategic counterpart was that deterrence no longer appeared effective, or, at best, seemed of uncertain effectiveness, when confronted by terrorism or states governed by fanatical rulers. Thus, pre-emption appeared necessary as a strategic means and goal.

A different set of cultural assumptions seemed at play when the USA considered China. The 2006 Quadrennial Defense Review described it as having 'the greatest potential to compete militarily with the United States and field disruptive military technologies that could over time offset traditional US military advantages'.[22] Reflecting 'realist' geopolitical competition,[23] China indeed aroused strategic concern, not least due to its economic growth and quest for resources, but there was not in the 2000s the sense of outrage or antipathy that much of American public opinion expressed in reaction to its perception of radical Islam. The 2010 controversy over the plan to locate a mosque near the site of the Twin Towers in New York provided another iteration of this response. Given the extent to which strategic priorities reflected domestic political assumptions, the different degrees of almost instinctive hostility aroused by the challenges posed by China and Islam were militarily significant.

Concern about China entailed for America a military focused on symmetrical warfare, and with weaponry and doctrine to match, notably high-tech naval and air power; while the concern about Islam meant a focus on a counter-insurgency capability and the army in particular. The implications of the political culture of threat and anxiety feed directly into military structures, while the latter, in turn, also help mould responses and priorities.

Conclusions

These structures cannot be readily separated from military culture in the shape of the assumptions of the military and expectations about its use. This issue was raised in the *Times* in 2010. On 25 November, the paper published a letter from Admiral Lord West of Spithead, a one-time First Sea Lord. Under the newspaper headline 'Korean crisis and UK strike capability', Lord West argued that Britain should be willing and able to support the USA in the defence of South Korea against attack from the north, which then seemed threatened. Two days later, a critical columnist, Matthew Parris, wrote in the paper 'the retired admiral is not off on some fanciful conceit of his own, but giving voice to an inherited mindset shared by millions of his countrymen, including many capable, brave and distinguished military men. They really do believe that post-imperial Britain can afford and manage a central, guiding role in the international disposition and use of military power'. Instead, Parris argued the realist case of limited British resources, concluding 'The next generation must learn to accept, as I fear much of my generation never will, that there exist future possibilities for which we cannot afford to cater'.

Parris' point about generational assumptions and impressions is an important one that can be matched in the consideration of other societies, as with discussion of radicalization among some Islamic youth. A focus on generational assumptions gives strength to the cultural interpretation by adding a degree of dynamism to it, but not such a degree as to invalidate the notion of culture. The 'unfixed' nature of cultural factors help explain their significance, as they can cause, reflect and incorporate change, or help to do so.

A similar point can be made about the perceived need to confront the future for technological reasons that make the past seem redundant. Cyber and space warfare seem prime instances of this process. They do indeed encourage an emphasis on the new and unexpected, but arguments relating to these forms of warfare also reflect cultural and psychological norms and notions. A focus on fast-moving change and unique and chaotic circumstances is currently fashionable, but this approach overplays the extent of change.[24]

7

Culture and Military Analysis

The idea of military analysis as itself a form of cultural activity is not one with which most commentators have engaged, although, as already indicated in this book, culture is a prime topic of theoretical discussion both in academe and in the military. Indeed, the second sentence of the introduction to Adrian Lewis' *The American Culture of War* (2007) states 'The thesis is that culture decisively influences the way nation-states conduct war'.[1] At the same time, there have been some calls to caution in cultural interpretations of war, notably Patrick Porter's thoughtful *Military Orientalism. Eastern War Through Western Eyes* (2009), which presses the dynamic and contested nature of culture, and thus the need not to apply it in a deterministic fashion.

The purpose in this section is to move from these uses of culture as a means of analysis, in order to discuss commentary on the military, both past and present, as a form of cultural activity. In doing so, I do not wish to repeat the chapter 'The Sound of Guns: Military History Today' in my *Rethinking Military History* (2004), but, as I cannot assume that readers have necessarily read this chapter, it is pertinent to summarize some of the major points. Moreover, as that book was written nearly a decade ago, it is appropriate to consider the situation afresh.[2] This is a particularly relevant task, because, since the book was written, there has been the challenge of responding to the great difficulties that faced coalition forces in Iraq and to the apparent reprise, in fact very different circumstances, in Afghanistan.

Presentism, or the imprint of present concerns and perspectives, does not only take this form. There is also the reconsideration of past episodes in the light of changing political emphases. This has certainly been the case in Eastern Europe since the end of Communist rule. For example, whereas the unsuccessful Soviet invasion of Slovakia in 1944 was seen as an heroic effort at liberation during the Communist years, Soviet actions have since been viewed more critically, not least with claims that Soviet interests were preferred to Czech and Slovak ones.

Popular Scholarship

Academics are apt to begin with their own activities and to see these as defining historiography, but that approach, which is problematic anyway,[3] would be mistaken in the case of military history because much of what is read is written by non-academics. The same is true of work on the present situation. Moreover, the work by non-academics does not depend on, and is not defined by, the intellectual advances by academics, nor on the research they undertake. Instead, work by non-academics is largely in relation to that by other non-academics. This is true not only in terms of the methods employed and sources used, but also, more significantly, with reference to the topics covered. In particular, the quest for market opportunity can encourage the search for new openings, although there is also a tendency to flock to similar subjects. Both established market preferences and significant anniversaries play a role in the latter. Thus, at present, there are the anniversary volumes for the American Civil War, and those for the First World War will follow. The commercial appeal of studies of the Second World War is such not only that publications on that book bear scant reference to anniversaries, but also that individual publishers, notably Allen Lane/Penguin, produce what can be seen as works that rival those they have recently published.

Much work by non-academics is first-rate by academic standards: based on an effective use of sources, well-written and thoughtful. Yet, frequently, there are also significant problems. The exigencies of the world of publishing combine with the practicalities of knowledge and research to lead, first, to a focus on Western Europe and the USA and, secondly, to a concentration on operational and tactical issues. War becomes a matter of campaigns and battles, more particularly battle and biography, with the emphasis on the familiar; and this is as true of the visual mediums of film and television as of the written word. Indeed, film and television increasingly help set the normative standards for written work. Much of the popular work is repetitive and responds to the market opportunities of the familiar topic, or, to take a more favourable tone, this literature is a matter of making established knowledge accessible anew.

This point can be readily seen in the treatment of the two world wars. As far as the First World War is concerned, despite good and successful work on the other fronts, the popular focus is overwhelmingly on the Western Front, and the emphasis is very much on the conflict as both deadly and futile. Incompetent generals and brave, but doomed, troops, 'lions led by donkeys', inhabit the narrative; and discussion of the war focuses on the same battles: Verdun, the Somme and Passchendaele.[4] These battles were indeed very important, and it is pertinent to discuss the themes above, but far less attention is devoted to the question of how the armies got from the apparent stasis of 1916 to the breakthroughs of 1917 and 1918, the collapse, successively, of Russia and of the Central Powers. The Allied offensive in the last hundred days is underplayed, or there is the *deus ex machina* of the tank.[5] In the latter case, discussion of the technological magic-bullet leads to an underplaying of the more complex issues posed by combined-arms operations

As far as the Second World War is concerned, the focus again is on the familiar topics, notably the war in Europe, especially if involving Britain and the USA,[6] and the relationship between the Allied leaders. Thus, air power is considered largely in terms of the Battle of Britain and the Combined Air Offensive on Germany, and far less attention is devoted to the use of air power on the Eastern Front and, even more, in the war in China. Moreover, there is disproportionately little attention on anti-aircraft warfare.

This focus on the familiar does not mean that the work is without considerable value, and that point extends to popular studies. To take a commercially successful book of recent years, in his *Masters and Commanders. How Roosevelt, Churchill, Marshall and Alanbrooke Won the War in the West* (2008), Andrew Roberts used the politics of strategy in order to throw crucial light on the superiority of Allied war-making, as well as specific light on the dynamics and, in particular, tensions of the Anglo-American coalition. Instead of making the mistake of assuming that superior Allied resources in some way determined the course and result of the conflict, Roberts presented debate over the use of resources and the strong constraints posed by the clashing yet also, to a point, accommodating personalities involved. Alanbrooke and Marshall emerge as effective professionals, but Roosevelt has a far more mixed verdict, in part because he did not really appreciate the nature of coalition politics at the international level. Churchill, who was difficult and also resolute, and could be foolish as well as outstanding, had far more experience, both from the First World War and as a result of the nature of the British empire. If such work helps explain Allied superiority to the Axis, it can scarcely be said that China or the Soviet Union participated centrally in the processes of coalition warfare, however much their contributions on the battlefield were crucial. On the other hand, both China and the Soviet Union benefited from coalition warfare, notably in terms of the supply of *matériel*.

Much of the popular writing on the war, however, repeats familiar points. To take a work advertised as revelatory, Gordon Corrigan's *Blood, Sweat and Arrogance. The Myths of Churchill's War* (2006) set out to challenge assumptions about the Second World War that, in practice, had been long queried, notably about the quality of Churchill's leadership, Montgomery's generalship, and the British contribution to victory. As such, Corrigan, who wrote with all the single-minded confidence of a retired officer, repeated the lack of originality and subtlety already seen in his treatment of the First World War, *Mud, Blood and Poppycock.*

That such work appeals to major publishers, in this case Weidenfeld and Nicolson/Orion Books, indicates what can be seen as a cultural and organizational aspect of the world of popular historical publishing, the appeal of certainty and the marked preference for mono-causal explanations. The tension between history as question/ questioning and history as answer/answering, a tension that overlaps with, but is not completely coterminous with, that between research and theory, is accentuated in the case of military history by the extent to which it appears to attract more than its fair share of assertive individuals not given to qualification or self-doubt, and apparently disinclined to cite the work of others except when the author as hero is castigating their folly.[7] The quest for allegedly new interpretations is another repeated feature of popular work. As far as popular historical publishing is concerned, it is worth noting features of the British situation, notably that special deals are offered for sales by newspapers that then always seem to carry favourable reviews of these books, while display space in bookshops is paid for.

The pressures of popular writing help explain coverage. The operational focus of popular writing is also readily apparent, and is matched by television history. Resources in the shape of what can be presented readily on screen play a significant role, but so also do assumptions about popular interests.[8] Authors who focus on such popular history are obliged to live by their pens, which encourages publication in a style that further marginalizes the subject in terms of the academy. These writers receive publishers' advances and have no teaching, but they rarely benefit from research grants and have to construct their projects in the likelihood that none will ever be provided. This situation lessens the feasibility of archival research and, definitely, the chances of work in foreign archives, without which it is impossible properly to appreciate the multiple interests that led to conflict, to compare military capability and effectiveness, or to understand 'both sides of the hill'. As a result, opposing forces are frequently presented in a misleadingly unproblematic fashion, namely as monoliths, the effectiveness of which can be discussed in terms of national cultural stereotypes.

Partly in consequence, the popular approach, moreover, is resolutely Westerncentric. Thus, *Decisive Battles. From Yorktown to Operation Desert Storm* (2010) by Jonathon Riley, who is ex-military, found decisive battles only on land, solely from 1781, and only involving Western powers. This selection left out many crucial engagements and entire types of battle. Typically for much of such work, what is covered is not tackled very well, and there are many better accounts of the individual battles. For reasons of language and resources, it is difficult for non-academic anglophobe writers to tackle the Second World War in China, which continues to be seriously underplayed, both as far as studies devoted to the conflict are concerned, and with regard to the coverage in general treatments of the war.

The focus, moreover, in popular work has been to highlight the experience of individuals, generally on one side, but often on both. Thus, at present, there is an extensive use of interview-based oral evidence, both in books and on television, with this evidence employed for recent conflicts[9] as well as earlier ones, notably the Second World War. War memoirs constitute an important part of military history publishing, overlapping, in part, with (fictional) war literature. The latter developed in its modern form from the early nineteenth century and helped to mould what was expected from memoirs, although the process was also two-way.

Contributing greatly to what Max Hastings termed 'romantic military history',[10] memoirs and biographies, unless they deliberately aim to attack their subjects, are frequently uncritical, if not downright eulogies, and the understanding of the 'other side' is very limited. To give some typical examples, without suggesting they are in any way bad books, Bob Cassey's *Upward and Onward. The Life of Air Vice-Marshal John Howe* (2008) is uncritical in the manner of all-too-much RAF history, while Ernest Powdrill's *In the Face of the Enemy. A Battery Sergeant Major in Action in the Second World War* (2008) provides an interesting account of the 1944–5 campaigns in which the author won a Military Cross, but is again uncritical. Similarly, for the

First World War, we have Christopher Burgess' *The Diary and Letters of a World War I Fighter Pilot* (2008).

Memoirs and oral history testify to the public and commercial appeal of the 'war and society' approach, as they are open to civilians as well as combatants. These forms of history also reflect the continuing appeal of the 'face of battle'[11] as there is a trend to hear the voices of veterans.[12] Despite the strength of some oral histories, much of the work, however, fails to ask testing questions of the memories, let alone dealing with the process by which such memories are constructed. However, such issues of validation are relatively unimportant for the many readers who are concerned with experiencing the vicarious excitement of war and seeking to understand it in terms of individual experience. Indeed, the overlap of fact and fiction is seen in the fictionalization of television and film accounts, the style and tone of books for the popular market, and much of the sales language employed to recommend books. At times, writers of biography show aspects of this overlap, as with almost mystical readings of generalship.

More generally, national partisanship can be an issue, both in what is covered and in the tone of the coverage. For example, *Power at Sea: I, The Age of Navalism, 1890–1918; II, The Breaking Storm, 1919–45; III, A Violent Peace, 1946–2006* (2007), a trilogy by Lisle Rose published by a university press, is interesting for the light it throws on high-brow popular naval history, in particular the contours of the latter in terms of what an American writer producing for an American readership can think it appropriate to offer. This remark is not intended to imply some sense of national superiority. In the British case, the Trafalgar bicentennial in 2005 led to a Nelson fest with books that contributed little still praised and prized. Rose is a naval veteran (1954–7), who served from 1978 to 1989 in the American Department of State's Bureau of Oceans and International Environmental and Scientific Affairs, and he has the clarity expected by his market. Rose's essential thesis is that others were unequal to the task that only the USA could confront: allegedly, for reasons of political system and/or class control ('rigid and cruel class distinctions defined and often smothered British democracy'), the other states could not adapt efficiently to the processes of industrial opportunity that provided naval strength. In contrast, the business, economy and society of the USA provided the correct infrastructure and imbued the appropriate virtues. This analysis shaped the narrative and pre-empted the conclusion which was one of courageous and creative American naval responses to challenges posed 'as much by parsimonious unimaginative Congress and administrations' as by maritime crises abroad.

A subtle analysis of the constituencies of political and economic interest that helped shape American naval power was not offered by Rose, nor an adequate assessment of their interaction with the tensions within the navy and between it and the other American services. Nor was there a searching comparison between the American and other navies. The language, instead, is of the type of 'killer resolve', 'shattered hulks', 'unforgettable ordeal', 'mounting horror', 'cold statistics', 'little respite', and so on, language seen with novels as much as academic studies; while the emphasis was operational without a necessary contextualization. Rose did not offer a study of the problems of adaptation, the difficulties of defining tasking, nor the dynamic nature of relative capability. More generally, national partisanship tends to ensure an emphasis on martial qualities and abilities rather than on the weaknesses of opponents, as in the Israeli account of success against the Syrians in the Yom Kippur War of 1973.[13] A similar pattern, albeit with the focus on the strategic faults of the Gauls, has also been seen with Julius Caesar's self-serving account of the Gallic Wars.[14]

War and Society

The emphasis in the popular literature is somewhat different to that in its academic counterpart where the stress, instead, is on what has been summarized as 'war and society' or 'new military history', a form that is no longer new. Before, however, considering this field, and what it suggests about the culture of academic scholarship, it is appropriate to note that there is also much work of quality, by both academics and non-academics, on operational and tactical history. Far from simply repeating existing studies, this work both corrects and reveals additional aspects. Caution emerges as a key characteristic and product of such scholarship, as with Ian Robertson's recent historical atlas of the Peninsular War (1808–14), which notes the inevitable 'measure of imprecision', the problems encountered, and the difficulty of assessing the timing of operations.[15]

Such operational work is very different to the 'war and society' approach, because the latter greatly reflects developments in other branches of history and, more generally, in the social sciences, and is thus an aspect of the porous character of the subject. For example, John Keegan's *History of Warfare* (1997) was influenced by anthropology. The German translation was titled *Die Kultur des Krieges* (1997). 'War and society' does not so much have parallels with a distinct 'war and culture', as rather overlapping it, as well as, in part, being an aspect of the 'cultural turn'. 'War and society' pursues the relationship between war and social class, gender, and other social factors, at one level, and, at another, asks how far war mirrors society: in what way the military and the exercise of military might reflect social constructs and images.[16] As a result, there is now an extensive literature on such varied subjects as conscription, memorializing war, the appearance of the military, the military and health, the environmental consequences of war, the gender aspects of military history, and war as a form of disciplining bodies and applying violence to the body. Each of these perspectives offers much, although they tend to share the Eurocentricity that characterizes so much of military history, and do not, in combination, amount to a full treatment of the subject.

The social dimension of the military as a subject for study is particularly valuable due to the emphasis, in much recent work, on comradeship as a key to understanding the thoughts, ethics and actions of soldiers and sailors. The links between fighting effectiveness, morale and unit cohesion, and their importance as opposed to tactical sophistication, underline the value of the study of comradeship,[17] and this study bridges 'war and society', the 'face of battle', and the 'cultural turn'. Differentiation between these approaches thus becomes difficult.

'War and society' began with issues such as recruitment, but, as an instance of what the 'cultural turn' could lead to, Joshua Goldstein's *War and Gender. How Gender Shapes the War System and Vice Versa* (2001) discussed the feminization of enemies as a form of symbolic domination, the role of male sexuality as a cause of massacre, sweethearts, nurses,[18] mothers, prostitutes, and the relationship between hunting and war. In his *The Culture of War* (2008), Martin van Creveld devoted a chapter to 'feminism', arguing that it threatened the culture of war, either by turning public opinion and norms against it, or by leading women to try to join the armed forces, which he saw as likely to weaken them.[19] In some respects, the chapter was perfunctory and ill-considered, not least because van Creveld failed to discuss adequately the many military tasks that women can ably fulfil. Nevertheless, it is instructive to see that the book included such a chapter. Women and children in combat have recently attracted scholarly attention.[20]

As another aspect of the 'cultural turn', seen again here as a new stage of the 'war and society' approach, work on the military and race has become more common.[21] Racial relations within individual militaries have become an important topic, and the experience of racial minority groups in these militaries has attracted those interested in memoirs and oral history.

The military and race also offers a way to approach Western policies towards the non-West. There is an older colonial and Orientalist pedigree, as the essentialist concept of 'martial races' and 'warrior peoples' strongly informed European colonial empires, and their large-scale recruitment and use of indigenous troops.[22] There is indeed a parallel between current interest in culture and the rediscovery of ethnography and 'racial traits' as factors by the British after the serious challenge posed by the Indian Mutiny of 1857–9. Both can be seen as a Western imperial or quasi-imperial response in times of crisis, and this approach to the present situation is instructive for it helps locate and explain the cultural interpretation in terms of a particular conjuncture.

Alleged or possible parallels between present and past activities, and contexts, came to the fore with Western military operations in the 2000s, not least the question of the role of racial stereotyping in affecting military conduct, for example the treatment of prisoners. Thus, the American treatment of prisoners in Iraq was discussed in terms of past instances. However, an historical reminder of the difficulty of judging such cultural issues was posed by the debate over American conduct in the war with Japan in 1941–5. The standard account presents this conduct in terms of American racialism, an instance of culture in action,[23] and that approach proved a way to provide an historical background to the situation in Iraq.

Nevertheless, it has also been argued that the mutual bloodshedding during the Pacific war was a product of the dynamics of the battlefield, rather than a consequence of outside cultural influences; and that an appreciation of this dynamic depends on an understanding of the process and context of surrender on the battlefield. In particular, the reluctance of the Japanese to surrender, and their willingness to employ ruses, notably pretending to surrender and then attacking their would-be captors, helped mould American responses. Thus, the issue of practicality was pushed to the fore in this account of the 'face of battle', rather than an emphasis on racialism and indoctrination.[24] There have also been attempts to incorporate both perspectives, the instrumental and the ideological, and this approach offers one that is properly grounded in conceptual and methodological complexities.[25] The extent to which racism played a role in pre-war Intelligence assessments of Japanese capability is instructive. Racist views were present but did not dominate the analysis. Interservice biases and rivalries proved more significant.[26]

The 'cultural turn' also covers the symbolic aspects of war and the military. The aesthetical characteristics of fortifications[27] have attracted attention, as has military display, not least in uniforms and music. Rather than treating display as non-functional, it played important roles within military society. Heraldry brought recognition, providing a means by which a warrior could be recognized 'as he performed great deeds and thereby enhanced his martial prowess and justified his membership of the martial élite'. Moreover, donning armour changed not only the wearer's appearance, but also the way he experienced his surroundings: 'The donning of armour may be seen as a transitional ritual marking the individual warrior's entry into a state of war. This was repeated on a collective level by the display of banners and the sounding of trumpets.'[28]

Turning to a later period, British army uniforms in the early nineteenth century were burdensome and frequently inconvenient, if not worse. The priority given to appearances hurt the service. For example, artillery drills emphasized the speed and dash important for ceremonial occasions, but the drill was altered for these shows, and exercises necessary for combat were neglected. Yet, military show fulfilled a number of functions. It overawed those outside the army, which definitely aided recruitment and was also important when troops were used to suppress civil disobedience. Uniform was a major attraction for some recruits because it embodied the martial image, at a time when the martial tradition of honour remained important, while uniform also projected a powerful aesthetic appeal. Moreover, the enticement of military dress encouraged men to serve as officers. Military imagery also played a crucial role in maintaining discipline. It helped to mark and mould men as soldiers, and to fit recruits into the life of their units. Soldiers were supposed to act as a unit, not simply for aesthetic reasons, but also so that they could fulfil their operational requirements in a disciplined and effective fashion. Training and uniform were designed to control soldiers' movements, and were more effective than harsh punishments. Uniform and other aspects of appearance were also intended to maintain and enhance morale and group solidarity. Uniform served as a crucial means of identification.

More generally, the order and organization of the army, notably the role of rank, seniority, precedence and honour, as with the order-of-battle, offered a vision of harmony in which society was free of discord, everyone had his own place, and the whole system moved and functioned with precision and efficiency. This was a potent and attractive image for a society facing major social disruption. It suggested that there was an alternative to the fluidity and discord of the *status quo*, an alternative that was at once effective and attractive.[29] Thus, symbolism was important both to readiness for combat and to other tasks.

Such work is important and throws light on factors that tend to be underplayed. However, these studies sometimes assert causes and consequences, links and reasons, that their authors can only demonstrate in very incomplete fashion. This is a problem by no means restricted to this type of history, but the socio-cultural analysis in which images and practices are presented in terms of control can be pushed too far. The aesthetic and the socio-political are not easy to interweave. Moreover, it is important not to drive out studies that deal with other aspects of campaigning, such as, in the case of the symbolism of medieval warfare, Laurence Marvin's *The Occitan War. A Military and Political History of the Albigensian Crusade* (2008) which presents Simon de Montfort as tactically adroit, albeit hit by a lack of local support, untrustworthy allies, and insufficient reinforcements.

Remembered conflict provides another aspect of the 'war and society' transformed into the 'cultural turn'. The memorialization of war throws light on the imaginative experience of conflict, and makes it possible to construct the cultural and social memory of war. At times, at the popular level, such attention becomes a work of *pietas*, as in *Last Dawn. The 'Royal Oak' Tragedy at Scapa Flow* (2008) by David Turner, whose uncle died in the sinking of the battleship by a German submarine. The roll call of the dead and the photographs serve a purpose but not that of scholarship.

Conclusions

A focus on the memory of war, however, is an aspect of what might seem to be a demilitarization of the discussion of war, and that can be regarded as an important aspect of the 'cultural turn'.[30] This 'turn' takes a role as part of the RAM, the revolution in attitudes to the military that has been so important in the West since the 1960s. Indeed, cultural factors can be seen as cause, course and consequence of this RAM. Individualism, hedonism, radicalism, the decline of deference, and feminism can all be regarded as significant elements of socio-cultural change from the 1960s and of the RAM. It can be all-too-easy reading some of the literature on military studies to forget that fighting was a prime concern of the military, its special purpose and function, and should therefore play a central role in military history and military studies. The avoidance of war through deterrence and/

or intimidation is also pertinent, but arises again through military strength and the perception of this strength.

The failure of much scholarship to deal with fighting provides an instance of the degree to which academic writers do not necessarily have a more profound understanding of their subject than their popular counterparts. Looked at differently, this tension between academic and popular approaches is part of a more general historiographical tendency.[31] At the same time, the unwillingness of much popular work to engage with conceptual, methodological and historiographical questions lessens its wider value. Whatever the style, there is a common need for a critical approach towards evidence and arguments. As James Corum has pointed out with reference to the German campaign of 1940, 'as long as there are generals who need to justify their poor performance and as long as there are enthusiasts peddling new concepts of war, the creation of military myths will flourish'.[32]

8

Conclusions

Cultural Turns

The standard discussion of culture and warfare demonstrates much about the culture of military history, and that remark is not intended as praise. A key element is an unwelcome degree of insularity, because the discussion often fails to note the extent to which there has, more generally, been a cultural turn in history as a whole, one sometimes referred to as the 'new cultural history'.[1] This development is subject to various definitions and explanations, but it is usually seen as a successor to the new social history that gathered pace from the 1960s, a successor that owed much to an interest in 'discourse', identity and language. Sometimes prone to vacuity, the 'new cultural history' is both contentious and not without serious disadvantages. The latter include a degree of preference for 'discourse' over action and theory over reality, as well as the extent to which the 'new cultural history' increasingly seems somewhat dated, rather like the 'new military history' which, in fact, dates from the 1970s.

The extent to which the 'cultural turn' in military studies and history reflected this more general intellectual development in history as a whole is clearer for academic studies than for the interest by military thinkers in cultural aspects of combat at the present day. Indeed, to turn to the latter, culture became a key way of explaining failure in Iraq and Afghanistan, with a cultural resistance, if not counter-revolution, seen as countering the technologically driven Revolution in Military Affairs. In many respects, this approach represented an engagement with anthropology, and, more particularly, a use of anthropological explanation to explain differences in fighting goals and style between Western forces and their opponents. That the term culture can be used to discuss all these changes, including the commitment to technology, indicates anew its flexibility and porosity, and, in doing so, its value as an interpretative device rather than as a precise analytical tool. In short, 'culture' takes on many of the characteristics of language, and thus its frequent use is an instance of what has been termed the 'linguistic turn'.

Frequent use scarcely equates with agreement on value. The value of strategic culture as a concept is a matter of particular controversy. To some commentators, it is profitably linked to strategic behaviour,[2] while, to others, it represents the primacy of theory over reality and one, moreover, that is resistant to change. Contention over the concept of strategic culture does not mean that cultural interpretations as a whole are flawed, but it does affect one significant instance of them.

Looking to the Future

The current use of language is far from fixed, and it is pertinent to look to the future and to consider the cultural turn in that light. This consideration has two aspects. First, what approach is likely to move to the fore in historical analysis? For example, will a 'new realism' supervene in the shape of a revived concern with material factors? Such a concern could take a number of forms, most obviously that of a new interest in class-based analysis. Issues of relative affluence and poverty might lead to such an interest and, in military terms, there might be a new emphasis on the availability of resources. Alternatively the focus of historiographical theory might move in another direction. Whatever is the case, it is unlikely, given the dynamic nature of this theory, that the 'cultural turn' will remain central to historical analysis. In light of the degree of autonomy provided by military concerns and commentators, the impact of this on military studies is likely to be indirect, but it may be a pertinent factor nevertheless.

Secondly, there is the question of changes in the character of military confrontation and conflict, with resulting consequences for doctrine, strategy and procurement. The new version of the US army's *Field Manual 3-0*, released in February 2008, emphasized the need to understand post-conflict stability operations as an important role by making them equal with traditional priorities. This situation is more serious because of the widespread distribution of firearms. In 2007, it was estimated that there were about 875 million firearms in the world, of which civilians own 650 million. However, the 'wars among the people' that seemed so pertinent a theme in the 1990s and, even more, 2000s, among both military commentators and scholars, may become less so, and, linked to this, the supposed civilizational clash with radical Islam may become less central as a theme. This change may lead to a decline in interest in cultural themes, which would provide an apt instance of the major extent of presentism in military analysis.

Alongside radical Islam, there are a number of other military challenges, all of which may rise in relative importance. For the USA, the key areas of challenge may become the Far East, specifically an unpredictable and dangerous North Korea and an expansionist China, and the greater Caribbean, notably Hugo Chavez's Venezuela, but including an unstable Mexico and whatever happens to a post-Castro Cuba. Resulting conflicts may include a counter-insurgency element, but this is unlikely to be conceptualized in terms of the cultural conflict depicted in Iraq and Afghanistan. Conversely, it may be the case that counter-insurgency operations involving foreign troops are automatically regarded in terms of the cultural clashes that appear to explain differences.

This point about the course of the future can be debated, but it also raises a significant methodological question, namely how far the conceptualization of war is driven by current and/or envisaged conflicts and, if so, whose conflicts? This question brings together realist and idealist strands, for the suggestion that ideas are driven by the reality of conflict, in others words presentism, is matched by the question of perception bound up in asking whose conflicts.

Western Perspectives

The last point indeed raises the issue of distorting Western perspectives. The most significant is that of the focus on the West itself. It is, for example, very difficult to know what to include in a War Studies Reader. The field of military history has changed greatly in recent years, or, rather, the range that was always there has become far more prominent. The change is overwhelmingly thematic, but there is also a greater range geographically, although there are still major lacunae in attention, notably South-East Asia, Madagascar, the Horn of Africa and Central Asia, none of which are properly integrated into global military history for the seventeenth to nineteenth centuries, let alone earlier. It is therefore very interesting to see what Gary Sheffield, a major and much-respected figure in twentieth-century British military history, chose to include in his *War Studies Reader. From the Seventeenth Century to the Present Day and Beyond* (2010). There is a pronounced tendency in this work, as in other collections, to focus on the West and readers would be hard-pressed to know from this book, or most others, that the Manchu conquest of Ming China was the most decisive large-scale conflict of the seventeenth century. On the whole, non-Western military history receives insufficient attention, as does the history of Western expansionism.

More attention has been devoted to the mispresentation of Asia summarized as Orientalism. From this perspective, it is instructive to note Peter Lorge's *The Asian Military Revolution: From Gunpowder to the Bomb* (2008). To Lorge, modern warfare first appeared in China during the twelfth and thirteenth centuries, and it was political and institutional developments, not technology in itself, that turned guns into effective military instruments, because Chinese institutions were the first to harness gunpowder to military use and to produce gunpowder weapons in large quantities. In Lorge's diffusionist model, it is Europe that is the recipient of an Asian military revolution, rather than the other way round. Drawing attention to points that are of more general relevance, Lorge suggested that European governments first had to evolve their bureaucratic institutions to the point where they could support an army in the Chinese manner before political and military leaders could organize an army in this manner. Attacking Western hubris in the case of China, Lorge also considered India, arguing that the British advantage there rested essentially on the bureaucratic governmental system of the East India Company, when opposed to the personal power of Asian princes, a thesis also advanced by R. G. S. Cooper in his coverage of the Anglo-Maratha wars.[3] Lorge, moreover, suggested that, although the European-commanded sepoy (native) army was better trained overall than its opponents, and usually better armed, these were not overwhelming advantages, and he concluded that the European military system changed South Asian military practice, but that it did not revolutionize it.

Lorge similarly argued that when Europeans first reached South-East Asia, they found a politically and geographically fragmented region already familiar with gunpowder, and that European weapons and trade accelerated pre-existing military and political developments without altering their trajectory very much. Moreover, in considering the arrival and departure of the West, Lorge put the emphasis on the political dimension, suggesting that the varying degrees and rates of

Western penetration of Asia were due not to Western technological progress, but to the varied stages of political activity in the respective Asian polities.

Alongside the critique of a misleading view of Asia in the shape of Orientalism, there should also be space for a comparable discussion about misleading perspectives about the West, but this approach has attracted fewer commentators, which is of considerable interest. Moreover, although it is easy to adopt a cultural classification of perception and misperception, it is also apparent that such processes can be seen within cultures. Looked at differently, multiple definitions of culture are possible if the focus is on perception and misperception.

The Second World War

To take the Second World War, a key element of misperception was apparent on the part of the Axis. It is possible to adopt a racial approach to this misperception and to refer to Nazi contempt for the Soviets and Poles as Slavs, and for the Americans as deracinated, with these countries also disparaged for the allegedly prominent role of Jews; but the situation was far more complex. For the Nazis, as for the Italian Fascists, the Japanese militarists, and allies such as Vichy France, there was also a contempt for democracy, capitalism and consumerism, and a belief that their impact on the Axis' opponents was such that there would be only a limited willingness to persist in any arduous conflict. The collapse of Third Republic France in 1940 appeared to vindicate this argument, and, indeed, the claim that France was defeated as a result of internal flaws long led to a failure to pay sufficient attention to more prosaic limitations in French warfighting in 1940, notably the strategy adopted. Scholarly attention among military historians has lately switched in order to put an emphasis on the latter, notably the allocation of reserves, rather than on the political culture of Third Republic France.

Returning to wartime attitudes, it was believed by Axis policymakers, thanks to a pronounced emphasis on the role of willpower, that cultural factors would trump the material resources of the Axis' opponents, particularly the USA, as well as the space of the Soviet Union. The course of the Second World War, however, revealed the flaws of this approach, both at the strategic level and in tactical and operational terms, for example with Japanese *kamikaze* (suicide) attacks by planes and ships failing to stop American naval operations, and with Hitler's willpower-driven insistence that German units not withdraw, making them vulnerable to Soviet breakthrough attacks, notably on the Eastern Front from late 1942.

At the strategic level, the Axis powers suffered from a frequent inability, as with the Japanese in China and the Germans in Serbia, to persuade the defeated to accept the verdict of defeat. This inability owed much to Axis harshness that reflected the degree to which opponents were despised. These, and other, failures of cultural perception have not attracted the critical attention devoted to Orientalism, in large part because the latter has been prominently used as a basis for attacks on American policy. As a result, in part, of the failure to devote sufficient attention to this issue in the Second World War, the widespread nature of misperception in warfare and international relations, and its importance for strategy, have been underplayed. Looking to the future, there is no reason to believe that such misperception will play a smaller role. Yet, partly for cultural reasons, many military commentators prefer to emphasize the fighting dimension.

National Styles

Alongside the perception and misperception characteristic of a specific political system, there is the issue of its relationship with a particular means of waging war, a relationship that brings into focus both the variety of the uses of culture, in this case political culture and strategic culture, their interaction, and the extent to which chronological conjunctures play a role. To take Germany, Robert Citino argued, in *The German Way of War. From the Thirty Years War to the Third Reich* (2005), that Prussia and Germany had been trying to keep their wars short since the days of the Great Elector (r. 1640–88) and Frederick the Great (r. 1740–86), because they believed, rightly or wrongly, that a short war was the only kind that they could win due to respective resources. Citino suggested that the tradition was carried on into the nineteenth century and that Moltke the Elder, in 1864–71, proved the short-war commander par excellence. However, the attempt to achieve a repeat in 1914 of Moltke the Elder's great victories came to naught.

In this approach, the German *blitzkrieg* (lightning war) operations of 1939–41 appear not as a consequence of the new availability of tanks and aircraft, as they do in interpretations predicated on technology and novelty; but, instead, of the attempt to return to the earlier tradition of military operations, an analysis that puts the emphasis on strategic culture. At the same time, it is worth probing the pattern of repeated German failure in 1914–45 as tactical skill and operational proficiency were not translated into strategic success. In part, this failure reflected the inability of the Germans to move from output to outcome, an inability that reflected their limited political grasp of the situation and the difficulty they experienced in getting the (temporarily) defeated to accept German views both on relative military capability and, as already indicated, on relative cultural and ethnic standing. This dimension has to be understood alongside that of battlefield effectiveness.

Future Weapons and Platforms

In the future, there will probably be the challenge of adapting to the increased use of different types of warriors. The present application of drones will be taken further, as unmanned 'smart' weapons are used more successfully and with higher specifications in other spheres, for example smart mines, torpedoes and submarines. There will be a development of advanced robotics, but also possibly a cloning of soldiers and, in the meanwhile, an enhancement of their capabilities through implants. In this and other respects, humans and machines may be melded to some extent.

These developments will pose a new series of cultural issues, some of which have already been ventilated in approaches to former developments in technology. One aspect of cultural concern, even angst, will focus on legality and the extent to which the laws of war can be adapted to respond to and shape new possibilities. There will also be the issue of the willingness to adopt new developments, which, again, can be understood in terms of cultural constructions, not least the degree of commitment to former methods.

The latter point can be seen in the continued commitment to the tank in the 2000s and in the response, at present, to the possibilities offered by missiles and unmanned aircraft, as, to a certain extent, this ordnance makes manned flight obsolete or potentially obsolete across a range of activities. Moreover, as unmanned aircraft can be fired at greater speed from vessels, so it is less necessary to have the through-deck carriers that are the usual means for launching manned aircraft at sea. Yet, the commitment to manned flight on the part of air forces and navies is strong, and the latter are particularly keen on aircraft carriers. The last may be a twentieth-century technology and platform, like the tank or the manned aircraft, but that does not mean that they cannot be of continued use late into the twenty-first century. At the same time, the developing military confrontation between China and the USA in the Western Pacific raises questions about the effectiveness of carriers in the face of ground-based missiles and submarines, in both of which China is making major advances in quality and deployment.

It is unclear how best the Americans can project power regionally if not by this means, but the American commitment to the use of aircraft carriers is as much due to institutional and cultural factors as to any rational response to the situation, a point that can also be made about air power as a whole. Looked at differently, the idea of a rational response is a realist concept that cannot be readily separated from these cultural factors, most obviously an instinctive conservatism and sentimentality on the part of many towards weapon types, at the same time as there is a strong commitment to the enhancement of the specifications of these particular weapons.

This interest in enhancement can in some cases be related to the opposite of an instinctive conservatism, namely an eagerness to embrace the new, as the means to gain a comparative advantage. This eagerness can be in weaponry, tactics and/or doctrine, but it also reflects a cultural disposition which, in these terms, is another way to refer to a preference in the collective psychology of the group in question.

Plotting the Future

Looking to the future as a conceptual issue is made more instructive by considering past efforts to do the same. To take, for example, Colin Gray's thoughtful book *Another Bloody Century. Future Warfare* (2005), Gray began by warning about the perils of prediction, provided political, social and cultural contexts for the importance of war, questioned the emphasis on technological determinism, assessed the likely nature of future regular and irregular warfare, and considered weapons of mass destruction, space-mounted weaponry and cyberwarfare, all of which were seen as different forms of weaponry, not paradigm-busters. Gray also argued that war was a constant feature of the human condition, albeit one of a highly variable nature that requires historicist assessment; that, although irregular warfare might be dominant for some years, a Sino-Russian axis was emerging to oppose the USA globally; that warfare was best understood in a political context, but that this needed to be considered in the light of cultural pressures; that war and warfare did not always change in an evolutionary, linear fashion; and that attempts to regulate war were problematic.

Like much of the literature of the period, Gray, who had close links with American military commentators, was good on the American side and on new technology, but was possibly not sufficiently interested in the problems posed by civil conflict, and the related issue of how best to define war. The latter is not an abstract issue if you are soldiers sent to deal with armed drug-dealers in a failed state. It was safe to predict, both then and now, that most conflict would continue to be in the 'Third World', much of it at the sub-state level. Yet, it is increasingly apparent that it is necessary to prepare both militarily and strategically for the consequences of great power confrontation.

The extent to which the future[4] is the proper domain of the historian has been queried, not least by Michael Howard, and it could be argued that historians find themselves in a very different position to the strategic theorists, such as Gray, whose business it is to help plan for the future. Indeed, much of the value of Gray's work derives from his hands-on experience. Gray's argument that the past provides valuable insight for the political scientist, whether as strategic theorist or in other roles, was a welcome and pertinent rebuke to political scientists who rely simply on models. His work was also a helpful reminder that historians do not own the 'past', as they so often imply, and that the perspectives of other branches of scholarship are instructive, if only in defining difference.

It is certainly clear that political scientists, like historical sociologists, risk making serious mistakes if they underrate the specificity, and both 'deep' and current context, of particular situations, whether past, present or future. To that extent, the future offers a particular challenge, as the specificities it poses are yet unclear, and therefore it is particularly likely that theory will dominate in writing about the future, whatever the background of the writer. A lack of known chronological conjuncture is a key issue when considering the future. Whereas the past can be assessed in terms of timing, of simultaneity or sequencing, those who write on the future face problems in considering this aspect of the situation. Instead of being able to anticipate simultaneity or sequencing, there is a relatively broad-brush approach to the future, or one simply divided in terms of near, medium and distant future. This approach faces several problems. Most seriously, it ignores the extent to which, far from being simply thematic or chronological, the future, like the past, is, in part, a series of action-reaction cycles. In these cycles, developments arise in response to particular crises, and the order of the latter helps define attitudes.

Themes therefore are played out in conjunctures, as events in the Islamic world in 2011 abundantly demonstrated.

Debating Strategic Culture

This situation is of particular importance due to the role of strategic culture in modern discussion of war, in part as an aspect of a wider scholarly interest in the role of cultural factors.[5] Some of the discussion is sophisticated, but there is, all-too-frequently, a tendency to treat culture, whether strategic or otherwise, in fairly rigid terms. This tendency ignores the extent to which culture is a sphere and form of contention, and that, partly as a result, it changes. Indeed, strategic culture can as much be seen as a vocabulary for framing responses, as it is a clear framework for these responses, not that the two are incompatible. Indeed, they are closely linked.

The extent of contention and mutability in strategic culture ensures that it will, in part, be moulded by events, and this situation has major implications for force structures, doctrine and preparedness. Militaries tend to be task-orientated, rather than capability-based, or, rather, the capability is heavily shaped by tasking, as are doctrine and training. As a result, the understanding of tasks reflects the perception of current problems and the experience of recent events. To take a simple example, the nature of Peruvian military doctrine in 2090 will be very different if Peru either has troubled relations with Brazil or is primarily faced by domestic discontent.

The example is taken advisedly because much of the writing on the future of war focuses on the USA, but the majority of conflicts will not involve the USA, other than indirectly, if that. Furthermore, these conflicts will be waged by militaries and NGOs that are armed very differently to the USA, and also in a military and political environment that is one of home conflict, and not force-projection. As a consequence, the trickle-down approach to military analysis – understand the leading power, the USA, and you will appreciate the international military system as a whole – is deeply flawed. This is one of the reasons why the USA, as subject of attention or, as in the case of Gray and many other writers, both experience and market for scholarship, is a highly problematic basis for writing about military affairs, whether past, present or future. The policy-community there necessarily focuses on the USA, as does the popular market, which is perfectly understandable, but deeply limiting, as any consideration of the nature of the popular market will show. The same could be argued of aspects of policy.

This limitation, moreover, is even the case if the range of attention extends outside the USA as, all-too-often the rest of the world is understood in terms of Western interests and also analytical conceptions. This is the fundamental asymmetry, an intellectual one that is much more profound than the asymmetry of different fighting styles or weaponry which currently engages attention. In that sense, there is a clear need to direct attention to the 'culture' of military analysis, in so far as that over-used word can be employed. The problematic nature of American trickle-down is the case whatever the trajectory of American military tasking, whether high-spectrum against China and/or Russia, or at lower intensity. One mistake, indeed, is to assume that lower-intensity American conflict offers much of a guide for the situation of most other states. This is not the case, not least because of the American option of terminating distant conflict. Militaries that have to face home-grown insurrections and/or terrorism, the vast bulk of militaries in short, have to consider the situation very differently to the USA.

It is the unpredictability of the future, an unpredictability stemming in part from chronological interactions, that needs underlining. A political science approach that skims history for examples, not least trans-chronological models, rather than considering the impacts of time, past and future, has only so much to offer.

Culture as the description of military challenge and aspiration may fade, in part because it is a loose concept that can be over-used. However, culture as an analytical category will probably continue. It will be most valuable if it is indeed understood in a somewhat loose fashion as changeable and thus malleable. In short, culture cannot be readily operationalized, but it is very helpful as a means of prompting thought. The most useful thoughts are those focused on the protean and varied nature of war, the extent to which conflict plays a differing role in particular circumstances, and the difficulties of moving from the output of force to a political outcome. The problems of appreciating the latter are significant for all participants, and are not culturally bounded.

The extent to which the cultural turn is helpful comes to the fore in military history because, by its very nature and the institutional investment in it,[6] the subject relates to present practicality as well as the past. Given the variety of the categories of culture involved, it is scarcely surprising that some are less controversial than others. In particular, organizational culture has not attracted much criticism. The situation is very different both for strategic culture and for the idea of culture as an essentialist guide to characteristics of conflict, such as the willingness to take casualties.

One of the most powerful attacks on strategic culture is that mounted by Hew Strachan, and his attack has considerable weight as he is a major scholar and also holds a significant post in the field, that of Chichele Professor of the History of War at the University of Oxford. At the same time, Strachan's work has very much been within the field of Western military history, specifically the British army and also the First World War, and this field does not encourage an engagement with the issue of cultural diversity in warfare. That, of course, is not the same as the question of strategic culture, but it seems likely that a willingness to engage with the notion of culture in one aspect will lead to an openness to that interpretative language in another. Strachan, however, chose to present strategic culture as a product of a disciplinary malaise, that of a security studies' field in which the study of strategy has been largely divorced from its historical roots. Strachan accepts that security studies involves the use of historical case studies, but he suggests that they lack context and are instrumentalized to prove a thesis. Strachan also argues that the notion and use of strategic culture represented a rejection of contingency.[7]

On the contrary, however, far from strategic culture necessarily being rigid, both the notion and its use rest on the idea that the response to contingency will be in line with pre-existing ideas. That situation is not the same as rigidity, but, instead, represents a guided contingency. Moreover, there is the need to distinguish between scales of response and to note the degree to which social assumptions are involved in the process of responding to crisis. As a result, strategy and policy are difficult to disentangle in practice, however much they can be distinguished in theory by claiming that strategy is the art of using military means to implement policy.

Strachan emphasized the unexpected Anglo-Argentinean Falklands' War of 1982 and the Iraq and Afghanistan commitments of the 2000s, presenting both as challenging in their unpredictability the longer term aspirations of strategic theory. Just so, but, of course, the values bound up in the latter also influenced tasking, doctrine and procurement, creating a set of assumptions that affected the possibility of contingencies as well as the response to them. The assumption among her politicians that Britain should play a major role in international crises was important to more detailed responses, and relates to the 2010 letter from Lord West discussed on pages 139–140.

The Display of Power

In considering strategic assumptions and their public grounding, it is instructive to consider the navalism and competition between Britain and Germany prior to the First World War. The rituals of fleet reviews and warship launches then provided a staging of power in terms of the definition of national identity in a competitive forging. Thus, along-side practical points about naval development, ritual, identity and the imagination of 'the other', all played a role, one in which assumption, entertainment and leisure were as significant and causative as govern-ment policy. The public celebration of naval power was both forum and force for identity. Charles Urban, one of the leading figures in the early British film industry, claimed that naval topics ranked highly among the most popular subjects in cinematography, with pictures of 'naval demonstrations' and the 'launching of war vessels' in espe-cially high demand. Cinema, like the press, helped ensure that such occasions could be seen by mass audiences, and contributed to their being public occasions. Indeed, in 1911, Emperor Wilhelm II, a keen proponent of naval power, and the German naval leadership openly acknowledged the extent to which their fleet reviews had changed, due to the influence of commercial and media forces, by deciding to give a prominent role to press and pleasure boats.

In Britain, the staging of unity involved much reference to the notion of the island nation. The navy was presented as the natural boundary, spectacle and defence for this nation. The naval stage played an important role in the construction of the empire, with fleet reviews, ship launches, and a range of other displays, celebrating the navy as a symbol of imperial unity and strength. This naval staging of the empire expanded greatly from the 1880s, with an increasing frequency and scale of displays, their greater costs, and the transfor-mation of old, and invention of new, ceremonies designed to foster imperial sentiment.

The sea and ships offered the British potent images of national mission and strength. Henry Newbolt's popular collections of poetry – *Admirals All and Other Verses* (1897) and *The Island Race* (1898) – linked maritime destiny with manly patriotism, as did Alfred, Lord Tennyson's poem *The Revenge* (1880), an account of heroic endeav-our from the reign of Elizabeth I. Rudyard Kipling, in his *Seven Seas* (1896) and *A Fleet in Being* (1899), displayed a shift in interest away from India and towards a maritime concept of empire. Less poetically, over 2.5 million visitors thronged the naval exhibition on the Thames embankment in London in May to October 1891. Three years later, the Navy League was formed in order to orchestrate public pressure for naval strength.

The political theatre of naval displays was designed to show power and deterrence. The Anglo-German antagonism was a dramatic game in which important cultural issues were bound up with strategic and diplomatic developments.[8] Moreover, political claims and strategic

assumptions were developed and deployed accordingly: 'The maintenance of naval supremacy is our whole foundation. Upon it stands
not the empire only, not merely the great commercial prosperity of
our people, not merely a fine place in the world's affairs. Upon our
naval supremacy stands our lives and the freedom we have guarded
for nearly a thousand years.' Winston Churchill's remarks, as First
Lord of the Admiralty, at the Lord Mayor's Banquet in London on 9
November 1911, would have surprised few of his listeners.

National Cultures

The difficulty of understanding such a situation so as to provide strategic advice useful in specific circumstances does not undermine the
value of the idea of strategic culture, because this culture, in practice, helps to create the resources that could be applied. For example,
in the case of Britain prior to 1914, that culture meant the world's
leading navy but no conscription. The circumstances of the resulting
conflict, the First World War, forced the development of a massive
army and then a resort to conscription in 1916; but strategic culture
is not unchanging. Moreover, the concept of strategic culture offers
much of value for understanding both peacetime and war, especially
the peacetime assumptions underlying the preparations and planning for war, including the strategy that is envisaged. If the friction
of wartime crisis forces change, that change is often in accord with
underlying circumstances.

A contrast between the American and Soviet responses to war in
1941–5 is instructive in this context, as the nature of social mobilization was very different. In large part, this difference reflected greatly
contrasting circumstances. Despite the shock of Pearl Harbor, there
were no Japanese or German tanks outside Washington, and thus the
sense of emergency in the USA did not equate with that of the Soviet
Union. Nevertheless, the contrast also reflected the character of Soviet
governance, notably the authoritarian and brutal nature of rule and
the cowed state of the Soviet population. The *gulags* remained very
active during the war years, as did the large-scale execution of those
the Stalin regime wished to purge. There was no comparison with the
situation in the USA.

Again, a contrast was apparent in the 1790s and 1800s. France
was invaded by Austrian and Prussian forces in 1792, as Austria and
Prussia were by French armies in 1805 and 1806 respectively, the last
a traumatic experience for Prussian military commentators such as

Clausewitz and Gneisenau. Yet the political response was very different, which provides an instance of the shaping of strategic culture, as the Austrian and Prussian invasion in 1792 helped consolidate the radical nature of the French Revolution, whereas change in Austria and even Prussia was more limited. At the same time, the Revolution also indicated the relationship between change and continuity in the case of organizational culture. There were many carry-overs from the earlier, *ancien régime*, French army and navy, but there were also important changes, notably an emphasis on merit divorced from birth. There was also, as later with the Russian Revolution of 1917 which led to the Communist takeover, a focus on youth in command. However, the election of officers was rapidly abandoned by the French Revolutionaries. The emphasis on republican virtue, seen in 1792–4, was replaced by one on professionalism, with merit not seen as a dangerous sign of individualism. There was also a more 'democratic' command structure, at least at battalion level: the social gap between non-commissioned officers and their superiors was less than hitherto.

Lastly, the French Revolution led to a cultural shift towards a consciously total form of war. Claims that this, and related changes, represented a new understanding of war, with an abandonment of restraints in favour of total commitment and revolutionary vigour,[9] are seriously flawed as they rest on a misunderstanding of *ancien régime* warfare. Nevertheless, the culture of warfare was at the very least repositioned in France. The ready recourse to violence in France owed something to a politics of paranoia. This had artistic echoes. In his painting *Marius Returning to Rome* (1789), François-Pascal-Simon Gérard had prefigured the iron determination of revolutionary violence when he showed a demonic Marius leading a column of troops of republican Rome with the heads of their victims on spears. Civilians are being slaughtered, and there is terror on the face of the people. Yet, Gérard's career also showed the extent to which circumstances and perspectives change. Born in 1770, he became a member of the Revolutionary Tribunal in 1793, but came to paint conventional battle scenes, notably Napoleon's victory at Austerlitz in 1805, before being made a court painter and baron by Louis XVIII.

The global dimension is also instructive. After the defence of the Revolution in 1792–9 against foreign and domestic opponents, power was seized by a general, Napoleon, in 1799. Viewed in a global context, however, developments in Europe were not exceptional. Napoleon can be compared to non-Western war leaders, such as Nader Shah, who dominated Persia in the 1730s and 1740s, Haidar Ali, who gained power in Mysore in southern India in the 1760s, holding it until his death in 1782, or the situation in Siam (Thailand). Parallels can also be drawn with Kamehameha I, the 'Napoleon of Hawai'i', the Merina rulers of Madagascar, and with the Zulu ruler Shaka, allegedly the 'black Napoleon' of southern Africa. Comparisons also draw attention to traditional elements of generalship. Thus, Nader Shah's seizure of the Peacock throne in Delhi after his victory over the Mughals at nearby Karnal in 1739 prefigured Napoleon's looting of Europe, including his taking of the Quadriga, the Goddess of Victory, from atop the Brandenburg Gate in Berlin in 1806.

As a reminder that a variety of national military cultures came into play and, again that it is necessary to give due weight to both the (contemporary) idea and the (subsequent) analysis of exceptionalism, republican America, where royal authority was overthrown in 1775–83, offered a very different pattern of development to that under Napoleon. Again, both strategic and organizational culture were at issue. Questions of expansionism and alignment were central to the strategic culture of the USA, while organizational culture focused on the desirability of a professional army as opposed to a reliance on militia which entailed a focus on individual states, rather than on the federal professional military.

These issues were highly contentious, and therefore it is possible in the case of America to see military culture not as a conservative force, but as one shaped and reshaped in political contention,[10] as well as with reference to developments. For example, recent belief in a RMA is in part a response to the socio-cultural changes in the USA that challenge the warrior ethos.[11] The call of national distinctiveness was, and is, also a call for a particular course of military development, and thus inherently political. In Brazil after the Second World War, the army's officer corps was divided between two factions, the nationalists who were wary of American control and multinational companies, and the internationalists who sought alliance with both in order to defeat Communism and pursue economic development. Rivalry led to violence and to the purging of the nationalists from the 1950s.[12] In Brazil and elsewhere, analysis of past developments sits as part of a wider politics of military commitment and change. That the present is scarcely free from this context, however, does not lessen the value of considering the cultures of militaries and war.

War and Business: Comparisons and Contrasts

At the same time, this contrast opens up the question of the danger of tracing differences to one factor only. In the case of the USA, cultural and other elements in war-making can be linked to a democratic politics and a populist society, but it is also pertinent to note America's role as the world's leading economy. This issue brings up the more general practice of comparisons between war and business, which are quite frequent in lectures, not least at leadership conferences, with military leadership and strategy providing obvious sources of inspiration. There is value in this approach, but comparisons should be drawn with more care than is often the case. This is because there are also obvious contrasts. The most important is not, in fact, killing, as modern militaries spend surprisingly little time doing that, which can be demonstrated, for example, by the Japanese armed forces, one of the biggest in the world over the last half-century. Taking this further, the key military function of deterrence is not shared by business, and no business would devote the resources spent on nuclear weaponry and then not use them. Industrial backup systems do not compare.

Whatever the situation as far as criminal groups in for example Mexico are concerned, not least if, as in Colombia, they overlap with terrorist and para-military movements, the military have a monopoly of organized, high spectrum force within their countries. This situation is a key contrast to business, as it means that there is not the effective competition in the provision or projection of force that businesses face in their activities. Terrorist organizations might seek to challenge the military, but comparisons with business competition are far-fetched, not least in so far as the institutional continuity of state forces is concerned.

Linked to this monopoly is a facet of military leadership that was isolated by Norman Dixon in his instructive book on *The Psychology of Military Incompetence* (1972). Dixon pointed out that the very bureaucratic factors that led to success in peacetime military leadership, such as worship of the system and being a safe pair of hands, were actively harmful in wartime; and vice versa. This abrupt switch between two different states is not seen in business. More generally as an aspect of the overlap between culture, psychology and leadership comes the degree to which many commanders are affected by a rigidity in thinking and acting beyond established patterns.[13] Norm-based conduct has detrimental as well as positive consequences.

Contrasts between military science and business management should not detract from some valuable parallels. A key parallel is the tension in the former over the emphasis on technology, and thus on effectiveness and change through technological enhancement. This is the approach very much taken by those who detected a Revolution in

Military Affairs in the 1990s and 2000s, and also by those who saw such a revolution on some earlier occasions, for example with gunpowder.

Other approaches towards development and capability, however, clash with this emphasis on technological enhancement. A key one is the argument that, rather than capability being set in the abstract, not least by the technological proficiency of the weaponry, it is necessary to draw attention to the variety in military and political environments faced by armed forces and the diversity of tasks they are set. This situation ensures that military forms and methods that may be pertinent in some cases may not be effective in others, and may indeed detract from effectiveness, whether combat or non-combat.

This task-based account of military capability has obvious applications in business management, as it leads to a requirement to focus leadership priorities and training very much on specific needs in particular conjunctures. Far from a 'borderless world', or isotrophic (equal at every point) surface, profitability, therefore, like military capability and proficiency, is in a dynamic relationship with changing circumstances, or, looked at differently, is endlessly redefined. Linked to this, there is a need to abandon systemic models and advances in favour of an approach orientated on fractured markets – geographical, social and cultural. This situation means that coping with uncertainty becomes a key method, and indeed goal, in both business and military training, ethos and operations. For both business and military, this coping has to be more rapid than that of opposing organizations, a process which is referred to as getting inside the decision loop.

To imagine a system without risk is inappropriate as that means an over-determining organization. Such an organization will not confront, first, the uncertain nature of its environment and, secondly, the way in which the organization must create a capacity to conceive of multiple solutions if the first tried does not produce the anticipated yield. Instead, a rapid action-reaction ethos and method is necessary as an integral part of the system, whether business or military. This may not be the lesson in terms of inspiring charismatic leaders that some seek, and indeed advocate in leadership classes; but such leaders can only operate if they also have and use intelligence. This is an underrated capacity at present, not least because of anti-élitist currents in culture as well as left-wing assumptions, even policies, that are frequently based on a denial of differential ability.

Yet, the need for intelligent (as opposed to charismatic) leadership cannot be pushed off onto the task of able staff officers and their business equivalents. Those at the top also need to be planners and with the informed scepticism that comes from appreciating that alternatives have to be considered, and even at the very moment that the dimension of morale, both military and civilian, cannot lead to public discussion of such an option. The key requirement is to be able to think, in order to replicate the mental dimension of coping with uncertainty and to plan, in terms of a purposeful goal illuminated by an informed scepticism about capabilities and methods. The extent to which the hierarchical practices of militaries can provide particular organizational cultures that encourage such thought and its application is a matter of continual tension. For example, the German General Staff has been faulted for lacking a Plan B in 1914.[14]

Scepticism

The amorphous and, often, nebulous nature of cultural terminology can discourage its use, and there is an understandable sense that there is something faddish about the concept(s) and language. Possibly these characteristics account for a lack of enthusiasm about 'the cultural turn' on the part of some military commentators. They are more content with the idea of strategic culture because the term includes a word that is understood, even if strategy takes the character of an adjective in this formulation. The disinclination to engage with culture as a concept also reflects the extent to which most military commentators are happier with the tactical and objective dimensions of war, and, in particular, focus on fighting as a professional skill, which is understandable, notably at the tactical level, yet insufficient. Such an approach does not preclude a range of interests, but does not readily lend itself to an explicit engagement with aspects of 'the cultural turn', although, ironically, this disinclination can itself be seen as a cultural product.

Nevertheless, that is not the sole reason why 'the cultural turn' had not been widely welcomed. There have also been specific concerns about aspects of it. In particular, 'the cultural turn' can tend to provide an account that has a misleading focus on a form of ethnic essentialism and/or cultural supremacy. If the situation is not generally that grave, there is the danger that the 'cultural turn' places too great an emphasis on national units and developments, rather than looking for other levels of depiction and analysis, such as those summarized as transnationalism. There is also the concern that 'the cultural turn' is better in explaining continuity rather than change, not least because cultural explanations tend to work better for analysing situations, rather than explaining their weaknesses, and, therefore, lend themselves to conservatism, and not radicalism.

These points have considerable merit, but it is also necessary to note two contrary issues. First, the very broadening out of the subjects of military history and military studies has led to a range of topics and issues, such as the impact of war on non-combatants and the nature of commemoration, many of which lend themselves to cultural interpretations and related questions. The treatment of these topics, however, frequently suffer from a focus on Western powers. Presentism can also play an unhelpful role. For example, in *The Barbarization of Warfare* (2006), four of the chapters were devoted to the discussion of recent American conduct. This collection offered too much on the twentieth century, on the Second World War, and on Guantanamo and Abu Ghraib, and insufficient, certainly, on other examples.[15] Despite criticism, it was not always, after all, the 'advanced' societies that experienced greater mobilization, as conflict among 'tribal peoples' could embody the essence of total war, and the slaughter and enslavement of civilians was widespread in pre-twentieth century conflict, even if the source material is often patchy. Aside from such instances of Central Asian campaigning as that by Timur at the cusp of the fourteenth and fifteenth centuries, in addition, in Africa, the elderly, women, and children were caught up in long cycles of raiding war every bit as much as fighting men.

Moreover, alongside concern about changes in Western warfare, notably the use of air power, other aspects of Western conflict have become less barbarous. Although Churchill subsequently wrote of the First World War, 'Torture and Cannibalism were the only two expedients that the civilized, scientific Christian societies had been able to deny themselves', in one light, these exceptions, which essentially remained the case thereafter, were aspects of the physical contact between combatants that had become less important in Western conflict. Furthermore, casualty figures in post-1945 counterinsurgency struggles did not approach those of such earlier episodes as the German suppression of opposition in South-West Africa and Tanganyika in the 1900s. In part, this was because, despite the impression sometimes created, the killing of large numbers of civilians by Western forces had become not only unacceptable to public opinion, but also relatively uncommon. The deficiencies of much of the use of cultural perspectives, however, do not mean that these perspectives are invalid, not least because such deficiencies as Eurocentricity are also seen with other approaches, and, indeed, frequently more so.

Contrasts

Secondly, it is difficult to consider the present situation without noting major contrasts that can be presented as cultural in character, and also that reveal the role of cultural perception. For example, the current crisis over nuclear proliferation in part rests on the assumption that different states would regard the potential of nuclear weaponry very differently. There is a widespread expectation that North Korea and, even more, Iran, would be far readier to use nuclear arms than states that already have them, such as China and Israel. This contrast can be presented in terms of policy, rather than culture, with the (unproven) claim, for example, that the bulk of the Iranian population is, in fact, reasonable, but, even if policy is considered, then the focus is on the collective assumptions that can be understood as strategic culture.

Moreover, although prediction is of course problematic, the degree to which different levels of casualties might be accepted lends itself to discussion in cultural terms, as does the process of discussion. So, indeed, does the attitude to casualties on the part of other combatants. An Israeli Lieutenant-General told me a decade ago that now he was expected to plan not only for as few Israeli casualties as possible, but also for causing as few Arab casualties as possible. As an instance of cultural differences, it is difficult to see any such reluctance to cause casualties on the part of Hamas or Hizbullah. Both in suicide bombing and in missile attacks, the emphasis, instead, appeared in these cases to be on the terror caused by unpredictable as well as heavy casualties.

The extent to which differences between armies in this respect can be traced to circumstances or culture is open for debate. Clearly, Anglo-American attitudes in 1944 to the causing of civilian casualties by bombing were very different to those of five years before. In 1939, the British government had been reluctant to engage in the bombing of civilian targets, but the situation was different by 1941, and, even more, by 1943. There had been no comparable change in German attitudes. Indeed, the indiscriminate nature of killing by means of V-1 and V-2 rockets in 1944–5 was fully anticipated in the German terror bomber attacks on Warsaw (1939), Rotterdam (1940), London (1940) and Belgrade (1941), as well as on a host of less prominent targets. The contrast between Anglo-American and German policy cannot be explained simply in terms of circumstances, because the Nazi attitude to the use of force was very different: the Nazis exulted violence, offering much to kill for and a sense of destiny to die for. There was also a contrast between the Soviet Union and (from 1941) its Western allies, as Soviet Communism politicized every sphere of public and private life and institutionalized violence.

The contrasts in national style in the Second World War were also contrasts in substance. The difference was readily apparent to soldiers who were judged unacceptable: thousands were shot by the German and Soviet military authorities, but not by the Americans or British. The atrocities against civilians committed by the German, Japanese and Soviet armies were far worse than those committed by the armies of the Western Allies, and so on. These differences can be traced to ideological factors, but also reflect those that can be termed cultural, for example the impact on military ethos of introducing conscription in a democracy. Given that these points can be observed for the past, it is unclear why similar contrasts should not be expected for the present and, indeed, for the future.

Conclusions

The use of culture in this fashion does not presuppose some unchanging, everlasting, inherent, national set of characteristics, let alone a common experience of war across time and culture.[16] That these characteristics have been unhelpfully employed as an analytical device by some writers deploying cultural arguments does not automatically vitiate the value of these arguments. Instead, this misleading usage underlines the need for care in taking any one set of factors and abstracting it from the more common need not only for caution but also for context. Factors operate in particular contexts and conjunctures, and cultural factors are no different in this respect. Having rejected technological determinism as inaccurate (as well as a product of a cultural preference), it would be extremely unhelpful to employ cultural factors as independent variables, and in a deterministic manner. Instead, when faced with descriptions and explanations that apparently cover all circumstances and developments, analysis of war and of the military should welcome a careful scepticism.

Notes

Preface

1 P. Porter, *Military Orientalism. Eastern War Through Western Eyes* (London, 2009), p. 6.
2 W. Murray and R. H. Sinnreich (eds), *The Past as Prologue. The Importance of History to the Military Profession* (Cambridge, 2006); J. B. Hattendorf, 'The Uses of Maritime History in and for the Navy', *Naval War College Review*, 66, no. 2 (Spring 2003), pp. 13–38. On military education, 'History Curriculum and the American Military Universities: The Role of European History and the Revolutionary Period', session in *Consortium of Revolutionary Europe Proceedings 1986*, pp. 96–125; G. Kennedy and K. Neilson (eds), *Military Education: Past, Present and Future* (New York, 2002).

1 Introduction

1 J. Shy, 'The Cultural Approach to the History of War', *Journal of Military History*, 57 (1993), 13–26.
2 P. Porter, *Military Orientalism. Eastern War Through Western Eyes* (London, 2009).
3 D. S. Showalter, 'Europe's Way of War, 1815–64', in J. Black (ed.), *European Warfare 1815–2000* (Basingstoke, 2002), p. 27.
4 M. Hastings, *Armageddon. The Battle for Germany 1944–45* (London, 2004).
5 S. P. Huntington, *The Clash of Civilizations and the Remaking of World Order* (London, 1996).
6 D. M. Pritchard (ed.), *War, Democracy and Culture in Classical Athens* (Cambridge, 2010).

7 P. H. Wilson, 'Defining Military Culture', *Journal of Military History*, 72 (2008), 11–41.

8 R. Morriss, *Naval Power and British Culture, 1760–1850. Public Trust and Government Ideology* (Farnham, 2004). For a less integrated use of culture, G. Dunlop, *Military Economics, Culture and Logistics in the Burma Campaign, 1942–5* (Leiden, 2009).

9 R. Holmes, *Churchill's Bunker: The Cabinet War Rooms and the Culture of Secrecy in Wartime London* (New Haven, Connecticut, 2010).

10 R. M. Citino, 'Military Histories Old and New: A Reintroduction', *American Historical Review*, 112, no. 4 (2007), p. 1082. For more recent work, S. Haugbolle, *War and Memory in Lebanon* (Cambridge, 2010), covering the Civil War of 1975–90, and E. Ben-Ze'ev, *Remembering Palestine in 1948. Witnesses to War, Victory and Defeat* (Cambridge, 2011).

11 K. Booth, *Strategy and Ethnocentrism* (London, 1979); C. G. Reynolds, 'Reconsidering American Strategic History and Doctrines', in his *History of the Sea: Essays on Maritime Strategies* (Columbia, South Carolina, 1989); C. S. Gray, 'Strategic Culture as Context: The First Generation of Theory Strikes Back', *Review of International Studies*, 25 (1999), 49–70; L. Sondhaus, *Strategic Culture and Ways of War* (London, 2006).

12 R. W. Barnett, *Navy Strategic Culture. Why the Navy Thinks Differently* (Annapolis, Maryland, 2009), p. 130. This book covers the American navy.

13 K. D. Johnson, *China's Strategic Culture. A Perspective for the United States* (Carlisle, Pennsylvania, 2009), p. 15. For continuity in distinctive features of Chinese war-making, R. D. Sawyer, *The Dao of Deception: Unorthodox Warfare in Historic and Modern China* (New York, 2007).

14 A. J. Johnston, *Cultural Realism: Strategic Culture and Grand Strategy in Chinese History* (Princeton, New Jersey, 1995); H. van de Ven (ed.), *Warfare in Chinese History* (Leiden, 2000).

15 F. W. Mote and D. Twitchett (eds), *The Cambridge History of China*, vol. 7. *The Ming Dynasty*, pt 1 (Cambridge, 1988), p. 376.

16 D. Robinson, *Bandits, Eunuchs, and the Son of Heaven: Rebellion and the Economy of Violence in Mid-Ming China* (Honolulu, Hawai'i, 2001); K. M. Swope, 'Bestowing the Double-edged Sword: Wanli as Supreme Military Commander', in D. Robinson (ed.), *Culture, Courtiers, and Competition: The Ming Court* (Cambridge, Massachusetts, 2008), pp. 63–7.

17 J. W. Lewis and X. Litai, *Imagined Enemies: China Prepares for Uncertain War* (Stanford, California, 2006).

18 J. Adams, *The Battle for Western Europe, Fall 1944. An Operational Assessment* (Bloomington, Indiana, 2010).

19 D. P. Colley, *Decision at Strasbourg: Ike's Strategic Mistake to Halt the Sixth Army Group at the Rhine in 1944* (Annapolis, Maryland, 2008).

20 J. Shy, 'The American Military Experience: History and Learning', *Journal of Interdisciplinary History*, 11 (1971), 227.

21 F. D. McCann, *Soldiers of the Pátria: A History of the Brazilian Army, 1889–1937* (Stanford, California, 2004).

22 H. R. Guggisberg, 'American Exceptionalism as National History?', in E. Glaser and H. Wellenreuther (eds), *Bridging the Atlantic: The Question of American Exceptionalism in Perspective* (Cambridge, 2002), pp. 265–76.

23 R. Weigley, *The American Way of War: A History of United States Military Strategy and Policy* (Bloomington, Indiana, 1977); A. Echevarria, *Toward an American Way of War* (Washington, 2004); C. Gray, *Irregular Enemies and the Essence of Strategy: Can the American Way of War Adapt?* (Washington, 2006).

24 A. Starkey, *European and Native American Warfare, 1675–1815* (Norman, Oklahoma, 1998); G. Chet, *Conquering the American Wilderness: The Triumph of European Warfare in the Colonial Northeast* (Amherst, Massachusetts, 2003).

25 J. Grenier, *The First Way of War: American War Making on the Frontier, 1607–1814* (New York, 2005).

26 T. G. Mahnken, *Technology and the American Way of War since 1945* (New York, 2008).

27 D. French, *The British Way in Warfare* (London, 1990); K. Neilson and G. Kennedy (eds), *The British Way in Warfare: Power and the International System, 1856–1956* (Farnham, 2010).

28 S. B. Schreiber, *Shock Army of the British Army: The Canadian Corps in the Last 100 Days of the Great War* (Westport, Connecticut, 1997).

29 R. O. Mayne, *Betrayed: Scandal, Politics, and Canadian Naval Leadership* (Vancouver, 2007).

30 J. Schull, *The Far Distant Ships, An Official Account of Canadian Naval Operations* (Ottawa, 1950); C. P. Stacy, *Six Years of War: The Army in Canada, Britain and the Pacific* (Ottawa, 1955); J. L. Granatstein, *Canada's War: Policies of the Mackenzie King Government 1939–1945* (Toronto, 1975).

31 M. Moss, *Manliness and Militarism: Educating Young Boys in Ontario for War* (Don Mills, Ontario, 2001).

32 C. Dueck, *Reluctant Crusaders: Power, Culture, and Change in American Grand Strategy* (Princeton, New Jersey, 2006); S. A. Brewer, *Why America Fights: Patriotism and War Propaganda from the Philippines to Iraq* (Oxford, 2009).

33 B. M. Linn, *The Echo of Battle. The Army's Way of War* (Cambridge, Massachusetts, 2007).

34 P. Robinson, *Military Honour and the Conduct of War: From Ancient Greece to Iraq* (Abingdon, 2006).

35 J. Black, *Why Wars Happen* (London, 1998).

36 R. Holloway, 'The Strategic Defense Initiative and the Technological Sublime: Fear, Science, and the Cold War', in M. Medhurst and H. W. Brands (eds), *Critical Reflections on the Cold War: Linking Rhetoric and History* (College Station, Texas, 2000), p. 225.

37   M. Smith, '"A Matter of Faith": British Strategic Air Doctrine Between the Wars', *Journal of Contemporary History*, 15 (1980), 423–42; S. L. McFarland, *America's Pursuit of Precision Bombing, 1910–1945* (Washington, 1995).
38   For example in M. van Creveld, *The Culture of War* (New York, 2008).
39   B. Gellman, *Angler: The Cheney Vice Presidency* (New York, 2008), pp. 249–50.
40   P. Robinson, *Military Honour and the Conduct of War: From Ancient Greece to Iraq* (London, 2006).
41   J. Lynn, 'The Embattled Future of Academic Military History', *Journal of Military History*, 61 (1997), 788–9.
42   M. Hastings, *Armageddon. The Battle for Germany 1944–45* (London, 2004). See the interview he gave in *Historically Speaking*, 6, no. 4 (Mar./ Ap. 2005), 15–19.
43   A. Converse, *Armies of Empire. The 9th Australian and 50th British Divisions in Battle, 1939–1945* (Cambridge, 2011).
44   J. E. Shircliffe, 'The Digital Battlefield. Preparing for Parity', *RUSI Journal*, 155, no. 6 (2020), p. 24.
45   K. L. Shimko, *The Iraq Wars and America's Military Revolution* (Cambridge, 2010).
46   J. Lynn, 'Embattled Future', pp. 775–89 esp. p. 782; V. D. Hanson, 'The Dilemmas of the Contemporary Military Historian', in E. Fox-Genovese and E. Lasch-Quinn (eds), *Reconstructing History: The Emergence of a New Historical Society* (London, 1998), pp. 189–20; 'Military History: A Forum on the State of the Field', *Historically Speaking*, X/5 (Nov. 2009), 10–19.
47   M. Hochedlinger, '"Bella gerant alii…"? On the State of Early Modern Military History in Austria', *Austrian History Yearbook*, 30 (1999), 245–58.
48   S. Call, *Selling Air Power: Military Aviation and American Popular Culture after World War II* (College Station, Texas, 2009); E. N. Luttwack, 'The True Military Revolution', in his *The Virtual American Empire: War, Faith, and Power* (New Brunswick, New Jersey, 2009).
49   William of Tyre, *Historia Rerum in partibus transmarinis gestarum* ed. R. B. C. Huygens (Tournhoult, 1986); English translation E. A. Babcock and A. C. Krey, *A History of the Deeds Done beyond the Sea* (New York, 1943), book 13: chapter 16.
50   B. D. Steele and T. Dorland (eds), *The Heirs of Archimedes. Science and the Art of War through the Age of Enlightenment* (Cambridge, Massachusetts, 2005), esp. pp. 87–133.
51   G. Agoston, 'Information, Ideology and Limits of Imperial Policy: Ottoman Grand Strategy in the Context of Ottoman-Habsburg Rivalry', in V. Aksan and D. Goffman (eds), *The Early Modern Ottomans. Remapping the Empire* (Cambridge, 2007), pp. 75–103.
52   J. Frémeaux, *De Quoi Fut Fait L'Empire. Les Guerres Coloniales au XIX Siècle* (Paris, 2009).

53 J. S. Arndt, 'Treacherous Savages and Merciless Barbarians: Knowledge, Discourse and Violence during the Cape Frontier Wars, 1834–1853', *Journal of Military History*, 74 (2010), 709–35.

54 D. R. Headrick, *When Information Came of Age. Technologies of Knowledge in the Age of Reason and Revolution, 1700–1850* (Oxford, 2000).

55 D. R. Headrick, *Power Over Peoples. Technology, Environments, and Western Imperialism, 1400 to the Present* (Princeton, New Jersey, 2010).

56 D. Parrott, *The Business of War. Military Enterprise and Military Revolution in Early Modern Europe* (Cambridge, 2011).

57 A. Colás and B. Mabee (eds), *Mercenaries, Pirates, Bandits and Empires* (London, 2010).

58 J. Black, *War Since 1990* (London, 2009).

59 D. Hoyos, *Truceless War: Carthage's Fight for Survival, 241 to 237 B.C.* (Leiden, 2007).

60 W. R. Pinch, *Warrior Ascetics and Indian Empires* (Cambridge, 2006).

61 C. C. Bayly, *Mercenaries for the Crimea: the German, Swiss and Italian Legions in British Service, 1854–1856* (Montreal, 1977).

62 J. E. Thomson, *Mercenaries, Pirates, and Sovereigns: State-Building and Extraterritorial Violence in Early-Modern Europe* (Princeton, New Jersey, 1994).

63 S. Chesterman and C. Lehnardt (eds), *From Mercenaries to Market: The Rise and Regulation of Private Military Companies* (Oxford, 2007); R. Mandell, *Armies Without States: The Privatization of Security* (Boulder, Colorado, 2002).

64 C. Kinsey, *Corporate Soldiers and International Security: The Rise of Private Military Companies* (Abingdon, 2006), p. 121.

65 S. Armstrong, *War PLC: The Rise of the New Corporate Mercenary* (London, 2008), p. 250.

66 R. Smith, *The Utility of Force: The Art of War in the Modern World* (London, 2005).

67 D. Pratten and A. Sen, *Global Vigilantes* (London, 2007).

68 A. Roberts, *The Wonga Coup: The British Mercenary Plot to Seize Billions in Africa* (London, 2006).

69 P. W. Singer, *Corporate Warriors: The Rise of the Privatized Military Industry* (Ithaca, New York, 2003).

70 Affidavits posed on website of the [American] Centre for Constitutional Rights, which is representing the Iraqi plaintiffs against Blackwater.

71 *The Times,* 6 Aug. 2009, p. 29.

72 I. Wing, *Private Military Companies and Military Operations* (Australian Land Warfare Studies Centre, Working Paper no. 138, Duntroon, 2010), p. 37.

73 S. Percy, *Mercenaries: The History of a Norm in International Relations* (Oxford, 2007).

74 J. R. Holmes and T. Yoshihara, 'China's Navy: A Turn to Corbett', *Proceedings of the U.S. Naval Institute,* 136/12 (Dec. 2010), 42–6.

75 C. S. Gray, *The Strategy Bridge: Theory for Practice* (Oxford, 2010).

76   D. A. Bell, *The First Total War: Napoleon's Europe and the Birth of Warfare As We Know It* (Boston, 2007), p. 284.
77   J. Shy, review on website of the Michigan War Studies Group. For an emphasis on counter-insurgency warfare, M. Broers, *Napoleon's Other War: Bandits, Rebels and Their Pursuers in the Age of Revolutions* (Witney, 2010).
78   A. F. Krepinevich, *The Army and Vietnam* (Baltimore, Maryland, 1986), pp. 274–5.
79   J. Black, *Defence: Policy Issues For A New Government* (London, 2009).
80   S. Schulman and H. Strachan, 'The Town That Weeps', *RUSI Journal*, 155 no. 6 (Dec. 2010), 76–85.
81   Strategic Trends Programme, Ministry of Defence, *Future Character of Conflict* (London, 2010).
82   M. Smith, *British Air Strategy Between the Wars* (Oxford, 1984); R. Wohl, *A Passion for Wings: Aviation and the Western Imagination* (New Haven, Connecticut, 1994); C. H. Builder, *The Icarus Syndrome: The Role of Air Power Theory in the Evolution and Fate of the US Air Force* (New Brunswick, New Jersey, 1994).
83   J. Kraska, 'How the United States Lost the Naval War of 2015', *Orbis*, 54 (2010), 35–45.
84   B. Schaffer (ed.), *The Limits of Culture: Islam and Foreign Policy* (Cambridge, Massachusetts, 2006).
85   P. Porter, *Military Orientalism. Eastern War Through Western Eyes* (London, 2009).
86   T. Farrell, *The Norms of War. Cultural Beliefs and Modern Conflict* (Boulder, Colorado, 2005).
87   C. Coker, *Barbarous Philosophers. Reflections on the Nature of War from Heraclitus to Heisenberg* (London, 2010).

2   The Culture of Gloire: The Royal Military

1   R. Gardner and K. Heider, *Gardens of War – Life and Death in the New Guinea Stone Age* (New York, 1968); K. F. Otterbein, *How War Began* (College Station, Texas, 2004); A. Gat, *War in Human Civilization* (Oxford, 2006).
2   I. Clendinnen, *The Cost of Courage in Aztec Society. Essays on Mesoamerican Society and Culture* (Cambridge, 2010).
3   A. Chaniotis, *War in the Hellenistic World* (Oxford, 2005); S. Dillon and K. E. Welch (eds), *Representations of War in Ancient Rome* (Cambridge, 2006).
4   M. Beard, *The Roman Triumph* (Cambridge, Massachusetts, 2009).
5   J. A. Brandão, *'Your Fyre Shall Burn No More': Iroquois Policy toward New France and its Native Allies to 1701* (Lincoln, Nebraska, 1997).
6   S. Carroll, *Blood and Violence in Early Modern France* (Oxford, 2006).

7   G. Hanlon, *The Twilight of a Military Tradition: Italian Aristocrats and European Conflicts, 1560–1800* (London, 1996); M. Hochedlinger, 'Mars Ennobled. The Ascent of the Military and the Creation of a Military Nobility in Mid-Eighteenth-Century Austria', *German History*, 17 (1999), 141–76.

8   J. D. Tracy, *Emperor Charles V, Impresario of War: Campaign Strategy, International Finance, and Domestic Politics* (Cambridge, 2002).

9   M. Rady, 'Rethinking Jagiello Hungary', *Central Europe*, 3 (2005), 15–17.

10 T. T. Allsen, *The Royal Hunt in Eurasian History* (Philadelphia, Pennsylvania, 2006); R. J. Knecht, *The French Renaissance Court* (New Haven, Connecticut, 2008).

11 P. Sabin, *Simulating War. Studying Conflict through Simulation Games* (London, 2011).

12 *Babur…Memoirs*, I, 152, 186.

13 N. Russell and H. Visentin (eds), *French Ceremonial Entries in the Sixteenth Century: Event, Image, Text* (Toronto, 2007); R. J. Knecht, *Renaissance Warrior and Patron: The Reign of Francis I* (Cambridge, 1994).

14 M. Bourne, *Francesco II Gonzaga: The Sober Prince as Patron* (Rome, 2008).

15 H. Duccini, *Fair voir, faire croire: L'Opinion publique sous Louis XIII* (Seyssel, 2003).

16 C. Pencemaille, 'La guerre de Hollande dans le programme iconographique de la grande galleries de Versailles', *Histoire, Economie et Société*, 4 (1985), 313–33; C. Mukerji, *Territorial Ambitions and the Gardens of Versailles* (Cambridge, 1997).

17 K. Friedrich and S. Smart (eds), *The Cultivation of Monarchy and the Rise of Berlin. Brandenburg-Prussia 1700* (Farnham, 2010), p. 57.

18 National Archives (hereafter NA) SP. 84/202 fols 73, 126, 84/207 fol. 124.

19 Robinson, *Bandits, Eunuchs, and the Son of Heaven*; Swope, 'Bestowing the Double-edged Sword', pp. 61–115.

20 On Philip, see also F. González de León and G. Parker, 'The Grand Strategy of Philip II and the Revolt of the Netherlands, 1559–1584', in P. Benedict et al. (eds), *Reformation, Revolt and Civil War in France and the Netherlands 1555–1585* (Amsterdam, 1999), pp. 215–32.

21 E. N. Luttwak, *The Grand Strategy of the Byzantine Empire* (Cambridge, 2009).

22 A. Hirsch, 'The Collision of Military Cultures in Seventeenth-Century New England', and R. D. Karr, '"Why Should You Be So Ferocious?": The Violence of the Pequot War', *Journal of American History*, 74 (1988), 1187–1212, 85 (1999), 876–909.

23 J. Axtell and W. C. Sturtevant, 'The Unkindest Cut, or, Who Invented Scalping?', and A. Lipman, '"A means to knit them together": The

Exchange of Body Parts in the Pequot War', *William and Mary Quarterly*, 37 (1980), 451–72, 65 (2008), 103–15.

24   D. Harrison, *Social Militarisation and the Power of History: A Study of Scholarly Perspectives* (Oslo, 1999), p. 194.

25   L. E. Grinter, 'Cultural and Historical Influences on Conflict in Sinic Asia: China, Japan and Vietnam', in S. J. Blank et al. (eds), *Conflict and Culture in History* (Washington, 1993), pp. 117–92.

26   R. B. Manning, 'Styles of Command in Seventeenth-Century English Armies', *Journal of Military History*, 71 (2007), 671–99, esp. 673, 699.

27   R. Irwin, 'Gunpowder and Firearms in the Mamluk Sultanate Reconsidered', in M. Winter and A. Levanoni (eds), *The Mamluks in Egyptian and Syrian Politics and Society* (Leiden, 2004), pp. 117–39; A. Fuess, 'Les Janissaries, les Mamlouks et les armes à feu. Une comparison des systèmes militaires Ottoman et Mamlouk à partir de la moitié du quinzième siècle', *Turcica*, 41 (2009), 209–27; C. Petry, *Protectors or Praetorians? The last Mamlūk Sultans and Egypt's Waning as a Great Power* (Albany, New York, 1994), p. 46. I have benefited from the advice of Albrecht Fuess.

3   Strategic Culture: The Case of Britain, 1688–1815

1   I would like to thank Oliver Letwin MP for discussing Conservative Party policy with me in July 2009.

2   T. D. Biddle, 'Leveraging Strength: The Pillars of American Grand Strategy in World War II', *Orbis*, 55 (Winter 2011), p. 5. See also J. Stone, *Military Strategy. The Politics and Technique of War* (London, 2011).

3   J. B. Hattendorf, *England in the War of the Spanish Succession: A Study of the English View and Conduct of Grand Strategy, 1701–1712* (New York, 1987); N. A. M. Rodger, 'The Idea of Naval Strategy in Britain in the Eighteenth and Nineteenth Centuries', in G. Till (ed.), *The Development of British Naval Thinking* (Abingdon, 2006), pp. 19–33.

4   R. J. B. Muir and C. J. Esdaile, 'Strategic Planning in a Time of Small Government: The Wars Against Revolutionary and Napoleonic France, 1793–1815', in C. M. Woolgar (ed.), *Wellington Studies* (3 vols, Southampton, 1996), I, 1–90.

5   R. Harding, *Amphibious Warfare in the Eighteenth Century. The British Expedition to the West Indies, 1740–1742* (Woodbridge, 1991).

6   The classic work, Edward Luttwak's *The Grand Strategy of the Roman Empire* (Baltimore, Maryland, 1976), is taken forward by E. L. Wheeler, 'Methodological Limits and the Mirage of Roman Strategy', and 'Rome's Dacian Wars: Domitian, Trajan, and Strategy on the Danube', *Journal of Military History*, 57 (1993), 7–41, 215–40, 74 (2010), 1185–1227 and 75 (2011), 191–219.

7   L. Loreto, *La grande strategia di Roma nell' età della prima guerra punica (BCE 273–229). L'inizio di un paradosso* (Naples, 2007).

8   J. R. Dull, *The French Navy and the Seven Years War* (Lincoln, Nebraska, 2005).

9   For another instance, for a term advanced in 1899, see J. Black, *Geopolitics* (London, 2009), and for the justification of the retrospective use of the term *Blitzkrieg* R. M. Citino, *Quest for Decisive Victory: From Stalemate to Blitzkrieg in Europe, 1899–1940* (Lawrence, Kansas, 2002).

10 H. K. Kleinschmidt, *The Nemesis of Power* (London, 2000), esp. pp. 114–70 and 'Systeme und Ordnungen in der Geschicht der internationalen Beziehungen', *Archiv für kulturgeschichte*, 82 (2000), 433–54; A. Osiander, *The States System of Europe, 1640–1990. Peacemaking and the Conditions of International Stability* (Oxford, 1994).

11 The size of the navy ensured that the armed forces were not small; possibly as many as 173,000 men in 1762.

12 J. H. Elliott, *Empires of the Atlantic World. Britain and Spain in America, 1492–1830* (New Haven, Connecticut, 2006).

13 C. Dueck, 'Hybrid Strategies: The American Example', *Orbis*, 55 (Winter 2011), 30–52.

14 U. Dann, *Hanover and Great Britain, 1740–1760* (Leicester, 1991).

15 P. G. Dwyer, 'Prussia and the Armed Neutrality: The Invasion of Hanover in 1801', *International History Review*, 15 (1993), 661–87, and 'Two Definitions of Neutrality: Prussia, the European States-System, and the French Invasion of Hanover in 1803', *ibid.*, 19 (1997), 502–40.

16 A. C. Thompson, *Britain, Hanover and the Protestant Interest, 1688–1756* (Woodbridge, 2006); B. Simms and T. Riotte (eds), *The Hanoverian Dimension in British History, 1714–1837* (Cambridge, 2007); Simms, *Three Victories and a Defeat. The Rise and Fall of the First British Empire, 1714–1783* (London, 2007).

17 K. Wilson, *The Sense of the People: Politics, Culture and Imperialism in England, 1715–1785* (Cambridge, 1998); D. Armitage and M. J. Braddick (eds), *The British Atlantic World* (London, 2002).

18 T. Claydon, *Europe and the Making of England, 1660–1760* (Cambridge, 2007).

19 C. G. Pestana, *Protestant Empire. Religion and the Making of the British Atlantic World* (Philadelphia, Pennsylvania, 2009).

20 M. Schlenke, *England und das friderizianische Preussen, 1740–1763* (Munich, 1963), pp. 171–225.

21 G. Yagi Jr, 'A Study of Britain's Military Failure During the Initial Stages of the Seven Years War in North America, 1754–1758' (Exeter, Ph.D., 2007).

22 I. D. Gruber, *Books and the British Army in the Age of the American Revolution* (Chapel Hill, North Carolina, 2010).

23 C. Cox, *A Proper Sense of Honor: Service and Sacrifice in George Washington's Army* (Chapel Hill, North Carolina, 2004).

24 P. Mackesy, *War Without Victory: The Downfall of Pitt, 1799–1802* (Oxford, 1984).

25 P. Mackesy, 'Strategic Problems of the British War Effort', in H. T. Dickinson (ed.), *Britain and the French Revolution 1789–1815* (Basingstoke, 1989), pp. 147–64.

26 T. Jenks, *Naval Engagements: Patriotism, Cultural Politics, and the Royal Navy, 1793–1815* (Oxford, 2006).

27 State of Forces in Great Britain, Feb. 1798, London, British Library, Department of Manuscripts, Additional Manuscripts (hereafter BL. Add.) 59281 fol. 15.

28 Thomas, Lord Pelham, 'Further considerations on the plan for a general enrolment of the people', 2 July 1803, BL. Add. 33120 fol. 135.

29 W. Seymour (ed.), *A History of the Ordnance Survey* (Folkestone, 1980), pp. 21–31; W. Ravenhill, 'The South West in the Eighteenth-Century Remapping of England', in K. Barker and R. J. P. Kain (eds), *Maps and History in South-West England* (Exeter, 1991), pp. 20–1.

30 Memorandum by George, 30 Nov., enclosed with George to Grenville, 1 Dec. 1794, BL, Add. MS 58858, fol. 113.

31 J. W. Strong, 'Russia's Plans for an Invasion of India in 1801', *Canadian Slavonic Papers*, 7 (1965), 114–26; H. Ragsdale, *Détente in the Napoleonic Era: Bonaparte and the Russians* (Lawrence, Kansas, 1980); O. Feldback, 'The Foreign Policy of Tsar Paul I, 1800–1801: An Interpretation', *Jahrbücher für Geschichte Osteuropas*, 30 (1982), 16–36.

32 P. W. Schroeder, *The Transformation of European Politics 1763–1848* (Oxford, 1994).

33 This emerges from the differences between the contributions on British warfare in L. Freedman, P. Hayes and R. O'Neill (eds), *War, Strategy and International Politics: Essays in Honour of Sir Michael Howard* (Oxford, 1992).

4 Organizational Cultures: Western Warfare, 1815–1950

1 A. Vagts, *The Military Attaché* (Princeton, New Jersey, 1967).

2 B. Rieger, *Technology and the Culture of Modernity in Britain and Germany, 1890–1945* (Cambridge, 2005).

3 P. Paret, *Understanding War: Essays on Clausewitz and the History of Military Power* (Princeton, New Jersey, 1992).

4 P. Paret, *The Cognitive Challenge of War: Prussia 1806* (Princeton, New Jersey, 2009).

5 D. Edgerton, *Warfare State. Britain, 1920–1970* (Cambridge, 2006).

6 E. Y. Park, *Between Dreams and Reality: The Military Examination in Late Chosŏn Korea, 1600–1894* (Cambridge, Massachusetts, 2007).

7 T. M. Knox (ed.), *Hegel's Philosophy of Right* (Oxford, 1967), p. 212.

8 A. Johansen, *Soldiers as Police. The French and Prussian Armies and the Policing of Popular Protest, 1889–1914* (Farnham, 2005).

9   M. Martin, *Images at War: Illustrated Periodicals and Constructed Nations* (Toronto, 2006).

10 M. Dorsch, *French Sculpture Following the Franco-Prussian War, 1870–80. Realist Allegories and the Commemoration of Defeat* (Farnham, 2010).

11 R. Chrastil, *Organizing for War: France, 1870–1914* (Baton Rouge, Louisiana, 2010).

12 G. Leggett, *The Cheka: Lenin's Political Police* (2nd edn, Oxford, 1986), p. 17.

13 D. Bloxham and R. Gerwarth (eds), *Political Violence in Twentieth-Century Europe* (Cambridge, 2011); M. R. Ebner, *Ordinary Violence in Mussolini's Italy* (Cambridge, 2011).

14 A. F. Parkinson, *Belfast's Unholy War: The Troubles of the 1920s* (Dublin, 2004).

15 S. Cronin, 'Importing Modernity: European Military Missions to Qajar Iran', *Comparative Studies in Society and History*, 50 (2008), 197–226, and 'Building and Rebuilding Afghanistan's Army: An Historical Perspective', *Journal of Military History*, 75 (2011), 56–7.

16 M. J. Bastable, *Arms and the State. Sir William Armstrong and the Remaking of British Naval Power, 1854–1914* (Farnham, 2004).

17 NA War Office (hereafter WO) 33/2816, p. 43, 2819, p. 26.

18 NA. WO. 33/2822, p. 93.

19 NA. WO. 33/2822, p. 10.

20 F. Patrikeeff and H. Shukman, *Railways and the Russo-Japanese War: Transporting War* (London, 2007).

21 NA. WO. 33/1512, p. 3.

22 G. F. Hofmann, *Through Mobility We Conquer: The Mechanization of U.S. Cavalry* (Lexington, Kentucky, 2006).

23 E. A. Huelfer, *The 'Casualty Issue' in American Military Practice: The Impact of World War I* (Westport, Connecticut, 2003).

24 H. R. Winton, *To Change an Army: General Sir John Burnett-Stuart and British Armoured Doctrine, 1927–1938* (Lawrence, Kansas, 1988); J. P. Harris, 'Obstacles to innovation and readiness: the British Army's experience 1918–1939', in W. Murray and R. H. Sinnreich (eds), *The Past as Prologue. The Importance of History to the Military Revolution* (Cambridge, 2006), pp. 195–216; M. Strohn, *The German Army and the Defence of the Reich. Military Doctrine and the Conduct of the Defensive Battle, 1918–1939* (Cambridge, 2010).

25 B. H. Reid, '"Young Turks, or Not So Young?" The Frustrated Quest of Major General J. F. C. Fuller and Captain B. H. Liddell Hart', *Journal of Military History*, 73 (2009), 147–75.

26 B. Bond, *Liddell Hart: A Study of his Military Thought* (London, 1977).

27 A. Barros, 'Razing Babel and the Problems of Constructing Peace: France, Great Britain, and Air Power, 1916–28', *English Historical Review*, 126 (2011), 75–115, esp., 75–7, 114.

28 W. F. Trimble, *Admiral William A. Moffett: Architect of Naval Aviation* (Washington, 1994).

29   N. Parton, *The Evolution and Impact of Royal Air Force Doctrine, 1919–1939* (London, 2011).
30   A. P. Wavell, 'The Army and the Prophets', *RUSI Journal*, 75 (1930).
31   M. S. Sherry, *The Rise of American Air Power* (New Haven, Connecticut, 1989); T. D. Biddle, *Rhetoric and Reality in Air Warfare: The Evolution of British and American Thinking about Strategic Bombing* (Princeton, New Jessey, 2002); R. G. Davis, *Bombing the European Axis Powers* (Montgomery, Alabama, 2006).
32   S. W. Palmer, *Dictatorship of the Air: Aviation Culture and the Fate of Modern Russia* (Cambridge, 2006).
33   W. W. Ralph, 'Improvised Destruction: Arnold, LeMay, and the Fire-bombing of Japan', *War in History* (2006), pp. 495–522.

5   Strategic Culture: The Cold War

1   NA. FO. 371/56763 fol. 24.
2   NA. CAB. 130/37.
3   O. M. Ulus, *The Army and the Radical Left in Turkey. Military Coups, Socialist Revolution and Kemalism* (London, 2011).
4   R. Buhite and C. Hamel, 'War for Peace: The Question of an American Preventive War against the Soviet Union, 1945–1955', *Diplomatic History* (1990), 367–84; G. Mitrovich, *Undermining the Kremlin: America's Strategy to Subvert the Soviet bloc, 1947–1955* (Ithaca, New York, 2000).
5   A. Statiev, *The Soviet Counterinsurgency in the Western Borderlands* (Cambridge, 2010).
6   M. Jones, 'Between the Bear and the Dragon: Nixon, Kissinger and U.S. Foreign Policy in the Era of Détente', *English Historical Review*, 123 (2008), p. 1283; J. Suri, *Henry Kissinger and the American Century* (Cambridge, Massachusetts, 2007).
7   E. Kurz, *The Kissinger Saga: Walter and Henry Kissinger – Two Brothers from Germany* (London, 2009). For continuing themes, H. Kissinger, *Does America Need a Foreign Policy? Toward a Diplomacy for the 21st Century* (New York, 2001).
8   I. Trauschweizer, *The Cold War U.S. Army: Building Deterrence for Limited War* (Lawrence, Kansas, 2008); S. Bronfeld, 'Fighting Outnumbered: The Impact of the Yom Kippur War on the U.S. Army', *Journal of Military History*, 71 (2007), 465–98.
9   F. Spufford, *Red Plenty* (London, 2010).

6   From the Cold War into the Future

1   L. C. Sebastian, *Realpolitik Ideology: Indonesia's Use of Military Force* (Singapore, 2006).

2   R. D. Ramsey, *From El Billar to Operations Fenix and Jaque: The Colom-
    bian Security Force Experience, 1998–2008* (Fort Leavenworth, Kansas,
    2009).

3   M. W. Daly, *Darfur's Sorrow. The Forgotten History of a Humanitarian
    Disaster* (2nd edn, Cambridge, 2010).

4   G. Prunier, *From Genocide to Continental War. The 'Congolese' Conflict
    and the Crisis of Contemporary Africa* (London, 2009); F. Reyntjens, *The
    Great African War. Congo and Regional Geopolitics, 1996–2006* (Cam-
    bridge, 2010).

5   S. Ellis, *The Mask of Anarchy. The Destruction of Liberia and the Reli-
    gious Dimension of an African Civil War* (London, 1999).

6   Amnesty International report, 21 Dec. 2010.

7   V. Cheterian, *War and Peace in the Caucasus. Russia's Troubled Fron-
    tier* (London, 2009); R. Asmus, *A Little War That Shook the World* (New
    York, 2010).

8   R. Johnson, *The Iran-Iraq War* (Basingstoke, 2011), p. 193.

9   For a self-consciously instructive historical parallel, G. Parker, 'The
    Limits to Revolutions in Military Affairs: Maurice of Nassau, the Battle
    of Nieuwpoort (1600), and the Legacy', *Journal of Military History*, 71
    (2007), 331–72.

10 R. H. Kohn, 'Tarnished Brass: Is the U.S. Military Profession in Decline?',
    World Affairs, 171 (Spring 2009), 73–83. For an attempt to meet the chal-
    lenge, D. Kilcullen, *Counterinsurgency* (London, 2010).

11 M. Clodfelter, *The Limits of Air Power. The American Bombing of North
    Vietnam* (2nd edn, Lincoln, Nebraska, 2006), pp. xi, 220–3. The lack of
    the political dimension is apparent in D. T. Putney, *Airpower Advantage:
    Planning the Gulf War Air Campaign, 1989–1991* (Washington, 2004).

12 R. W. Leonard, 'Learning from History: Linebacker II U.S. Air Force
    Doctrine', *Journal of Military History*, 58 (1994), 267–303, esp. 269, 303.

13 D. Priest, *The Mission: Waging War and Keeping Peace with America's
    Military* (New York, 2003).

14 S. Biddle and J. A. Friedman, *The 2006 Lebanon Campaign and the
    Future of Warfare: Implications for Army and Defense Policy* (Carlisle,
    Pennsylvania, 2008), p. 87.

15 J. Miller, S. Engelberg and W. Broad, *Germs: Biological Weapons and
    America's Secret War* (New York, 2001); J. A. Lockwood, *Six-Legged Sol-
    diers: Using Insects as Weapons of War* (Oxford, 2009).

16 R. Clarke and R. Knake, *Cyberwar: The Next Threat to National Security
    and What to Do About It* (New York, 2010).

17 E. Seedhouse, *The New Space Race: China vs the United States* (Chiches-
    ter, 2010).

18 For the role of air power in opposition to insurgency and terrorism,
    J. Hayward (ed.), *Air Power, Insurgency and the 'War on Terror'*
    (Cranwell, 2009).

19 A. J. Bousquet, *The Scientific Way of Warfare. Order and Chaos on the
    Battlefields of Modernity* (London, 2009); K. E. Haug and O. J. Maaø
    (eds), *Conceptualising Modern War* (London, 2011).

20 N. Cigar (ed.), *Al-Qa'ida's Doctrine for Insurgency: Abd Al-Aziz Al-Muqrin's 'A Practical Course for Guerrilla War'* (Dulles, Virginia, 2008).
21 I. Daalder and J. Lindsay, *America Unbound: The Bush Revolution in Foreign Policy* (Washington, 2003).
22 *Quadrennial Defense Review Report* (Washington, 2006), p. 29.
23 J. J. Mearsheimer, *The Tragedy of Great Power Politics* (New York, 2001).
24 Z. J. Alach, *Slowing Military Change* (Carlisle, Pennsylvania, 2008), esp. pp. 65–8.

7 Culture and Military Analysis

1   A. R. Lewis, *The American Culture of War* (Abingdon, 2007), p. xvii.
2   See also M. Moyar, 'The Current State of Military History', *Historical Journal*, 50 (2007), 225–40.
3   J. Black, *Using History* (London, 2005).
4   B. Bond, *The Unquiet Western Front: Britain's Role in Literature and History* (Cambridge, 2002).
5   For a different focus, see J. Black, *The Great War* (London, 2011).
6   For a history of the war by an Eastern Front specialist, E. Mawdsley, *World War II. A New History* (Cambridge, 2009).
7   For example, J. Mosier, *The Myth of the Great War: A New Military History of World War One* (New York, 2001) and *The Blitzkrieg Myth: How Hitler and the Allies Misread the Strategic Realities of World War Two* (New York, 2001). For criticism, see G. Sheffield, 'John Terraine as a Military Historian', *RUSI Journal*, 149, no. 2 (Ap. 2004), p. 72; D. Showalter, 'Comment on Mosier's *War Myths*', *Historically Speaking*, vol. 6, no. 4 (Mar./Ap. 2005), 9–10.
8   F. J. Wetta, 'Battle Histories: Reflections on Civil War Military Studies', *Civil War History*, 53 (2007), 232–3.
9   S. Naylor, *Not a Good Day to Die: The Untold Story of Operation Anaconda* (New York, 2005).
10 D. A. Yerxa, '*Armageddon*: An Interview with Sir Max Hastings', *Historically Speaking*, vol. 6, no. 4 (Mar./Ap. 2005), p. 18.
11 Good recent work of this type includes G. Daly, *Cannae: The Experience of Battle in the Second Punic War* (London and New York, 2002).
12 A. D. Gilbert, *Voices of the Foreign Legion. The French Foreign Legion in its own Words* (London, 2009).
13 J. L. Young, 'The Heights of Ineptitude: The Syrian Army's Assault on the Golan Heights', *Journal of Military History*, 74 (2010), p. 850.
14 P. Richardot, *Les Erreurs Stratégiques des Gaulois face à César* (Paris, 2006).
15 I. Robertson, *An Atlas of the Peninsular War, 1808–1814* (New Haven, Connecticut, 2010), p. 2.

16 A. Corvisier, 'Aspects divers de l'histoire militaire', *Revue d'histoire moderne et contemporaine*, 20 (1973), 1–9; W. Wette (ed.), *Der Krieg des kleinen Mannes. Eine Militärgeschichte von unten* (Munich, 1992).

17 A. Forrest, *Napoleon's Men: The Soldiers of the Revolution and Empire* (London, 2002).

18 On whom see, recently, K. D. Vuic, *Officer, Nurse, Woman: The Army Nurse Corps in the Vietnam War* (Baltimore, Maryland, 2010).

19 M. van Creveld, *The Culture of War* (New York, 2008), pp. 395–409.

20 R. Pennington, 'Offensive Women: Women in Combat in the Red Army in the Second World War', *Journal of Military History*, 74 (210), 775–820; O. Kucherenko, *Little Soldiers. How Soviet Children Went to War, 1941–1945* (Oxford, 2011).

21 R. Scheck, *Hitler's African Victims: The German Army Massacres of Black French Soldiers in 1940* (Cambridge, 2006).

22 W. Lee (ed.), *Empires and Indigenes: Intercultural Alliance, Imperial Expansion, and Warfare in the Early Modern World* (New York, 2011).

23 J. M. Dower, *War Without Mercy: Race and Power in the Pacific War* (New York, 1986); C. M. Cameron, *American Samurai: Myth, Imagination, and the Conduct of Battle in the First Marine Division, 1941–1951* (Cambridge, 1994); P. Schrijvers, *Bloody Pacific: American Soldiers at War with Japan* (Basingstoke, 2010).

24 E. Bergerud, 'No Quarter: The Pacific Battlefield', *Historically Speaking*, III, 5 (June 2002), 8–10.

25 M. Hughes, 'War Without Mercy? American Armed Forces and the Deaths of Civilians during the Battle for Saipan, 1944', *Journal of Military History*, 75 (2011), 93–123, esp. 122–3.

26 J. Ferris, *Intelligence and Strategy: Selected Essays* (London, 2005), pp. 120–7; G. Kennedy, 'Anglo-American Strategic Relations and Intelligence Assessments of Japanese Air Power 1934–1941', *Journal of Modern History*, 74 (2010), 772–3.

27 M. Pollak, *Cities at War in Early Modern Europe* (Cambridge, 2010).

28 R. W. Jones, *Bloodied Banners. Martial Display on the Medieval Battlefield* (Woodbridge, 2010), pp. 177–8. See also, M. G. A. Vale, *War and Chivalry: Warfare and Aristocratic Culture in England, France, and Burgundy at the End of the Middle Ages* (1981).

29 S. H. Myerly, *British Military Spectacle. From the Napoleonic Wars through the Crimea* (Cambridge, Massachusetts, 1996).

30 For an example, J. Winter and A. Prost, *The Great War in History: Debates and Controversies, 1914 to the Present* (Cambridge, 2005).

31 J. Black, *Historiography. Contesting the Past, Claiming the Future* (London, 2011).

32 J. S. Corum, 'Myths of *Blitzkrieg*', *Historically Speaking*, vol. 6, no. 4 (Mar./Ap. 2005), p. 12.

8   Conclusions

1   L. Hunt (ed.), *The New Cultural History* (Berkeley, California, 1989); V. E. Bonnell and L. Hunt (eds), *Beyond the Cultural Turn: New Directions in the Study of Society and Culture* (Berkeley, California, 1999); M. A. Cabrera (ed.), *Postsocial History: An Introduction* (Lanham, Maryland, 2005).

2   C. Gray, *Strategy and History: Essays on Theory and Practice* (Abingdon, 2006).

3   R. G. S. Cooper, *The Anglo-Maratha Campaigns and the Contest for India: The Struggle for Control of the South Asian Military Economy* (Cambridge, 2003).

4   See also 'The Future of War: A Forum', *Historically Speaking*, vol. 7, no. 3 (Jan/Feb. 2006), 25–38.

5   W. Murray, 'Does Military Culture Matter?', in J. F. Lehman and H. Sicherman (eds), *America the Vulnerable. Our Military Problems and How to Fix Them* (Philadelphia, Pennsylvania, 2002), pp. 134–51.

6   D. A. Charters, M. Milner and J. B. Wilson (eds), *Military History and the Military Profession* (Westport, Connecticut, 1992); W. Murray and R. H. Sinnreich (eds), *The Past as Prologue. The Importance of History to the Military Profession* (Cambridge, 2006).

7   H. Strachan, 'Strategy in the twenty-first century', in S. Scheipers and H. Strachan (eds), *The Changing Character of War* (Oxford, 2011), pp. 503–7.

8   J. Rüger, *The Great Naval Game. Britain and Germany in the Age of Empire* (Cambridge, 2007).

9   D. A. Bell, *First Total War. Napoleon's Europe and the Birth of Warfare as We Know It* (Boston, 2007).

10   R. H. Kohn, *Eagle and Sword: The Federalists and the Creation of the Military Establishment in America, 1783–1802* (New York, 1975); T. J. Crackel, *Mr Jefferson's Army: Political and Social Reform of the Military Establishment, 1801–1809* (New York, 1989).

11   C. Coker, *The Warrior Ethos: Military Culture and the War on Terror* (Abingdon, 2007).

12   S. C. Smallman, *Fear and Memory in the Brazilian Army and Society, 1889–1954* (Chapel Hill, North Carolina, 2002).

13   R. Pois and P. Langer, *Command Failure in War: Psychology and Leadership* (Bloomington, Indiana, 2004).

14   A. Mombauer, *Helmuth von Moltke and the Origins of the First World War* (Cambridge, 2001).

15   G. Kassimeris (ed.), *The Barbarization of Warfare* (New York, 2006).

16   For the latter, M. B. Cosmopoulos (ed.), *Experiencing War: Trauma and Society in Ancient Greece and Today* (Chicago, Illinois, 2007).

Selected Further Reading

Booth, K., *Strategy and Ethnocentrism* (New York, 1981).

Booth K. and R. Trood (eds), *Strategic Cultures in the Asia-Pacific Region* (Basingstoke, 1999).

Brooks, R. and E. Stanley-Mitchell, *Creating Military Power: The Impact of Culture, Society, Institutions, and International Forces on Military Effectiveness* (Palo Alto, California, 2007).

Cassidy, R. M., *Counterinsurgency and the Global War on Terror: Military Culture and Irregular War* (London, 2006).

Coker, C., *Waging War Without Warriors? The Changing Culture of Military Conflict* (London, 2002).

Creveld, Martin van, *The Culture of War* (New York, 2008).

Dull, I., *Absolute Destruction: Military Culture and the Practices of War in Imperial Germany* (Ithaca, New York, 2005).

Farrell, T., *The Norms of War: Cultural Beliefs and Modern Conflict* (London, 2005).

Glenn, J. D. Howlett and S. Poore (eds), *Neorealism versus Strategic Culture* (Aldershot, 2004).

Hanson, V. D., *Carnage and Culture: Landmark Battles in the Rise of Western Power* (New York, 2001).

Huntington, S., *The Clash of Civilizations and the Remaking of World Order* (New York, 1996).

Johnston, A., *Cultural Realism: Strategic Culture and Grand Strategy in Chinese History* (Princeton, New Jersey, 1997).

Lee, W., *Barbarians and Brothers. Anglo-American Warfare, 1500–1865* (Oxford, 2011).

Linn, B. M., *The Echo of Battle: The Army's Way of War* (London, 2007).

Porter, P., *Military Orientalism. Eastern War Through Western Eyes* (London, 2009).

Schaffer, B. (ed.), *The Limits of Culture: Islam and Foreign Policy* (London, 2006).

Snyder, J., *The Soviet Strategic Culture: Implications for Nuclear Options* (Santa Monica, 1977).